Praise for *When Your Heart Sa*

"As Judy Reeves goes lightly and quickly across
for losing her husband sharply interrupts the journey. This diary-like
haunted by his death and the nagging refrain that Reeves is unsure she's a writer
while she journals her wonder, often in exquisite detail, at the undiscovered
world. Her 'search for meaning and connection' is to find and let go of connection, to begin asserting her feminist self, and to finally own the necessity of being
alone—a précis for the writing life that is and that also awaits her."

—Thomas Larson, author of *The Memoir and the Memoirist*

"In scenes of quiet brilliance, Judy Reeves crafts a dazzling memoir of a woman
in search of herself after the death of her husband. As she travels around the
world—Paris, Athens, Moscow, Bombay—we discover the geography of her
life, with its griefs, sensual joys, challenges, and dreams. This is *Eat, Pray, Love*
for women who know that the greatest journey of all is the one that points
inwards. I savored every page."

—Mary Reynolds Thompson, author of *A Wild Soul Woman*
and *Reclaiming the Wild Soul*

"Never have I felt so carried off inside a dream with all the sensual details,
encounters with fellow travelers and citizens of society than when reading
When Your Heart Says Go. Both a love story and a tale of grief Judy writes
with achingly provocative descriptions of her around-the-world trip, taking
us along on her intimate journey to heal from a tragically lost love. I fell in
love with every word, just as she fell in love with who she would become."

—Amy Wallen, author of *How to Write a Novel in 20 Pies*
and *When We Were Ghouls*

"There are many compelling travels in Judy Reeves's captivating memoir. She
introduces us to people, places, trains, and moments that define her year of
travel. More so, she takes us up close into her inner journey of grief, loneliness
and deciding who she was going to be and how she was going to live her life
after the death of her husband. Reeves's writing speaks to something universal about loss, longing, and the human spirit. While reading her story, I was
drawn into myself—a sign that a gifted writer is leading the way."

—Lynda Monk, Director, International Association
for Journal Writing, IAJW.org

"Written in luscious poetic language by a master wordsmith this memoir is filled with exquisite sensory details, colorful settings, and interesting personalities she encounters along the way. I highly recommend it!"

—Jill G. Hall, author of the Anne McFarland Series

"Through eloquent and finely articulated details of her travels, painting images from words and hoping to insulate herself from the depth of heartbreak, Reeves realizes that no matter how many different landscapes she traverses, outer change is a futile substitution for inner healing and freedom from unbearable loss. *When Your Heart Says Go* captures the meandering lostness of losing one's beloved, and the compassionate joy which eventually emerges to hold it. Reeves's book is a reminder of the truth of life creating itself newly."

—Laura Basha, PhD, author of *The Inward Outlook*

"Reeves shares from her heart as she processes the death of her soulmate, taking us along on an adventurous around-the-world journey. She writes deftly and poetically from exotic cities where she not only discovers herself again but ultimately her calling in life."

—Leslie Johansen Nack, author of *Fourteen*

"What an inspirational journey! In her memoir *When Your Heart Says Go*, Judy Reeves's vivid descriptions take us with her as she encounters the places and people that help her open up and become a fuller person. Reeves's beautiful book is a testament to the power of writing as well as the human capacity for resilience."

—Sandra Marinella, author of *The Story You Need to Tell*

"Go on a mind-expanding, heart-expanding journey with Judy Reeves as she recounts her worldwide journey of exploration after the death of her husband."

—Eric Maisel, author of *The Coach's Way*

"*When Your Heart Says Go* by Judy Reeves, is one of the most hypnotic and lyrical memoirs I've read. Judy weaves memory seamlessly—the blue skies of Delft, the seascapes of Dubrovnik, childhood moments, the highlights of Moscow and Paris. The love of her husband and the still sharp bare landscape of losing him are threads throughout, inviting us to join her inner journey to Self. Her memoir reminds us to reflect on our inner and outer journeys to discover the core of who we are. Highly recommended!

—Linda Joy Myers-founder of The National Association of Memoir Writers, author of *Don't Call Me Mother, Song of the Plains,* and the historical fiction novel *The Forger of Marseille*

WHEN YOUR HEART SAYS GO

My Year of Traveling
Beyond Loss and Loneliness

Judy Reeves

SHE WRITES PRESS

Published 2023
Printed in the United States of America
Print ISBN: 978-1-64742-563-0
E-ISBN: 978-1-64742-564-7
Library of Congress Control Number: 2023907746

For information, address:
She Writes Press
1569 Solano Ave #546
Berkeley, CA 94707

Interior Design by Kiran Spees

She Writes Press is a division of SparkPoint Studio, LLC.

To Tom
"For the Good Times"

and

To my father
Don Gray
Who opened the world when he opened that world atlas

Is there an odyssey the female soul longs to make at the approach of fifty—one that has been blurred and lost within a culture awesomely alienated from the soul? If so, what sort of journey would that be? Where would it take me?

—**Sue Monk Kidd,**
Traveling with Pomegranates

SPRING 1990
San Diego

After Tom died, I moved from our house in San Diego's backcountry to the beach where I felt most at home. The condominium I bought overlooked an estuary where I could sit on the balcony and watch seabirds come and go, tides shift in and out. I wanted to live to a different rhythm than the Santa Ana winds and tule fog that marked the seasons in Jamul.

It didn't happen just like that—Tom alive, whistling as he worked with Jesús in the orchard, laying irrigation pipe and stomping dirt around newly planted avocado trees, then Tom dead and me living alone in the condo overlooking the estuary. For a few years in between I kept our business running, had an off-and-on affair with a man I didn't trust, traveled to New Zealand and Australia with my best friend, Camille, and to Europe with my daughter, Amy.

Despite the loss and grief and confusion, I'd created a new life, a full life. In fact, too full. When I stopped long enough to reflect, to be still and listen to my body—to close my eyes and become conscious of my heartbeat and my breath—tears would invariably form; an ache lodged in my throat that was different from the physical manifestations of grief I'd experienced. The sensation seemed to come from a deeper part of me. Buried beneath the surface of my too-full life was a mysterious kind of longing, though I sensed it wasn't *more* I wanted. God knows I already had more than I could handle. What I wanted escaped definition or category or even language—an ineffable yearning of the kind I imagine has set many blind seekers on a path to they know not where.

One spring day in 1990, three years after Tom's death, as I sat on my balcony, sun glittering the water, shorebirds flying in and flying out, I heard his voice from a time long before, from when we'd first found each other. We were at my home in Cardiff-by-the-Sea. He'd built a fire in the fireplace and tossed in sprigs of juniper that crackled with an aroma he said summoned Canada, his home. Then, with a voice that preachers pray for and actors envy, he leaned close and whispered in my ear, "Now, when your heart says, 'Go.'"

The idea came on a sea breeze, as though dropped by one of those winging seabirds. It came fully formed and utterly irresistible—sell the business, sell the condominium, sell the car, get one of those around-the-world airline tickets, and go.

Just go.

JULY 31, 1990
San Diego to London

The little commuter plane—dear God, it seems so insubstantial—trundles down the runway and makes a turn at the end. I look out the round window and see Amy's truck parked just outside the fence. Of course she can't see me, but I smile in what I hope is a reassuring way.

The plane straightens, speeds up, and lifts off. I get a swooping feeling in my stomach, an off-centered, momentary dizziness. Out the small window, as if looking through a camera, my view of San Diego zooms out—Mission Hills flattens into the bay, there's Fiesta Island, and there's the estuary that used to be my view from the condo. We continue to climb, then sail north along the coastline. Outside it's all blue Pacific.

I blink into the Southern California sunshine that's dulled to the color of sand by the notorious LA smog. The international terminal seems miles away, and I haul my newly purchased, fully packed, too-heavy suitcase across never-ending blacktop and through an echoing parking garage that smells of exhaust and overheated engines. July at LAX: my definition of purgatory.

At last I reach the enormous, hectic terminal where a football field of look-alike airline check-in counters stretches before me. Ducking around other travelers, I trudge along, at one point bumping my bag into a business-suited, square-shouldered, silver-haired man whose glance warns of damage that could be done, and finally locate the Pan Am check-in, get in line, and set my bag down. My shoulder aches with relief. Clearly, I've overpacked; I always do. Besides, though the nifty suitcase-cum-backpack combo I bought at REI is cleverly designed, I'm not the backpack/youth hostel type. I'm nearly forty-eight years old, I've never worn a backpack in my life, and I haven't slept communally since Girl Scout camp.

Not an hour from home and already I'm met with a situation that calls for rapid improvisation. After I get my boarding pass, I stop at a traveler's store along the corridor of shops and buy a set of strap-on wheels for my bag.

I find a pay phone and call Camille. It has become our custom to call each other from airline terminals no matter where we are.

"You sound far away," she says, and I know she doesn't mean in miles.

Ensconced in the calm that comes with reaching cruising altitude, which we'll sustain for the next ten hours, I relax back in my seat with a sigh. I can do anything I want for the next year, anytime I want. Sleep. Eat. Write. See people, places, things. Wander, stay, go. I have Time and the absolute freedom to use it, spend it, squander it, save it, give it away—any way I want. This is the most extravagant gift I have ever given myself. But gifts often have two sides, and there is about this one something that also carries the weight of a burden.

My seatmate, an older woman in a pink velour outfit and matching lipstick, smiles an invitation to chat. But small talk would most likely include trying to explain myself, which I can't imagine doing. I smile in return, turn slightly away from her, pull down my tray table, and open my journal to a blank page.

Pen in hand, ready to write the first words that will record what I have done—am doing—I hesitate. With some effort I resist looking back at the other choices I could have taken and instead resolve to look forward. I close my eyes and imagine myself as *traveler*.

Visions of me writing. Me, in cozy, semi-frumpy rooms, pensions, and two-star hotels, writing. Me on some sunny beach, tan and healthy and writing. At the theater in London, sitting at cafés in

Paris, on trains along borders between countries, eventually on sun-drenched South Pacific beaches. I see me as *tourist*—open to others, talking, friendly, curious. I also see the me who wants to be alone, who savors solitude, knowing full well that within solitude lies sorrow and something even deeper, shadowy and questioning.

As I consider these visions of the new places I will see, experiences yet to come, I raise the little shade to glance out the airplane window. The vastness is pink and mauve and soft; the sun bright as it teases its way through clouds piled on the horizon.

I hope I will be a good guest of the places I visit. I ask myself what I mean by *good guest*. Writing at last, a list helps my thoughts take shape in my journal:

Giving rather than taking.

Saying thank you in whatever language is spoken.

Respecting the customs of the place and the people.

Being teachable and open to learning.

Being present in the present.

AUGUST 1–9, 1990
London

Propped up on thin pillows in my bed at the Leicester Garden Hotel where I've taken a room for a few days, I write of escalators—first at the airport in LA, then, ten-plus hours later, the escalator at South Kensington station in London.

There I was ambushed by a deep sense of loneliness; lost among so many people—serious people in serious clothes, people in a hurry, people going about their everyday lives. I left that everyday life in California and can't even say why. Because it wasn't enough? Because it was too much?

So there I was on a blistering August day in an unfamiliar place—not the me that was and not the me that will be but a limbo me, an outline.

Think of the morning sun and the shadow that trails you; the late-afternoon sun and the shadow that precedes you. But in the middle of the day when the sun is high, you don't cast a shadow. I am the middle of the day.

I awake too late for the meager hotel breakfast and go out, squinting and a bit dazed, into the hot morning to get, if not some food, at least a cup of coffee. Not far away I find a small patisserie. Brightly lit, with a wide window onto the street and several plain wood tables and chairs, the place isn't crowded at this late-morning hour.

Someone's left an *International Herald Tribune* at my table and I read the bold headline that yesterday Saddam Hussein's Iraqi forces invaded Kuwait. Still foggy-headed and jet-lagged, I don't know how significant this might be. The size of the headline indicates Significant. I order breakfast and read on: the UN has levied sanctions on Iraq and President Bush has ordered navy ships to the Persian Gulf. Serious? Or another of those fracases that flare up enough to make headlines, then fade back to the usual Middle East tensions? A cup of coffee arrives, weak though it is. I turn the page to distract myself with other news.

I read that at Madame Tussauds Wax Museum the staff have removed the Queen's head from her royal body and put it in the fridge for the duration of this record-breaking heat wave.

I'm on the move, looking for beauty. Improvising once again.

The Leicester Garden, a traveler's hotel recommended in *Frommer's*, is too plain, too basic—the carpet's thin and the bed uncomfortable. So I set off on this scorching day to my new hotel, the Garden Country Hotel on Kensington Gardens Square.

The gravel path through the Kensington Gardens makes wheeling my too-heavy pack difficult. No, not difficult, but rough enough that I am conscious of having to drag it along. My feet are swollen in huaraches, my skirt clings to sweat-sticky legs, and I am lost. Or, if not lost, at the very least I don't quite know where I am. And it's bloody hot.

The trees are tall and grand and spreading and the lawns lush and green on either side of the gravel path. Benches line the way and on one a man leans back, face to the sun, shirt off. His bare chest fairly gleams in the bright light. I'm drawn to stare at his whiteness, that bit of belly above his trousers, the small and roundish pink of his nipples, his hairless chest. I don't know when I have seen a whiter body.

No birdsong disturbs the still air; the birds must be drowsing, too, like the man on the bench. We are all, to use a British expression, knackered. The verdant aromas of late summer, grass thick and lush and tempting, if I stop here under this grand oak, in plain sight, in bright daylight but in the shade . . .

Planting myself on the grass, skirt under my legs, I remove my shoes. The contrast of my aqua skirt against the deep emerald pleases me. I rub my bare feet in the grass. Is there a better sensation for a girl with Missouri roots? This, I think, is what home feels like.

Pack placed behind me, I lean back, then slide a little farther down until I am nearly supine. My eyes can't help but close against the branch-dappled sun, and, stranger in an unfamiliar place, single woman on the grass under a tree in a public park, I fall asleep, deeply and completely.

Every day at some news shop or another I find the *Herald Tribune* and read page by careful page with my coffee at a local café or lunch counter as I wander around London, blisters on my feet and head full of questions about what the hell I'm doing. Though the paper continues to be filled with news about Iraq and Kuwait, in these first days I am focused on myself, filling my journal with page after page of self-examination and self-consciousness and notes that record how I spent my day.

Who can say why a certain memory, a particular image, comes when so many others don't? My first week in August in London I went most every day to Piccadilly Circus and bought half-price day-of tickets, sometimes for both matinee and evening performances. I walked neighborhoods, strolled off the main streets where huge oaks and London planes shaded lanes, and wandered in tucked-away squares brightened by window boxes full of summer flowers. I took the Underground, vowing to get off at a different stop every day. I attended AA meetings, visited historic sites, museums, galleries, and Harrods department store, where I remember only still-feathered fowl hanging from the ceiling. Why, in all of this grand city with its rich variety, is my most vivid memory of the afternoon I napped in Kensington Gardens beneath a great spreading tree? Why this memory and not another, seemingly more impressive one?

"Judy, you always make things so complicated," my mother told me.

Remembering this and other scolding voices still echoing inside my head, I think, Can't it just be a memory? Can't it just be like a tiny box that holds the warm air, the summer smells, the dappled light, the compelling need to stop and rest?

Was it all that, the green park, the humid heat, the sensation of dense grass on bare feet, the broad and leafy tree, that brought an old and deep understanding of being where it was—where *I* was—safe? Was this the kind of Proustian experience in which sensory details of the present ferried me into the past, where I had a response of safety so complete I could actually fall asleep under a tree in a park in a foreign country?

Or it's possible I was simply drugged by the whole of it—the temperature, the aromas, the leaf-veiled light—like Dorothy in a field of poppies.

Still, I wonder, *why this memory, this scene and not another, appears so vividly.*

I do make things complicated; I've never been able to simply let them be. This is one way of trying to grasp control when the whole thing—existence itself—is just a free fall into the void and I'm afraid to let go.

AUGUST 9, 1990
London to the Netherlands

On the train from Liverpool I take the final place in a four-seat arrangement with a family trio, nodding hello to Mr. and Mrs. and hello to the boy sitting next to the window, wiggly in his seat. I attempt to be nonchalant with my bottled water and tuna sandwich from the kiosk at the station. The boy wrinkles his nose and says something to his mother. I recognize the language—German—but not the words; still I know it is about my sandwich. The mother reaches into her shopping bag and gives him an apple.

I try not to notice their attention and pull my book closer. I'm reading D. H. Lawrence, *Women in Love*, found in a used bookstore while on a day trip to Cambridge. The prose is very romantic, lush, and wordy; I've read it before, but so long ago I don't remember much. More familiar is the "how to eat a fig" scene from the movie. I want to compare the two scenes, though it has been years since I saw the film. I'm curious what a writer can do on the page compared to in a film. After all, the film has not only dialogue but also setting, actors, lighting, music. All the writer has is language.

The lights of London fade behind us as we rattle along. A young man—thin, wearing shorts, bare legs exposed—comes down the aisle and suddenly yells out, bends down, and grabs his ankle. When he takes his hand away there is blood. A lot of blood. He has sliced his leg against something sharp on the seat in front of us. His lips pull tight in obvious pain. My stomach lurches and I turn away. Digging in my paper bag from the kiosk, I find a clean napkin and give it to him.

Someone calls the conductor, who looks at the young man's injury, blood seeping through the napkin. Then he bends down to inspect the place where the seat connects to the floor of the train—something is not fitted right or is somehow broken.

"It's not supposed to be like that," the conductor says to the aisle.

The injured man limps through the car and crosses through the sliding doors at the end. The conductor stands, hat in hand, and looks at the place that caused the injury. I put what is left of my tuna sandwich in the bag. The Germans and I are silent.

Lots of things happen in life that aren't supposed to be like that.

On the ferry across the North Sea I share a room with Maggie, a Scottish woman from Australia who lives in Cambridge. Maggie is crossing to meet her husband who works in Rotterdam; she met him when she was in the UK on a yearlong work-travel journey and never returned home.

"Be ready for that," she warns.

I wonder how one goes about becoming ready for that kind of love to strike or appear or descend—or whatever love does to us when it finds us.

NOVEMBER 4, 1978
Cardiff-by-the-Sea

I was in mid-production on an audiovisual project for the nonprofit I worked for and needed a voice-over talent to narrate the show. Tom came to audition: tall and slim, wearing a black turtleneck that emphasized both, eyes the brown of polished mahogany, and a voice like I'd only heard on radio and TV. He sat behind my desk where the light was best and read the script. He held the pages with long, strong fingers, what I came to describe as *man hands*.

That night at home, alone in my bed, I dreamed about him—all legs, lanky in a white suit lit by a single spotlight on an empty stage. His dark hair with auburn highlights; his voice resonating still from our afternoon encounter.

He got the part.

AUGUST 10, 1990
Tiel

The hotel in Tiel is crowded with recovering alcoholics from all over Europe—expats, military, seekers, and travelers who heard about this English-Speaking European Intergroup AA Conference or, like me, made it a destination on an otherwise empty itinerary.

An enthusiastic member of AA, a regular at three or four meetings each week, and a sponsor of several women—that was me. It may sound selfish, since one of AA's basic tenets is about giving it away to keep it; that is, by helping others we help ourselves to stay sober, but sponsoring so many women had become draining. You can give away and give away until there's not much left. I didn't know it at the time, and wouldn't have admitted it if I did, but somewhere under all my enthusiasm I knew I needed to take time for myself. For all the self-examination and therapy, all the step work and journaling, I didn't know I was starved for solitude.

At all big AA events we smoke (some of us still do, though not me, finally), consume copious cups of coffee, and eat barrels of ice cream. In addition to the many scheduled meetings, panels, and speakers, spontaneous meetings happen in hallways, hotel rooms, and stairways.

Which is where I find myself on Saturday night. The after-banquet dance is in full swing in the ballroom, where lights are low and the music loud. I don't have a dancing partner and am not looking for one, so I take a place on the open stairway leading from the ballroom up to the mezzanine. I'm not the only one stationed here—several of us are sprinkled all along the wide stairway.

A young American woman, only a few days sober, traveling in

Europe during summer break from college, sits beside me. We share a few general exchanges. I tell her I am eleven years sober. Muted lights from the ballroom circle red and blue and green against her blond hair as she puts a match to her cigarette and exhales smoke in a sigh.

"I'm heartless," she says. She's looking down at her shoes. "I strangled my cat." The words themselves are strangled. "I can't believe I'm that cruel."

She's crying, sobbing really, and all I can do is put an arm around her and let her cry. The two of us an island of intimacy on some stairs in a hotel in a city neither of us has been before or probably ever will be again. Strangers, but connected for just that long in a way that, when we allow ourselves, defines humanity.

Another young woman comes to sit beside me later that evening. Also newly recovering, new to AA, new to her own anger. She tells me she has horrifying images of revenge she wants to enact on her boyfriend.

"I want to put broken glass in my vagina," she says, "so when he fucks me, his penis will be ripped to shreds."

There is no forgiveness, no penance given this night, or ever, in these exchanges. As many others have done for me over the years, I offer only a silent witness to their confessions, an arm around shaking shoulders, a suggestion of AA's Twelve Steps. What do you say to a woman who tells you she believes herself to be heartless? "Why would I strangle my cat?" Or a woman so consumed by rage she imagines putting broken glass inside herself?

My mother never allowed my anger. She didn't allow her own. And you, grandmother, and grandmother before you? How far back must we go to find the woman who allowed her own rage? Who railed against the night, against the man who raped her, the god who deserted her, the light that never existed?

Later that night, still on the stairway, another bloodletting. A young woman is cut by a sharp edge of an ice cream cart, her calf sliced, like the man on the train. She releases a sharp yell of pain and surprise; there is blood. A flurry of activity and noise below me, someone put salt on her wound—I don't know why—another shout of pain, and she is taken off to a nearby hospital emergency room.

The music continues, the couples dance, and the women, one by one, come to sit on the smoky stairs and tell their secrets.

AUGUST 12, 1990
Tiel to Amsterdam to The Hague

I board the train for Amsterdam, where I plan to stay for—well, for however long I'll stay. Traveling without a reservation, trusting in the luck of the traveler.

But there was none to be had at the traveler's assist desk in Amsterdam Centraal station. "Nothing," the broad-shouldered man at the counter tells me when it's finally my turn.

SAIL Amsterdam 1990, a celebration of tall ships from all over the world at the height of the season, made rooms more than scarce and crowds impossible. The train station is a brick palace of a place: vast, high-ceilinged, and echoing with travelers from all over Europe.

I consider a couple of choices: go to the 7:00 p.m. AA meeting that's listed in the international English-speaking AA meetings pamphlet I carry with me and hope for a couch at someone's house, or get back on a train and go somewhere else.

The man at the traveler's assist desk suggests, "Go to The Hague. It's close and you'll find a place there."

AUGUST 12–16, 1990
The Hague

The Hague. Not famous like Amsterdam, with its canals and flower markets and museums, Van Gogh and Anne Frank, its music and sex shows and cannabis cafés. The Hague: political capital of Holland, home to the International Criminal Court and the Peace Palace, situated on an edge of land that runs along the North Sea; long beaches, narrow, winding streets, gracious brick homes with lace curtains and colorful window boxes.

I do find a room here. Room 24 at the Bali Hotel. Stained glass windows, graceful teak furniture in the lobby, potted plants.

After a night's dreamless sleep in my single bed I pack my daypack with a notebook, pens, the D. H. Lawrence, and set out on a sunny morning to find a café. What a surprise when, walking down the promenade, I come upon Marty, Vladimir, and Karen, friends from the conference I'd just left in Tiel the day before.

Karen is sturdy, blond, blue-eyed, and tan; a lively woman who lives in The Hague. She seems to always be moving. And talking. And talking. Vladimir, from Moscow, is tall and long-legged, with a shot of wavy hair that hangs over his brow and an unhealthy pasty look to his skin, especially compared to the robust Karen. He's wearing a Beatles T-shirt.

Something about Marty reminds me of Tom. Not physically. Where Tom was tall and almost too thin, Marty is shorter, stockier, with a roundish face and green eyes. But like Tom, he's intelligent, quick-witted, at ease with language. He's from Manitoba, so it's also his Canadian-ness. I don't even know what I mean when I say that.

Some might think Americans and Canadians aren't so different from each other, but to my mind we are. Americans have all that rebellious independence, a kind of swagger; Canadians don't swagger but may have a sense of being a little superior to Americans. After all, they have royalty on their side; often we Americans don't even have each other. Marty also has a background in radio and TV, like Tom. Like me.

Marty is bright, funny, easy to be with. While Karen and Vladimir go to the Soviet embassy so Karen can apply for a visa, we two settle in at an outdoor café. We may be flirting, Marty and me. I don't even know; it's been a long time since I flirted with anyone.

Later that evening, after another AA meeting, Marty and I go to dinner at the *pannenkoekenhuis*, where they serve pancakes bigger than my face, bigger than a dinner plate. We eat, we talk, we close the place down, and after, we amble down the darkened streets to the still-open Burger King and order American coffee and keep talking. That's another thing that reminds me of Tom—the talking, the storytelling, the charm of it all, the charm of him.

Sometime during our long evening of stories and revelations, Marty tells me about his marriage and an affair he'd had.

I must have reacted to that because Marty stops his story, looks at me, and says, "Something just happened. Your eyes changed."

"What changed?" I ask. We're still at the Burger King, in one of the Naugahyde booths, our coffees between us on the Formica table, its shiny too-white top with a strip of chrome around the edge reflecting the too-bright overhead glare.

"From wondering to knowledge," he says.

He may have seen in my eyes the consideration of us having an affair. Is this what I've been thinking?

I'm ambivalent about affairs. I know too many marriages that have been devastated, women who have been broken, but I understand the excitement and titillation that often precede an affair and the need and longing we humans sometimes experience, which some of us act upon. I will confess to a few affairs in my previous life, before sobriety, before Tom. But since his death I have had only the one off-and-on relationship that's currently off.

When the Burger King closes at 1:00 a.m., I invite Marty to my room where we sit on my bed and talk until 4:00 a.m. By then, he says, it's too late to go to Karen's, where he is staying.

"Her door would probably be locked," he says. "Besides, I need some space from her. She's too bossy."

And so we spend the rest of the night together. In bed—that small single bed in Room 24 at the Bali Hotel, sharing a single pillow, spooning together.

We don't take off our clothes. We don't have sex. We don't even kiss. We simply curl together and sleep.

The next morning we return to the pancake house for breakfast.

"I had a dream about your penis last night," I tell him as we sit at our wooden table, the sweet aroma of maple syrup making the air seem sticky. "It was really big."

"You should see it in real life," he says.

Love this guy. Not in a romantic, falling-in-love way, not at all like Tom but a friendly, companion-on-the-journey way. Sleeping with Marty in that small single bed in a foreign country on a journey of I don't know what—exploration, discovery, grieving, healing, search-ing, all of the above—sleeping with him and not having sex: this is part of the journey too. Being in a larger world than the one I have known, behaving in ways that are new to me, different.

I am curious about who I might be as a single woman approaching fifty, alone and independent, a cauldron of emotional soup concocted of fear and excitement, dread and anticipation. Like characters in the D. H. Lawrence novel, are we contradictions or merely complex? Or like Tom's hero in the Kris Kristofferson song, *partly truth and partly fiction*?

AUGUST 16–18, 1990
Amsterdam

While I drink a morning cappuccino at a table by the window at Caffé La Strada in Amsterdam, a gorgeous, loud thunderstorm assaults the day. Lightning mangles the sky and pellets of rain the size of nickels bounce knee-high off the sidewalk.

After one refill of coffee and writing about the wet onslaught for a page in my journal, the storm passes, leaving the streets gleaming and the sky appropriately Delft blue. I pack myself up and transform into tourist to take a boat tour of the old city on its canals in the freshened August air.

Amsterdam is houseboats with fancy curtains; tall, thin, pastel-colored buildings with contraptions at the topmost point above the window where furniture is hoisted up, the stairs too narrow for passage of beds and chests and tables. We glide along past thick old trees and quiet streets where bicyclists and strollers make their way. I hardly listen to the tour guide's descriptions, picturing myself living in one of those tall buildings, bicycling here and there. I do this—gaze out train windows as we pass fenced backyards and amble along cobbled streets in old cities and wonder who I would be if I lived there. Would my Southern California self, with its residual traces of Midwest-simple, be transformed into someone more sophisticated, more worldly?

After the canal tour, still in tourist mode, I walk from Centraal station to Rijksmuseum to the Van Gogh Museum where I can't help but weep upon seeing the originals of paintings that have been replicated ad infinitum on postcards and umbrellas and tote bags. "Vincent," I say to the hallowed walls, "I love your sunflowers and your irises." I may appear the fool standing before these paintings, hardly breathing, tears large and splashing as the morning's rain. But still I say aloud, "Thank you for your round and golden suns, your starry nights."

I often see myself this way, self-conscious and awkward, foolishly crying at the sight of a burst of bright bougainvillea on a neighbor's fence, a fat cat lazing on a Sunday twilight doorstep, the opening notes of a remembered song that brings back a remembered time.

Call me sentimental (I am), say I'm too sensitive (I am), but of all the things I want to change about myself—my insecurity, my vanity, my inability to confront—that I am frequently and unexpectedly wounded by beauty is not one of them.

During the day of wandering and wondering I come upon an open-air tulip market. Rows and bins of bare bulbs and shelves of glorious blooming tulips. I simply stand and breathe the earthy smell in this shaded place. Memories of Midwest gardens and irises along root-cracked sidewalks take me back and back to a childhood where the freedom of first roller skates and then bicycles set me on a road toward *away*. Where my first temptation to travel was born: Daddy and I, side by side on our scratchy brown sofa, reverently turning pages in a pre–World War II world atlas, our fingers tracing roads and rivers and the borders of countries whose names he would say as if casting a spell—Argentina, Czechoslovakia, Tanganyika, and then to the heavens, where we recite the names of planets, and beyond even that. "The universe," Daddy says, inching a finger along the inky expanse. "No one can say how it came to be or how big it is or where it begins or ends."

Everywhere I go in Amsterdam I notice beautiful young people—on foot, on bicycle, alone and in twos and threes—smoking, laughing. I admire the open-faced, blond beauty of the Dutch women. Their smooth skin, their robust bodies and generous breasts, their easy style. These European women in their casually put-together outfits—scarves draped just so—look so together, so cool, so how I want to look. If I had the perfect pink scarf, I'd look cool too; I'd look together. I'd look like I belong.

I recognize this thinking for what it is. If I confessed it at an AA meeting, I'd be laughed at. I know the obsession to find that pink scarf, or the perfect bag or shoes, or dreaming out train windows of living in a different place—this *if only . . . then* thinking will never lead to any kind of happy ending. I know these attempts to change the outside is what I do in a futile effort to change how I feel inside. But just being aware of my flaws and foibles doesn't lead to change; I need help.

I was seeing a therapist after Tom died. (I was also consulting psychics, going on journal retreats, reading tarot cards, and hanging out with a few self-identifying witches.) In one session my therapist, Charlie, took me through a backward journey of hypothetical events where, one by one, my communities, my work, my friends, and my family disappeared.

"What would happen then . . .?" Charlie asked as each support and connection disappeared and I tried to keep my head above the emotional waters that were engulfing me.

Finally, after every person, every identity, every defense was gone, Charlie asked, "What would happen then?"

"I would be alone," I said. Through my tears I saw the image of a little girl standing by herself on a long, empty country road.

"What would happen then?" he asked once more, his voice soft.

"I would die," I said, overcome with a sad truth about myself: alone, I was not enough.

Someone else might have turned to religion here, or at least faith in some kind of God. I packed my bag and turned to the road.

AUGUST 19–20, 1990
Vastradastraat

I awoke with memories of the soft Dutch night—fog surrounding a castle in a small town near here. *Here* is Vastradastraat, Netherlands, where I stay overnight with Sandy, whom I met at the conference in Tiel, her husband Bill, and their family.

In memory the night held a hint of lilac, an essence, a secret you just knew. The castle was large and rambling. Its towers rose high, but the castle was solid to the ground, like the Dutch themselves. This part of Holland—the lower corner that sits between Germany and Belgium—isn't flat like the north but hilly. Farmland. Cows graze in fields outside Sandy and Bill's home, which is filled with people—little kids, adolescents, friends—sharing stories around a big dining room table. There's much smoking, copious refills of coffee. Bill is a just-retired army officer, "A spy-catcher," he says, "military intelligence." Tall and robust, he smokes a pipe and occasionally breaks into song.

Conversation stops when they listen to the news on the radio. It matters in this house; they need to know the events in Saudi Arabia. *The desert*, Sandy and Bill call it. They have two sons in the army, one stationed they don't know where exactly, just *the desert*, and another leaving in two weeks. My grasp of the situation comes only from what I have read in the *Herald Tribune*.

In the morning I stay abed late after waking from a dream of making love with someone I don't know—or, in writing of it in my journal, can't remember—though it must have been someone I trusted; it was a lovely and gentle dream. Outside my window church bells resound, calling worshipers to mass.

Except for the bells, the room is a quiet place. The bed, with its high head- and footboards that, the night before, held me like a cradle. From downstairs I hear Bill singing scraps of Kris Kristofferson's song, "Sunday Morning Coming Down."

Tom was a late-night DJ at a country radio station when we first met. Sometimes I'd sit in the booth with him while he played music and talked to callers on the phone, women he'd call *darlin'* while he winked at me. He loved Kris Kristofferson's songs and "For the Good Times" was one of his favorite recordings. In our bed he'd whisper to me in that deep radio voice, *Hold your warm and tender body close to mine.* Even now I hear Tom's voice and recall the look of him in the morning, waking to the tule fog outside our bedroom window, a glimpse of lavender against the hillside.

Tomorrow morning I'll take a train to Cologne, where I plan to catch the Nord Express for Copenhagen, but for now the bells continue, dogs begin to howl in response, the aroma of pancakes comes up the stairs. I want to get up and join the family, yet I am reluctant to leave my borrowed bed.

AUGUST 20, 1990
Aachen to Copenhagen

I like overnight journeys on European trains. Sleeping in compartments with polished wood and crisp white sheets, porters who've turned down the bed, the rocking movement, the muffled *clack-clack* of metal wheels on metal track. I like awaking in the night to pull back the swaying curtain to see—nothing. Darkness. It's safe. Nothing to do but go from here to there; waiting but not waiting. It is movement; it is *en route*.

The time with Sandy and her family has me recalling the years when, as young marrieds with young children, my sisters and I, our husbands, and our little ones would descend upon our parents on Sunday afternoons. I was married to my first husband then, the father of our children—a son, Chris, and a daughter, Amy. After dinner the played-out cousins slept—two and three to a bed, like puppies—and we adults played charades or games. One evening we set up a board game that pitted me against my mother. We'd gotten to the place where all it would take was one move on my part to wipe out my mother's advantage and win the game.

"You wouldn't do that to your mother, would you?" she said from her side of the game board, barefoot and in her cotton shirt, no makeup, still young in those days.

I'd like to think it was my normal competitiveness, which is quite strong, that made me enjoy making the move that did, in fact, eliminate her from the game. On the surface it was all done in the good-natured spirit of winning, but now looking back at that evening I see me and my mother facing each other across the board and me making the move that defeated her. I see myself slyly triumphant and know it wasn't just competition that caused that sensation of triumph. I'd been straining against my mother's cautions for decades—*don't show off, don't think so much of yourself, don't be conceited*—that the sense of victory at winning the game was surely some kind of metaphoric response to that restraint of self-expression.

The Cathedral of St. Peter, a magnificent twin-spired medieval building, sits across a wide boulevard from Cologne Central Station. This is where I take refuge from the afternoon wind and rain as I await my connecting train to Copenhagen.

Inside the massive prayer-laden place old wooden pews and glossy stone floors bear witness to centuries of worshippers. Stained glass windows that, even without sunlight to jewel them, are stunning in their intricacy. The gift shop stocks black-and-white photo postcards of Cologne bombed out during the Second World War. In all the wars, in all the bombing, in all the wreckage of what we do to each other, this glorious cathedral has stood nearly unscathed for centuries. Not so the worshippers. Twenty thousand civilians were killed in the bombing of Cologne.

I don't climb the stone steps to the spire as I've done in so many other churches and castles in other places, other times. On this rain-soaked August afternoon I come in from the wet and gray and buzz of the train station to this quiet and holy place.

Finding a seat in a pew, I close my eyes and abide.

AUGUST 20–25, 1990
Copenhagen

The smorgasbord sandwiches I buy at a kiosk and sit beside the water to eat are delicate open-faced constructions involving meats and cheeses and pickles and sometimes capers. Unlike the overburdened, outlandish deli sandwiches of America, these Danish sandwiches are graceful, composed, and delicious. I eat several along with rich dark coffee as I watch the parade of bicycles that passes before me. Bicycles everywhere and ridden, it seems, by everyone—old, young, and in-between—each of them rosy-cheeked and healthy.

The early evening holds the light, sunny and blue after the clouds and rain that ushered me to this city. I came anticipating whatever Copenhagen held for me. The welcoming warmth and friendliness I experienced with Sandy and Bill and their family in Vastradastraat overrode the traces of loneliness I carry, warming me even in the chill and wet of Cologne and extending its glow into the chill and wet of my arrival here. But here beside the water a melancholy that lurks just below the surface comes upon me as dusk overtakes the day. Now, on my first day in Copenhagen, though the late sun is promising, the sights in this square alluring—Tivoli across the street on one side, the imposing brick facade of city hall with its massive clock tower on the other, and all the robust bicyclists—I am here again with myself.

All my life, since I can remember, I have wanted to be a writer. Dreaming myself Brenda Starr, reporter, after that beautiful woman with voluptuous red hair, who, in the Sunday comics of my youth, traveled the world to exotic places, chasing after stories for her newspaper. Basil St. John, who wore a patch over one eye and raised black orchids, added to the story's mystery and romance. After my adolescent Brenda Starr phase and a few years of writing heavily plotted stories and sentimental rhyming poetry, I suffered a crush on Lillian Hellman. Not the person Lillian Hellman, but a black-and-white photograph—her deep in concentration, trails of smoke rising from the cigarette held between her lips, a squat tumbler of what must be scotch on the table beside her typewriter. Somewhere in the shadowy background, her lover, the dashing Dashiell Hammett. The two of them living a noir, romantic, alcohol-fueled literary life.

This image and others—Dorothy Parker at The Algonquin, Anaïs Nin and her many journals and many lovers, Isak Dinesen and her farm in Africa—I carried jumbled in my imagination of me as *writer*: garrets in Paris may have been involved, stilted huts at a tropical water's edge. Instead, married young, children early, Pop Warner football Mom and Bluebird leader; I worked in newspapers, in radio and TV, PR and marketing. Every job I've ever had included writing, but I never said, "I am a writer." Instead I said, "I work for . . ." or "I do PR," because truth be told I didn't believe what I did was writing even though the better part of my days were ass-in-chair, fingers-on-keyboard. Now, months after selling the business Tom and I shared, I have no way to describe myself even to myself.

Walking the twilight streets back to my hotel, I remember a quote from Rilke about being a writer in his *Letters to a Young Poet*: "You must be able to stand the solitude." I don't know if I can.

The tender intimacy in that single bed in Room 24 at the Bali Hotel with Marty, the warm familiarity of friendship and family with Sandy and Bill just days ago erased the loneliness for a time, but somewhere deep inside I know that neither of these is what I long for. I have no name for this yearning, no recognition of its deeper internal origins, so it might be easy to mistake it as simply a longing for companions during the hours and days of solitude my journey offers, or to fill pages in my journal with words of loneliness while at the same time I write letters home telling of my excitement and wonderful adventures, describing to hell and back the details of places I've been, things I've seen, events I've witnessed.

Having a wonderful time, I write. *Wish you were here.*

Truth is, I am both of these—the single woman longing for what she can't name and the brave traveler off on an extended solo adventure. This journey is my attempt to reconcile the two and create or discover a patched-together new woman—someone at home with herself and at home in the world.

Street musicians perform all around Copenhagen, and as I continue my way back to my hotel, I come upon an intense and dark young man playing classical guitar. I stop and listen and take note of his intimacy to his instrument, how his body bends to it, eyes closed, lips open, hands flashing on the strings. He doesn't acknowledge the kroner I drop in the open guitar case that leans against his stool where some change and a few bills scatter against a small stack of CDs. I want to take a photo but it's too dark for natural light, and I'm concerned the flash would break his concentration, though I'm pretty sure he is not present here on the sidewalk but someplace else, a place his music has taken him. I want to go there too. So I don't stay as an observer, recording with photograph, noticing with words; I allow the night and the music to carry me away and at the same time keep me exactly where I am.

I am tourist-ing this afternoon, visiting Rosenborg Park, the royal gardens, where paths are laid out in orderly lines like the neat little sandwiches I've come to crave. Shrubs and bushes and great green linden trees and statues posed along the way. The day is warm and gentle and I am easy in my strolling. Here and there are other strollers, more bicyclists, of course; we all seem at ease.

Along the path I come upon an old woman whose job, self-assigned I imagine, is to shoo the pigeons from the heads of statues of these long-ago kings and queens. In a long dark skirt gathered at her waist, an apron tied around, she works her broom, sweeping and shooing.

Perched on a bench outside the invisible circle the old woman has made with her broom, I breathe deeply to shake loose my imaginings and take in the sweet scents of the gardens—still-blooming roses, pink and lavender stock, bright-headed daisies. No wonder we call certain fragrances intoxicating—all that oxygen to the brain, now I'm a little dizzy.

Here in Denmark I'm in the presence of fairy tales, especially those of Hans Christian Andersen, stories of old crones who are witches who cast spells upon on those whose dreams and desires lie beyond their grasp. *What spell might be cast upon me,* I wonder; *what tests must I go through to find happiness.* Or, as in so many of Andersen's cautionary tales, there may be no happy ending but rather lessons to be learned.

Rosenborg Castle, constructed in the early seventeenth century, rises tall and many towered inside the royal gardens. Continuing as tourist, I pay the small fee and go inside the polished ornate halls where silver fenders stand against fancy fireplaces. I amble through a tile room, a mirror room, rooms where my huaraches scuff intricately designed floors. A royal dining service is displayed on a long table with golden dishes. Next an array of dozens and dozens of jeweled boxes. I imagine royal underwear carefully folded and placed in these glittering boxes.

Silver lions as large as carousel horses guard a throne also made of silver. And all manner of things fashioned of gold—dishes, crowns, button boxes, book covers, letter openers, scissors, glasses, pens, inkwells, eating utensils and service pieces—solid gold, gold-plated, gold filigree, and pearls of gold strung together on golden threads. Necklaces and pins and earrings set with stones so large they look unreal. Opals and pearls and sapphires, a smoky topaz as large as my fist. A necklace, brooch, and ring of diamonds and emeralds, another of pearls, another simply diamonds—except there is nothing simple about this collection.

Among all this wealth, all these treasures, used and worn by those born into it through no effort of their own except that they came through the royal birth canal and into the royal cradle, I reflect on my own birth into a Midwestern working-class family and consider what I label myself, *lucky*.

In AA meetings we say, "I am here by the grace of God." Or, "But for the grace of God, I would be out on the street, still in jail, locked up, crazy. Dead." Grace: a state of well-being derived out of nothing and given through no effort of our own. Given or granted or arrived at against what seems to be the natural evolution of circumstance. Arrived at despite our own worst thinking and bad behavior. Grace cannot be explained or reasoned or created. No tests are given by magical crones who sweep the dirt at the feet of stone statues in a royal garden. We allow it to be God-given because we have no other explanation.

The mall is brightly lit and shop windows flaunt their temptations—dresses and sweaters and skirts, jeans and pants. The weather is getting cooler now and I decide I should get some tights to wear with my skirts.

Along with all the clothes, this ultra chic store where everyone is younger than me offers a tempting array of scarves. Stacks in all colors folded together in a display that reminds me of a Pantone color chart. Reds bleed to oranges that fade to yellow. Greens, greens, greens, and blues, from the palest *it's a boy!* baby blue to the deepest indigo of the waters I crossed to get here. I want them all and I want just one—the perfect one. The one that will complete the look I've been longing for since I noticed it on those lovely Dutch women. A blue that compliments my eyes? Something in pink, a pastel to make my blond even blonder? Not the lightest shade of pink, that pale blush that reminds me of something virginal, which is not a look I can carry off. I need something bolder. I run my fingers along the stack and stop at the scarf shaded a pink that's left its innocence behind and is moving toward something deeper, heading toward dangerous but not in a hurry to get there.

I jockey the scarf from the stack and am pleased to discover that it ends with a couple inches of fringe. I wrap it around my neck, let the ends drape in uneven symmetry over my breasts. The fringe is a little flirty but with clear limits—like me with Marty that night in Room 24 at the Bali Hotel.

Watching myself in the mirror, I wrap the scarf once around my neck, draped and casual. Twice around and it takes on a bit of the cool, together European look I'm aiming for but haven't quite attained. Turning, studying my reflection, I consider that look may be possible. I shake the scarf open to its pink fullness and drape it around my shoulders and it becomes a shawl.

Yes, this scarf. I buy it along with a pair of black tights and ask the pretty young saleswoman to clip the tags. "I want to wear it," I say.

Leaving the glitter of the mall, I emerge into the evening, my pink scarf wrapped just so round my neck, and back onto the streets, narrow and cobbled and lined with aged buildings and streetlamps that cast a golden glow. It's like leaving one world and entering another. I'm different too. My back straighter, my strides longer and more confident. I smile as I picture the old woman in the park—perhaps she did cast a spell upon me.

The Little Mermaid poses on a rock near the harbor where I've come for an afternoon respite and where some grand celebration is taking place. A tall ship sails out to sea accompanied by cannon-fire salutes and escorted by fireboats; plumes of water shoot into the azure summer sky. The Danish America's Cup team is here. Beautiful boats. Gorgeous seafaring men. A brass band plays while an announcer goes on and on. This is the thing about not understanding the language—language becomes simply background noise. I don't pay attention because it would be maddening—listening and not understanding, straining to recognize a word here or there. Instead my mind is an open book turned to a blank sheet and I notice sights, sounds, colors, people and how they look, how they interact. Details of how they dress, sit, sip, spit, and smoke. How they wander through the grass or stay to paths.

All these things I write in my journal. It's what I have always done when I'm alone, traveling or otherwise. Too often in my shared life my journals were closed, my private voice silenced not by request of another but by a lifetime of subtle influences.

I study the mermaid sculpture again and consider the Disney version of the story, which, as an American girl, is the one I was taught; the one about happily giving away your authentic self to find your true love and be complete (is this what Mother meant when she said, "I just want you to be settled and happy"?). In the Hans Christian Andersen story the mermaid bargains with the sea witch, willing to sacrifice her voice and mutilate her body for the chance to have true love and get an immortal soul, not even one of her own but a shared soul that can come only through the love of another.

In Disney's "happy ending" version Ariel and the prince marry and sail off into the sunset. Andersen tells it another way: the prince marries another and the mermaid dies and turns into sea-foam. But Andersen's original has its own version of a happy ending. After three hundred years as an ethereal spirit who brings goodness to the world, the mermaid does receive her very own soul. Some interpret Andersen's version as a cautionary tale, teaching children to be good so they can earn their way to heaven.

Today, sitting beside the sculpture of *The Little Mermaid* on this bustling, celebratory summer day in Copenhagen, I choose my own interpretation—sing with the voice you were given, love the body that is your own, and if there is a heaven, this should be good enough to earn you passage.

Tivoli is flowers by day, lights at night. Tivoli is acrobats, bands—a military band, a big band, a jazz band—ballet dancers, marionettes, and carnival rides and games, all set among casinos, food pavilions, and fancy restaurants. I buy a bag of popcorn and wander amid the nighttime fairyland of forty thousand bulbs.

The lights outline pathways and arch above them. Buildings are sketched in lights and, between the outlines, more lights. I am transported. I do believe in magic. I do.

Lights hang in the many trees like bunches of gorgeous grapes. Generous, full red-orange globes droop from branches. One tree is decorated in incandescent candy canes and another draped with clusters of long, glittering streamers. Each curve of the path takes me to yet another luminescent dreamscape. In one, stained glass glows beside a pool where underwater fountains shimmer in soft pastels. In another, metal-sculpture fireflies flicker above a goldfish pond lit under their wings by twinkling white glitter.

I stand beside a little lake with amethyst lamps planted around like so many irises. These fairy-tale lavender lights bring me to tears.

I don't know why I am crying and I don't know why I am thinking of my mother. I only know at this moment I want her to see this, to experience it. Not with me now—mother and adult daughter—but mother as a little girl long before she could even imagine me, young enough to still believe in magic and in herself, who she is and who she can be. Through my tears I gaze across the pond and almost see her there on the other side of the glowing make-believe flowers. I'm crying for her and for me and for Tom and our lost dreams and what could have been and also for the exquisite beauty of this place on this warm late-summer night.

AUGUST 25, 1990
Copenhagen to Stockholm

Copenhagen to Stockholm is an eight-hour train ride that includes a ferry crossing on another rainy day. Except for London and The Hague, each new location I have traveled to so far has greeted me with rain. I want to make something of it but I don't; I just notice.

Before we left the station in Copenhagen, I bought a copy of *Time* magazine; now I read reports of events in the Middle East. The UN Security Council has condemned Iraq and demands it leave Kuwait; hundreds of thousands of Pakistani, Egyptian, Palestinian, and Filipino guest workers have fled; the Indian government begins air-lifting Indian nationals from the country. On August 20 eighty-two British nationals were taken hostage in Kuwait.

All this happened while I toured palaces and gazed at riches, meandered the bicycle-filled cobbled streets of Copenhagen, ate smorgasbord sandwiches, and wept at the magic of Tivoli.

My cabinmate for the journey is a Danish man about my age, I'm guessing. Small-hipped, bit of a beer belly, but attractive in a healthy kind of way. Our eyes meet and we smile at each other.

"Do you mind if I smoke?" he asks in English, his accent thick.

"Please," I say, "go ahead."

Beyond that we don't speak. He smokes.

I look out the train window and remember Sandy and Bill and their sons somewhere in *the desert*. Outside, instead of the brown of Middle Eastern deserts, I see lush green trees—chestnuts and maples—interspersed with rural fields and farms, quiet ponds and bucolic lakes. A peaceful countryside. The difference between here and there, life and death.

Tom and I quit smoking together on his birthday in June 1983. I never started again. He did after only a few months. I wonder for the hundredth time whether he would have had lung cancer if he hadn't returned to smoking. Foolish *what if* thoughts. The third of Kübler-Ross's stages of grief: *bargaining*. Besides denial, bargaining may be the least serviceable of all the stages. Anger has its place and provides a sense of power. Depression is a given. Acceptance is the ideal that I've found to be the most ephemeral. There's not much solid footing on that rock, at least for me.

The Dane and I ride together. He smokes. I gaze out the window.

AUGUST 25–28, 1990
Stockholm

At Café Gråmunken in Stockholm, another city whose street names I can't pronounce, I drink a cappuccino so delicious it prompts an out-loud *mmm*. Self-conscious, I glance around to see if anyone noticed. The two young women at the next table, blond and fresh-faced, don't look up—if they did notice they don't react. Nor does the thick-shouldered man with his newspaper.

I have come to love these cafés—their small marble-topped tables; wooden chairs, many of them bent-wood and most of them well used; racks of newspapers or shelves of books; lamplight glowing off scuffed hardwood floors or nickel-sized black and white tiles; plate glass windows open to the street, or sometimes windows of small squares framed by dark wood; displays of pastries in clear glass cases; stacks of ceramic cups and saucers and orderly lines of tall, thin glasses; sugar in misshapen lumps in pretty containers or sometimes wrapped in paper imprinted with the café's name. Tiny silver spoons. In these cafés are the ambiance of history and a comforting familiarity. Which is why in each city I visit I find a typical café where I can settle in, sometimes for hours, and write. For me, heaven is a wooden-floored, golden-hued European café.

I *mmm* into my cappuccino again and consider where to head next, though I have just arrived. I won't stay in Stockholm long. Next will be Oslo. It's close and something about Norway interests me. Sweden and Ingmar Bergman, Norway and Henrik Ibsen.

I am drawn to writing plays and screenplays. I'd attempted a few plays in high school and even before, as a young girl, given dialogue to my paper dolls. Along with dreaming myself Brenda Starr, reporter, I fantasized my future self a kind of Lillian Hellman creating my own *Little Foxes*. Me and a typewriter, my cigarettes and scotch.

"Take typing," Mother said. "You'll have something to fall back on." As if what I could look forward to if my marriage didn't work out (unsaid but implied) was a life as someone's secretary. I would have taken typing anyhow; I knew being Brenda Starr, reporter would require that skill. Any kind of authorship would require that.

Tom used to say nothing felt better than "having written," and I still say, "Nothing is scarier than the blank page." Writing is risky. Being a woman alone in the world is risky. At the time of this journey I haven't done much of either. Yet here I am, half a life gone (more for all I know), setting out on a dicey path to I don't know where. Some kind of longing propelling me, a familiar fear nagging at my coattails. Superstitious me, wearing my pink scarf and chasing after magic.

My nearly gone cappuccino beside me, I consider my next direction after a few days in Stockholm, a few days in Oslo. I won't go outside the city in either of these countries. Though I generally love road trips—the first month of my yearlong journey was cruising the West Coast, San Diego to San Francisco to Seattle and back—this time I don't want a car even though I'm intrigued by the countryside. The deep woods of Bergman's films and the fjords of Norway might both be on my itinerary were I traveling with a companion.

"What say we go to Vancouver, babes?" Tom would ask, or Baja, or a fishing camp in some far distant place. "What say we get a camper to go on the truck?" he'd said, and that silver camper atop our Ford truck with dually wheels became *the rig*, good for a few trips down to Mexico and up the coast to British Columbia and finally for one last road trip across the US and Canada on a journey to say goodbye to friends and family.

Alone in countries where I don't know the lay of the land or the language spoken, I find myself staying to the cities—those whose names Daddy brought to life as we sat on the sofa with the big green world atlas spread across our laps—London, Paris, Copenhagen,

Salzburg—places I can immerse myself in historic sites and stories other than my own.

Budapest is writ large in my notebook and I decide this is where I will go after Scandinavia. It's time to stay in one place for a while and something about Budapest calls. Two months on the road and I'm tired of the constant movement, yet have not been able to settle in any place for more than a few days.

I finish my cappuccino, pack up my daypack, and go out into the blue-sky sunshine world of Stockholm. The old town—Gamla stan—is more cobblestoned, winding streets lined by four- and five-story buildings in pastel shades with shops I name *charming*. I find a copy of Lillian Hellman's *Pentimento* at a used bookstore, which is good because I left a half-finished Henry Miller on the train. I pass boutiques, cafés, and restaurants; stop for gorgeous views of bridges and harbors and a few of the fourteen islands that make up the archipelago of Stockholm. I get a much-needed haircut and have lunch at a place on the Hamngatan, then find myself in a lovely square where a politician speaks in English about workers' rights. Tourists, Swedes, and all the rest of us listen. People go from place to place, gathering here, settling there, making community wherever they go.

I circle around, cross over, touch down, looking for a place to land. In reality I could stay in any of these places and join a community, become a part of something.

But not yet. Not yet.

At the Central Station where I go for the train to Oslo, something has happened or is threatening to happen. Stockholm police in full riot gear stand in knots along the walkway, armed with menacing guns, clear masks pulled down over their faces. I am two selves—the reporter taking mental notes of it all and the present self, anxious to the point of fearful. I don't sense immediate danger, but a tension settles deep in my body like a sleeping animal you wouldn't want to waken. Around me others go about the business of buying tickets, shopping the newsstand, shuffling suitcases and backpacks, hardly taking notice. Dragging my wheeled pack along, I fast-walk into the station. Once safely inside and breathing a little easier, I visit the bathrooms where the attendant, an old drunk, tries a few pickup lines. I don't know whether to be offended or complimented, such is my state.

AUGUST 28–29, 1990
Oslo

In Oslo, too early to check in to my hotel, I discover The Broker, where I order a coffee, page through a travel guide, and make notes in my journal. Soft classical music comes from unseen speakers, a few thick-leafed potted plants here and there among the familiar marble-topped counters and bent-wood chairs. I and a few others have our drinks, eat our pastries, sitting quietly apart/together. Rain welcomed me to yet another city, this time a soft mist that grays the sky and veils the view out the window of old stone buildings, watercoloring the sidewalks and shapes of people passing by.

In each new place I follow certain settling-in rituals that mark the transition from one location to another: change money, locate a café, eat a meal, and, of course, find a room at a hotel or pension where I can shower and change. Something about getting the money, café, meal, hotel, and shower all accomplished means I am present where I am.

As I read and make notes—underlining, circling the names of places in the travel guide, opening pages to maps of places both near and distant—the idea of a tour from Greece to Egypt begins to take form. I want to go to Istanbul, too, but I'm hesitant to travel there alone. Same with Morocco; an immediate yes followed by a shy *but not alone.* I want adventure, I want foreign, I want exotic, but I'm discovering I have limits on how much adventure I'm up for solo. What do I consider safe, I ask myself, and when does adventure edge into risk and risk push me back to safe?

Push/pull.

I want to be a traveler like the Swiss adventurer and writer Ella Maillart, who said, "You do not travel if you are afraid of the unknown, you travel for the unknown, that reveals you with yourself." But I don't have that kind of courage. Instead I've gone to places my more recent ancestors knew—where something in my DNA recognizes familiarities. In London, The Hague, Amsterdam, Copenhagen, or Stockholm, until I speak I am my commonality—with my fair skin, blond hair, blue eyes, I can go unseen or, if seen, viewed as "one of us."

A decade earlier in Bali, on assignment for the nonprofit organization where I worked, I'd gone out early to sit on the steps outside my room. I had my coffee, my journal, and was writing as I do every morning. Birdsong filled the banyan trees, and not far down the path was an altar fragrant with flowers and sweet cakes—another gentle, perfect morning. Soon a gaggle of young girls approached. In Bali children of a compound care for each other, the older for the younger, and they stay together as they roam the village. Sweet and shy and lovely, the girls gathered nearby, tended to the flowers, and spoke in quiet whispers to each other. All five or six of them, dark hair, dark eyes, skin a warm brown. Barefoot, they wore little dresses of cotton in colors as soft as the morning.

I smiled at the girls, welcomed them, then went back to my writing. One girl, four or five years old, approached and watched as I wrote. Gradually she came closer and closer still and soon sat beside me, her bare feet slightly dusty, a pink barrette holding back her straight black hair. She didn't look at me or speak but after a few moments shyly reached out and touched my arm with a small tentative finger, giving me a few gentle strokes. Her finger on my skin was fairy-light, a butterfly kiss in what may have been an attempt to discover whether the texture or temperature of my skin was different from hers.

Something of the same happened in Bolivia a few years later. We'd traveled along the Tahuamanu River in the Pando region—the jungled area that borders Brazil—stopping at health posts along the river. At one I'd found a bench in the shade where I could tend to the business of changing film and cleaning lenses. Soon a small group of boys gathered in a circle around me several feet away. Some kneeled on the dirt, some stood back, whispering and observing. In thin mismatched T-shirts and shorts, mostly barefoot, they, too, like the little girls in Bali, were curious. I smiled a welcome but then went back to my work. One young boy approached from the side, coming closer and closer, until near enough to reach out and touch my hair, which he did shyly, as some of the other boys giggled, hands over their mouths, poking one another with bare elbows.

Somewhere I have a photo of that moment. Me on the bench, the circle of young boys; me, pale-skinned, and them, brown; my blond hair bright as some solstice sun among all their dark heads.

In each of these instances I was the odd one, I was different, I was looked at, even stared at—much as I stared in curiosity and fascination at the bright birds and howler monkeys in the rubber trees along the river. We were what each of us had seldom seen. I wasn't unsafe in either situation, and the time in Bali was as sweet and tender a moment as I can remember. The children were curious, that's all, and I understand this. I was once a curious child, too, and part of that is still alive in me. But the idea of standing out, being looked at, considered an object, a curiosity—this is what causes me to reflect while planning my adventures at The Broker this rainy morning in Oslo.

Fear for my own safety may be a part of it—a single woman traveling alone without the shelter of a job, a role, or being part of an organization. As I consider and probe deeper, as writing can cause me to do, I imagine bazaars and marketplaces; labyrinths of passageways; language even more foreign to my ear than Swedish or German; musical tones and rhythms that my body doesn't know; food eaten, prepared, sold packaged or not—all these exotics that would tempt a true traveler—I find myself turning away, and I judge myself for this hesitation.

How does a woman of a certain age—of any age—navigate the world alone? I haven't really been alone since moving out of my family's home after high school; even then I lived with roommates those few years before I first married at the age of twenty. How do I make my way not just on this journey but when I return home? Alone and without an identity. My introduction of myself has been "I'm Judy Reeves and I . . ." followed by my job title or some other identifying fact of my life. Now I am simply Judy Reeves, and I don't know if that's enough.

After checking in at the Anker Hotel, unpacking, and showering, I must shop for a nightgown; I've left mine in the sleeping compartment on the overnight train. Imagine the attendant who discovers that nightgown: Will he tell stories? Daydream lovers? Or simply mumble something about distracted travelers and toss it in the trash bag he carries with him?

I wander streets with their buildings of brick or stone built smack against one another, a wrought iron balcony here, fancy crowning there. I've carried some laundry with me to leave at a nearby laundromat I spotted. I have no idea what the money is here in Norway. I hold out a handful of change and the kind man who operates the machines takes what I have and tells me what might be something like "No, no, don't worry, this is fine, your loads are small." I interpret all this from his smile, his crinkly eyes, his gentle tone. He may recognize me as the kind of woman who would leave her nightgown in the rumpled white sheets of an overnight train.

Farther downhill toward the harbor, I find I can't take the tour to Bygdøy peninsula; it's too misty for a trip to see the Viking ships. On I wander and come upon the grand buildings of the Royal Palace, the Parliament, with spacious grounds and open plazas. At the National Theater I pick up a program for the Ibsen Festival, which will begin the next day. I won't stay for the festival; much as I would love to see *A Doll's House*, which is among the festival's repertory this season, it will be in Norwegian. As a pilgrimage to the playwright, a literary homage of sorts, I take a photo of the enormous Henrik Ibsen statue. My vantage point is far below the bronze sculpture, looking up into the playwright's strange, wing-shaped beard, weathered green.

Strolling Oslo's central area along Karl Johans gate, I arrive at

Dronningparken still abloom with lush rosebushes and find a place to sit under linden trees whose leaves have begun to change colors. The moist air releases the sweet fragrance of the roses, and the idea comes that if I stay long enough, if I am patient, I might be able to see the leaves changing, a time-lapse view of fall approaching on this misty day.

Pack beside me on the bench, glad for my sweater and the tights I bought in Copenhagen, I gaze up into the spreading trees and try to imagine a time-lapse view of myself changing—my habits, my beliefs, the way I peel and eat an orange, make love, wrinkle, and age. Can I see myself as the little girl in the photo on my dresser, all blond curls and excited eyes? Or time-travel forward and see myself semi-settled in a house where I've created a room for my writing and where there's a view of a river or a deck overlooking a backyard with many rose-bushes and an orange tree. Maybe there's a cat.

On the long trek back up the hill to my hotel I find a shop where I buy a new nightgown, a white cotton thing with smocking at the neck. Not sexy but serviceable. It will go into my bag with my other things, and who can say what will be left behind in the next place.

AUGUST 29, 1990
Oslo to Frankfurt

As I leave Norway by train, a low sun lingers in the sky, gilding the pines golden and warming the parade of white-barked birches. Long, green-black inlets of water dotted with an occasional island. Rolling wheat fields and farmhouses, yards abloom with fall flowers. Apples ripen golden and red on trees where wooden ladders lean against dark trunks.

I'm in a plush compartment with dark carpeting and wood-grained walls. We rock along as I daydream, write a letter to my son, make a picnic of a baguette, ham, and cheese. The uniformed young attendant teases me about drinking water.

"This is a German train. We drink beer."

"Not for me, thanks," I say. "I've had enough."

"You can never have enough beer," he tells me. "It is the very sustenance of life."

Oh, if he only knew. Drinking beer as early as high school, vodka in our cokes at slumber parties, learning martinis in attempts to be sophisticated (failing badly), then wine—terrible wine like Thunderbird and Boone's Farm—Bloody Marys in the morning to cure the gin and tonics of the night before, always more beer. Accompanying all that in the seventies with plentiful marijuana. If he only knew.

Out the train window rosy tinges hover above the pines. It seemed the sun had finished for the day, but here are lingering fingers of pink. *Pink lingerings*—I play with words in my journal.

We stop for yet another small Norwegian town. I reconsider going outside the cities to the countryside. To truly experience Norway, one must go out into the magnificent, wild country. Yet I have not. I nudge aside regret and continue gazing out the window.

Tom would have liked Norway. I envision him buying shrimp off the boats in the harbor, talking fishing with the men, eating Norwegian salmon he caught himself. He would have found a man with a boat and paid to be taken out to sea to spend time out of time, line in the water, watch cap pulled down tight, that one eye squinted against the light that flickered on the water. He would have been happy. He would whistle.

Maybe Tom was the one who told me God doesn't count the time on earth a man spends fishing. Probably not; he never believed in God. But he did believe in fishing.

In one of those half-created/half-real stories about Tom and me, we were fishing on a small quiet lake in the untamed mountains of British Colombia. As the sun set the water became still and dark, reflecting a bronze sky lit with shades of violet I didn't know existed. I rowed while, in the story, he trolled his line over the side.

"So this is what they mean about Canadian sunsets," I said.

He squinted at me in that way he had, favoring his good eye. "You're only allotted one of these in a lifetime."

"Oh yeah," I said, "how many have you seen?"

He recast his line into the mirroring water. "This is my third."

The train continues along. Darkness brings only my face when I look out the window and I turn away. I have been reading *Pentimento*, Lillian Hellman writing about love, and I've been crying, realizing the loss of love; knowing love and losing it. Some part of me wants to read these stories, to experience the loss, to cry. This is what good writing can do, touch those tender places that hold the pain, the loneliness, the grief. Sometimes I go to sad movies just so I can cry—I want to use the word *legitimately*. As if crying during a sad movie is legitimate crying whereas sitting alone on a train in tears is not. Still here I am, alone in this compartment on this night train to Frankfurt in this comfortable seat, the movement of the train gentle, the overhead lamp illuminating only the pages of the book, my hands. It's private here; the muffled *clack-clack* of metal wheels on metal track is soothing and sad and melancholy.

I stay overnight in Frankfurt because I can't get a flight to Budapest for another four days, but a train goes to Salzburg tomorrow; convenience determines agenda. As I've traveled along I've torn pages from my travel book of places I've been or places I've decided not to go. In Oslo I left behind pages on Salzburg and Vienna. Never mind, more travel guides are available at the train station. Or I can just get lost and found and lost again. The story of my journey so far. Maybe my life.

In Frankfurt I do get lost trying to find my way to an AA meeting. I ask a woman in the metro station about the Bethel International Baptist Church. She doesn't know the place so she turns me over to a kindly old guy who smells of booze and looks like he might have slept in the station, all grizzled beard and rumpled clothes. She might be thinking, Well, he could use an AA meeting too. He leads me astray and soon turns me over to a woman in an army uniform, who directs me to two separate buses, neither of which is the right bus. I finally take a taxi to the church, where I discover the women's meeting that's listed in the international directory isn't happening; it's scheduled for Saturday night. Oh well. I stay for the meeting that is scheduled even though it's not what I expected, and isn't life like that anyhow. Lost and found.

The first AA meeting I ever attended, at Tom's persuasion, wasn't there when we arrived either.

Tom had been in and out of AA for a few years and knew an alcoholic when he saw one, let alone lived with one. A few weeks into our relationship he introduced me to *Alcoholics Anonymous*, the "big book," and suggested portions I might want to read. He didn't exactly say so, but I know he thought the passages would illustrate certain, um, telltale behaviors and the bulb would light up for me. But it was one particular night in Mexico that caused me to, as they say, "put the cork in the bottle."

I was a daily drinker and had been for many years. In the newspaper business in those days, then radio, TV, and PR, it's what we did—drinking at lunch, happy hour, press parties, and other occasions of "liquid" socializing—and I did it better than most. But I always had a job and went to work every day, so certainly I didn't have a problem, which is the kind of denial that keeps many an alcoholic from getting the treatment she needs for her disease.

When Tom and I met in the fall of 1978 I wasn't so much trying to control my drinking as I was trying to control my blackouts. It was finally on a trip to Mexico, both of us drinking but me drunk to the point that, at our hotel in the middle of a long, wet day and night, Tom said, "I'll take you back across the border, but then you're on your own. I can't stay with a woman who drinks like you do."

They say alcoholics have to hit bottom before they'll quit drinking. Tom saying that to me was my bottom. We both went back across the border and to AA.

On the night of my first meeting in February 1979—the meeting that wasn't there—we eventually found another one in the neighborhood and went in just as it was ending. Another church, another basement, and a group of twenty or so people standing in a circle holding hands and saying the Lord's Prayer. That's not what I expected either. But Tom didn't give up and neither did I; both of us were eight years sober when he died.

The meeting in Frankfurt in the Bethel International Baptist Church basement, with its linoleum floor and metal folding chairs, around a beat-up table is "12 Steps to Happiness." A dozen of us sit around the table—the usual suspects at these English-speaking AA meetings: Americans, Brits, a military guy from Idaho or Wisconsin, an English-speaking Dane or Swede on the road like me. The cigarette smoke is dense, the coffee weak or burned. An American guy unfortunately named "Stick Dick" responds to everyone's share and lectures us and passes out an obscene cartoon about being stuck in a crack (you can imagine) and hands out copies of the "speech" he gave when he got his twenty-seventh anniversary token the previous week.

I don't know how Stick Dick got his name, probably his appearance—twig-thin with a crew cut growing out in uneven brownish fronds. In my mind he appears like one of those tall palms that line Santa Monica Boulevard.

We don't give our last names in AA—that's the anonymous part. Instead we tag each other with descriptors so we all know who we're referencing in our stories and gossip. At the AA clubhouse in Lemon Grove where Tom and I attended most of our meetings everyone knew who we meant when we mentioned Sweatshirt Jerry or Gucci Phil or Wheelchair Chris. Tom was Radio Tom and I was Nice Judy. I didn't like "Nice Judy." The name, I mean. I didn't want to be described that way. It sounded so, well, *nice*, which is not the way I thought of myself, not first thing anyhow. The tag "Crazy Judy" was already taken, and besides, compared to the woman who got that name, I wasn't. Still something other than *nice* would have suited my ego better. Something with a little more character than *nice*. Mysterious Judy or Judy Blue (in reference to my eyes).

How would I be tagged now, I wonder as I traipse these old cities with my single suitcase and my sad eyes. Maybe Journal Judy or California Judy. I'd like to be known as Writer Judy before I'm Old Judy and then Dead Judy. "You remember her," they might say, "Writer Judy." I hope they do anyway. For a while.

An hour later, when I leave the "12 Steps to Happiness" meeting, my two copied pages of Stick Dick's speech remain on the table. A nice person would not have left them.

AUGUST 30, 1990
Frankfurt to Salzburg

I wish American trains were more like European trains. If they were, I would ride the rails more often. At home I'm a road trip kind of woman—top down, music up, cruising the blue highways. After Tom died I sold his four-door maroon Mercedes sedan with the darkened back windows that always reminded me of a mobster car and bought a never-mind-the-stop-sign red Mercedes convertible and took to the road. Riding a train doesn't hold the exhilarating thrill of freedom that a full tank and an open road make for. Instead, traveling by train— closed compartment, plush seats, window blinds open to the passing scenery—is easy: no navigational decisions to make, no gas-gauge-to-miles calculations to consider, no need to pay attention to potential hazards that might be on the road ahead. On the train we'll get where we're going when we get there, usually on time—in Europe, anyhow. So all I need to do is just rumble along with no mind to the outside world except to notice the scenery. Sometimes easy trumps exciting, especially when what's needed is time to get a new perspective.

AUGUST 31–SEPTEMBER 3, 1990
Salzburg

On a cool, gray Saturday I stay late in my slightly gloomy third-floor room at the Pension Goldene Krone near the river in the Linzergasse district in Salzburg. Lying in bed, pillow behind my head, journal on my knees, I consider the thick walls of the pension and how old the building is—built in 1480. Five hundred years have passed since the stones in these walls were placed. I wonder how many travelers have slept in this room before me and what of them remains. Not physically, like the nightgown I left on the train, but an essence, something on a psychic or energy level, an imprint of some sort. I rearrange my pillow, adjust it behind my head, mark the lamp switch with my fingerprints, and wonder what sign of my presence might be left.

If it is possible that something of us stays even after our physical bodies are gone, I want to believe Tom's fingerprints are still on my skin. But if his are, then there are perhaps also the fingerprints of all the husbands and lovers and affairs and one-night stands before him. My mother's when she held me as a baby. My father's when he picked me up and danced me to Benny Goodman's "Blue Moon" on the hardwood floor of our dining room. I wonder if these fingerprints retain their individual shape or whether they merge and muddy; no doubt some sort of sensor detector a millennia in the future will read our skins and see a palimpsest of prints and spin stories of who we were and how we lived.

A memory of my wedding day—the first one. October 27, 1962. A gorgeous sail-blue San Diego day amidst the uncertainty of the Cuban missile crisis. I am twenty years old and stand with my father at the great doors just inside the entrance of the Immaculata at the University of San Diego. As we pause at the far end of the long aisle that leads to where my soon-to-be husband awaits, I wonder if I'm doing the right thing. The traditional wedding march begins, the music rising up to the church's great dome. I take my handsome father's arm and we begin the slow walk toward my future.

This is the place in my remembering when I want to stop and say, "What if . . .?"

What if I hadn't taken that first step? What if I had listened to the intuitive voice, that little bell as Tom called it, that questions decisions and choices. I don't think about what I wouldn't experience—a son, a daughter, grandchildren, friends—instead, on that golden Saturday when I paused just as the music began, what if my father had turned and whispered a question in my ear or told me I could change my mind. "What if . . .?"

It may be a worthless use of time, this imagining. What can come of it except discontent? Because who would create a *what if* life in which she becomes an alcoholic, marries and divorces twice, and her beloved third husband dies a terrible death; a life in which she behaves selfishly, even heartlessly, at times?

No, the *what if* life of my imagination would be more like those made-up past lives fortune tellers give you for a quick ten bucks and a read of your open palm. In those tellings we were always someone famous or beautiful or both. We were historic figures—never just the wife of the shoemaker with seven children to care for or the shoemaker himself.

Still, even now, all these years after that wedding day, it might be interesting to play *what if . . .?* I can take the road not taken and on that mental journey learn things about myself I can like, even love, and possibly discover something important that matters to me and bring it into my life to carry with me along a road I have yet to choose.

Though the weather is still gloomy, I go out for exploration and reconnaissance—the public telephone, the American Express office, the post office, all necessary places I search out in each city as I settle in for a few days or a week. My route takes me across the Staatsbrücke, one of ten bridges that cross the Salzach into the old city to find Humboldtstubn, a café just down the street from the AA meeting that's listed for that evening at Kirche Saint Blasius.

Shoulder-to-shoulder buildings line the foot-worn streets, each fancied up with painted wall decorations and baroque wrought iron fixtures that display the names of shops and restaurants. Some still bear names of the guilds that used to occupy them—blacksmith, woodworker, printer. Strolling along Getreidegasse with fellow tourists, I come upon another ubiquitous band of Andean musicians. Hearing the lovely song of their flutes and drums and rattles echo through the narrow streets, I recall when I first heard this music years ago in Bolivia during a stop-over in La Paz before heading out to Pando in what seems another lifetime. Nostalgia for me is made up of loneliness and longing.

I toss a few schillings into the musicians' open guitar case and look up *nostalgia* in the pocket dictionary I carry in my daypack. The word is from the Greek *nóstos*, "return home," and *algis*, "pain," and comes to mean "acute homesickness." *Homesick* is not the word for what I feel. *Lonely* fits better. Aching for someone who knows me. Is that home for me, a place someone cares about me?

My sister has a devout and absolute belief that God knows her and cares about her personally, individually. What a comfort that must be. Why can't I believe that too?

In AA we say, "God as I understand him." Noah, Tom's AA sponsor, once told me, "We can never understand God. If we could, we'd be gods ourselves."

"Let the group be your higher power," they tell us nonbelievers. "Borrow my higher power until you find one of your own." A temporary fix and for some just what they need until they do find their own. But others of us remain seekers, traveling the lonely road to a place we don't know and may not even recognize.

Strolling the paths of the Mirabell Gardens, I come upon gargoyled sentinels guarding the way. Strangely misshapen and odd-looking statues darkened with age and moss, they're about waist-high to me. A stone growth neck to shoulder lumps one, a smirking grin on another is marred by missing teeth, and look at the nose on that one! They could be characters from fairy tales. Whatever they are, I must take some photos.

When I left San Diego I was given several gifts from friends wishing me bon voyage: a pair of earrings decorated with green and blue enamel in the shape of the continents, several blank journals and many pens, a miniature copy of the first sixty-four pages of *Alcoholics Anonymous* where the heart of the program is related, and a tiny doll-companion small enough to fit in my palm. She has strands of bright yellow yarn-hair to her shoulders and wears pink trousers and tiny white painted-on shoes. I named her *Travel Girl*, and carry her with me in my daypack and pose her in various places along my way, taking photos to send home. She sat upon the pull-down tray on my flight to London, posed surreptitiously among the cheeses in Harrod's, and dangled her feet into the sink in the pretty bathroom at the Bali Hotel in The Hague. Now I set her atop the head of one of the goofy-looking trolls, her yellow hair bright against its mossy green-brown stone.

How I must appear to the two matronly women who come along the path dressed in sturdy shoes and thick hose. Me, posing Travel Girl, stepping back, taking a photo, changing her position, and taking another. To continue on their way the women have to cross between Travel Girl atop her statue and me and my camera. I nod and smile. They cluck their tongues and look at me warily. As they continue out of earshot they whisper something that might be "Americans!" Or maybe to them I'm just some eccentric woman taking a photo of a kid's toy atop the head of a troll.

When my first husband and I were in the process of separating all those years ago, he said to me, "I never know when I come home if I'm going to find you climbing a tree or cooking dinner." After a moment of thoughtfulness he continued, "That's what first attracted me to you—what I loved about you. I didn't know what to expect. And then I tried to change you."

Rosalio, a high-school boyfriend, once said to me as we were goofing around at some forgotten event, "You're the funniest girl I know." I'm not sure what I want to say about that except that somewhere along the way, following my mother's admonishment to "just settle down" with her hand settled firmly on my ten-year-old head and the remark from that boy in high school—along with my first husband's comments and other such instances through another couple of decades—I did "just settle down." Over years of such comments and observations from others who held influence over me, it's possible I became, as Clarissa Pinkola Estés suggests, "over-domesticated," until finally I was "Nice Judy."

Now I cause clucking tongues and sibilant whispers among strangers on a shaded path in Salzburg's famous Mirabell Gardens, posing a tiny doll on the mossy head of a garden gnome. Here I am on a solitary journey, searching, not to return to that little girl vibrating with excitement under her mother's hand, or the high school clown, or any other past incarnations, but something unnamed and elusive— who I am now.

Julia, a young American expat attending acting school in Switzerland, has a summer job with a traveling circus. Not a circus in the trained elephants and young men on a flying trapeze manner, she tells me, but a "sensory circus."

"A sensory circus?" I ask.

She explains over coffee at Café Rupertinum in the old town after the AA meeting where we met. Her emerald eyes gleam bright with excitement. "One of the guys who developed it wants to tell the world about the importance of being aware of our senses and using them to achieve balance in our lives," she says.

That's me—born under the sign of Libra, so of course I am always trying to find balance in my life and achieve the near-impossible feat of sustaining it. Julia's description of the sensory circus intrigues me. And I like her. Another woman, though years younger, with whom I'm comfortable and with whom I can talk about my wanderings, my search for what I can't explain. After all, she ran away with a circus. I decide to go to the circus the next day.

The weather clears overnight, bringing a bright, sun-saturated morning. After breakfast I make the easy walk to the park where the circus is encamped. It isn't hard to find: before I even get inside the park I spot what looks like several—five or six—circus wagons posing in the shade of great spreading sycamores. Exploring, I find Julia at work in the café wagon with its bright colors and benches padded with woven fabric. The light inside is jeweled and the aroma is bakery. Julia treats me to tea and strudel. We settle on a many-cushioned daybed. Julia, in a deep green sweater that makes her eyes even more emerald, her lips bright in vivid red lipstick, smiles as she tells how she became involved in this entertainment/experiment.

"I knew his partner in theater school," she says, speaking of the men who dreamed the project. "The two of them teamed up to create this." She sweeps her arm in a generous arc that includes the café wagon and what lays beyond—an invitation to something magical, from the way her eyes dance as she talks about it. It being the circus wagons, the people, and the exhibits that have been traveling around Europe all summer and are in Salzburg for a couple of weeks.

"It's a manifestation of their dreams," she says. "One dreaming of how the world could change if we were aware of our senses and used them to achieve balance in our lives, and the other with the idea of creating a circus."

How is it done, manifesting dreams? After all those school years being scolded for daydreaming, all the admonishments to calm down when my enthusiasm was too much, can I still create something out of my dreams? *What are my dreams?* I wonder, the sweet taste of strudel filling my mouth.

"Let's go," Julia says as she bounds from the daybed and removes our empty cups and licked-clean plates from the small table. And we're off.

Julia's café wagon is one of several where a few dozen other volunteers live and work and tour with the circus. Farther out curving gravel paths lead through tall grass to an array of open-sided tents grouped in a semicircle.

"Each exhibit focuses on a different sense," Julia explains as we walk along. She says hello to the few others we pass on our way. Young travelers and a family or two with excited children. Inside I'm an excited child myself, that giddy bubbling in my chest, a grin spread across my face. I'm loving the anticipation.

Dozens of black ceramic pitchers line tables around the perimeter of the first tent we enter. I lose count at twenty-seven, each container filled with a different element.

"Touch," Julia says. And I do. Texture after texture inside each pitcher—grains of sand; loamy earth (the rich smell that always reminds me of my young Midwest years); cool, clear water; corn husks; long strands of something silky. I reach in again and again, open and close my hand, aware of my palms, my knuckles, my fingers and nails against rough, smooth, silky, hard, round, sticky, liquid, cool, warm, dry, soft. I circle the display and close my eyes at each container to better experience the sense of touch.

For weeks after Tom died I would linger in our closet, open-palmed, fingers stroking the rough texture of his favorite brown tweed jacket, the smooth cotton of that red shirt with the pearl snap buttons I washed so many times that it had the comforting softness of old bedsheets. And those jeans, still unwashed from the last time he wore them; the jeans I brought home from the hospital. The boots he wore in the orchard. His glasses. His wedding ring, which I put on my finger and still sometimes wear.

We leave the touch exhibit and I am aware of my body, the ground solid beneath my feet, the warm air on my skin, the weight of my pack on my shoulder. Julia leads me to the sound exhibit in an adjacent open tent. Here an enormous brass gong three-quarters of my height hangs like a great dull sun from a sturdy wooden frame. As I stand behind the gong, Julia in front, she taps it with a small mallet and the sound rolls over me, low and deep. I understand for the first time *sound waves*. Sound comes like the motion of the sea, wave after unending wave, until it fades and I no longer sense it bodily but know it continues. Were our old dog Boozer beside me his Labrador ears would still hear it—and so it goes on into the universe, wave upon wave upon wave, ad infinitum.

The sound waves of the gong resonate in my belly, but the tone of the prayer bowl where we go next resonates higher. Julia circles the brass bowl with a wand, and with eyes closed my chest opens, and I know the sound there. I breathe into the ringing. Julia takes my hands and brings them close to the prayer bowl. Vibrations resonate against my palms. I am holding sound.

The vibrations stay with me as we leave the sound experience, and for just that long it's as though touch and sound have joined together in my body, somehow spread into or onto one another and created a more complex sensory mosaic, the way watercolors and rainbows bleed colors one to the other.

In the center of the next exhibit stands a human-size kaleido-scope—three full-length standing mirrors pushed together to form a triangle. Julia slides aside an opening and I step inside and for twelve minutes—she timed me—I am with versions of myself. Me in a circle with me reflecting me. I see myself—blond, blue-eyed, my turquoise T-shirt, dark skirt; I am wearing the enameled earrings with the shape of the continents embossed upon them. I see me looking to me for direction, a question on my face. I smile at me. I am friendly. I touch fingertips to fingertips, toe to toe in those old, worn huaraches. I hold hands with myself, touch arms, me times six, twelve, eighteen, and beyond. I am all the Judys that might ever be. For twelve minutes or no time I am infinite, multitudes, endless.

Outside the mirrors I am singular once more and glad for Julia beside me. She doesn't ask, "How was it?" She's been escorting visitors into the world of sensation all summer and recognizes my inability to find words beyond "Wow!" to describe my experience. It's too soon to use language; I want to stay with feeling.

We follow the path to the next station—this one outside in an open area. Three tall, thick poles have been set up to form a triangle, a sort of tepee structure, only higher and more narrow. From the center, wrapped several times by rope as big around as my wrist, hangs a smooth greenish-gray boulder. "Six hundred pounds," Julia tells me, nodding toward the stone. In the circle beneath the hanging rock is a human-size indentation in the earth rather like the wide groove formed by children's feet beneath a playground swing and lined with fine gray pea gravel.

"Lie down on your back," she says, "face toward the rock."

Leaving my pack beside me on the grass, I slide beneath the massive thing; though I'm aware of the gravel, it's fairly smooth and not uncomfortable. The rock hangs a scant few feet above my belly. Above me endless sky.

Julia instructs me to close my eyes. And for some reason—trust beyond reason—I do.

With a small tug, Julia puts the boulder in motion. It swings above me, slow-motion, back and forth along the length of my prone body. The sun is bright and I welcome the shadow of the stone across my closed eyes. The shadow regulates my breath and I find I am breathing with its rhythm. After a few minutes of this calm breathing—shadow/no shadow, just pink behind my eyelids—the motion of the rock changes. Without opening my eyes, my body notes the difference. Instead of the smooth back-and-forth sweeping, the movement is now more circular. My breathing changes from calm to ragged and I remember or realize I am lying on my back on the ground while above me a six-hundred-pound rock circles. A kind of panic rises inside my body: my heart itself is stone; my stomach is a plunging elevator. Breathe. Breathe, I tell myself. My single, fragile self. I am not multitudes. I am only this—a small body in a hole on the ground beneath a swinging boulder. I am only flesh and bones and a barely beating heart.

I open my eyes and see Julia above me, silhouetted by the bright sun. She steadies the rope with her two hands, gradually slowing the swinging of the rock until it stills. I roll out of the cleft under the rock and stand, dizzy and blinking in the light. I hold her arm and take a few deep, steadying breaths, nose lifted like an animal.

The outline of branches against azure sky—I identify a beech tree; feet solid on the grass, Terra firma, I think, grounding myself with knowledge.

"There's more," Julia says after a moment. "Are you ready?" And after a moment I say I am.

We enter another tent. Here sight experiments are set up—light and shadow, black and white merging on a screen to become silver. I try to return to my willing, curious self, open and interested, and part of me does, but the cool breath caused by the slow passage of the stone just above me lingers on my body.

Outside again, we follow a path that leads to a giant wooden wheel positioned a few inches off the ground and tipped to one side. It reminds me of a playground merry-go-round.

"The object is to find balance," Julia says.

We climb onto the structure, stand across from each other, wide-legged and smiling, and almost immediately do hit a balance, the wheel turning freely.

"Too bad it's not that easy in real life," I say.

"This *is* real life." She smiles, eyes shaded against the sun.

We find a place to sit on rough-hewn logs around a campfire encircled by sturdy rocks. Here I'm invited to gather corn, salt, and water from a supply station a few feet away, then grind the corn on the flat stones also provided, and mix in the salt and water. An herb garden grows nearby so flavors can be added—basil, rosemary, thyme, others I don't know. The bread mixture is cooked on another flat stone on the fire. The aroma is delicious: cedar fire, baking dough, and beneath those an undercurrent of the earthy scent of summer grass. Julia brings cold apple juice from the café. We sit side by side on the log and sip. I can't say when a cool drink has ever so aroused my mouth.

All around us light and color and scents and the motion of leaves; of fire dance; of smoke rising and making ever-changing shapes; the taste of sweet, sharp apple juice; a far-off drum from another exhibit; the murmur of children and their parents along the way; the log I sit upon; my sun-touched skin. Lovely green-eyed Julia smiling at me.

"The purpose of this place—the whole experiment," Julia says, "is action and reaction. The effect of one thing upon another and from two or more things something new is created."

Two or more things. I drink my apple juice, consider: Tom's death, this solo journey—a new me is being created. One of those Judys in the mirrors or the recognition of my fragile animal self under the rock; the wandering, lost-and-found single woman with no place to go and no one to see. For me, for now, this search is about going beyond the familiar into the unfamiliar, not the same known and unknown as Ella Maillart's brave travelers, but a journey into the self or selves, known or unknown, the physical as well as the mind; searching, seeking, exploring.

Tomorrow I go to Budapest.

SEPTEMBER 3, 1990
Salzburg to Budapest

I have always wanted to ride the Orient Express. Me the romantic. All the stories, those noir films. Mystery. Intrigue. Romance. Now I'm aboard the Orient Express, Salzburg to Budapest. I've never been to Budapest, but like the Orient Express, the mere name of the place is seductive.

The train turns out to be just a train, of course. Not a long, romantic journey of fine dining with candles, linen tablecloths, embossed china, and weighty silver. Not a roomette with polished trim, a comfy bed, a porter to turn down clean, crisp sheets and leave a foil-wrapped Austrian chocolate on the soft pillow. Instead I will ride six hours in a second-class seat next to a person I don't remember talking to.

Only occasionally do I glance out a smoke-stained window into a repetition of backyards and train-side gardens. I write in my journal some but mostly read the new travel book I bought—*Let's Go Europe*.

"It's important to have Western money, especially in Yugoslavia," I read. "The train from Budapest to Belgrade to Split is best. . . . Eurail is not valid in Yugoslavia. . . . A ferry goes from Dubrovnik or Split to Corfu. . . . Yugoslavia is as amenable to travelers as Italy or Greece. . . . Budapest is a wondrous, sensuous place."

My trip on the Orient Express is an altogether forgettable train ride until, halfway into our journey, we approach the Austria/Hungary border. Guards, stoic men in green uniforms who carry large, complicated, and scary-looking guns, pass through the slowing cars.

Outside, signs are written in a language I can't decipher. Of course, I couldn't read Austrian or Swedish or Norwegian or German or Dutch or Danish either, but at least in those languages all the letters are familiar. Here, outside my train window, is a different alphabet. I recognize some of the letters but their construction baffles me—I have no idea how to begin to pronounce these words.

For the first time in my travels I am truly anxious. Underlying most every day of my travels is a kind of light anxiety. My journals carry evidence of that. But here on this train with these men who don't smile, who carry no welcome on their faces or in their demeanor, I experience fear. Because of the guns. Because of the strange-looking alphabet. Because I can't decipher what I'm supposed to do.

All my life I have been able to model my behavior from the clues I get from watching others: this is the correct fork to use; this is how we serve ourselves at a buffet; this is how girls sit, walk, dress; this is how women smoke. (*Never while walking down the street*, my mother told me.)

I watch people in the seats in front of me. I hand over my passport as I've seen them hand over theirs. A tall guard with a pale face and visible pores stands wide-legged beside me and pages open my passport. He looks at my picture, looks at me, then both again. I don't smile. Or maybe a small smile. *Tremulous* is the word that comes.

Apparently my imitation of others satisfies the guard. He gives me back my passport along with some official-looking forms that I can't read but know from my experience at other border crossings must be completed before we go through customs at the station where we disembark. I return my passport and the papers to my pack, breathe in a sigh and with it, a kind of desperate hope for a patient and helpful person on arrival. The Orient Express rolls on and we begin the second three hours of our journey into Budapest.

SEPTEMBER 4–12, 1990
Budapest

Keleti, the international train station in Budapest, is another grand, many-columned, high-ceilinged, cavernous place filled with the noise of travelers going/coming/waiting. My sighed breath of hope must have been interpreted as a prayer by some benevolent traveler's angel because my passage through customs is relatively smooth. After all the rubber-stamping and nodding, I go to the counter where travelers can ask assistance in making hotel reservations and find out about various sites and local transportation.

I have arrived in Budapest as I have in every other stopping place without a reservation. I don't know where I'll sleep tonight, but I do know I want to rest for a while. I want an apartment, not just a room in a hotel or pension. Mornings I want to sit in my nightgown with my fresh-brewed coffee and write. I want the ease of preparing my own meals and to eat when I want, not have to dress and be at the hotel table between six-thirty and eight for a breakfast of bread and jam, watery juice, and watered-down coffee.

The man at the counter in his white shirt and tie speaks thickly accented English. I tell him what I want. "An apartment," I say. "Or rooms. With a bath. A kitchen."

"How long?" he asks.

"A week, maybe two." I shrug.

"How much?" He's looking at some stapled-together papers with listings impossible to read upside down even if I could decipher the language.

I calculate—American dollar to Hungarian forint—and come up with a number.

The agent is on the phone speaking rapidly in a language I haven't heard—at least not in the kind of long sentences he's using. But I do recognize the word *simpatico*. Of all the strange-sounding words of Hungarian as it is spoken with all the noise echoing around me, I recognize that one word, and for the first time since the afternoon at the sensory circus in Salzburg with Julia, I feel like I am seen.

By nature I'm a friendly person—gregarious, extroverted, and easy to make friends with. But on this journey I am mostly solitary, a loner. I don't invite conversation, don't ask to join others at a table or comment at museum exhibits or chat with seatmates on a train. Julia was an exception. Sandy and Bill in the Netherlands, Marty in The Hague. Mostly I read. I write in my journal. Write postcards or letters. I am not used to myself this way, but for reasons I don't understand I am introverted, closed, solitary. Often I am lonely, yet I'm unwilling to step into a persona who interacts with people.

I leave Keleti station with an address in one hand and enough forints in the other to take a taxi across the Danube—from Pest to Buda, the city separated by the river into two sections—where I have secured an apartment owned by a couple who I hope will find me *simpatico*.

Tuesday past noon and still I am lounging in bed reading *On the Road* and sticky with guilt. That old naggy voice of conscience, remnants of my Midwest upbringing, is judging me, calling me lazy, telling me I'm sloughing off. But still I don't get up, don't change out of my nightgown, don't stop sloughing. The Road—both Kerouac's and my own—is moving too fast for me.

The bed is a corner nook in the main room of an apartment in Buda's twelfth district, which I've taken for ten days. All thanks to the kind man at Keleti station who wrote the address on a slip of paper, which I then gave to a taxi driver, who drove me here in the violet Budapest twilight. A semitransparent beige curtain separates my nook from the rest of the room. The walls behind and beside me—the corner of the alcove—are hung with patterned rugs that make the enclosure even more cozy. One large pillow, a smaller pillow, and a white duvet comfort me. A bedside table draped with a green-and-gold scarf provides the nightstand where coffee I made in my own kitchen grows cold as the afternoon wears on.

I have found a resting place here in the wooded hills of Buda. Outside my carpet-walled retreat, the windowed end of the room faces the city across the river; my view filtered through filigreed curtains yellowed with history and, probably, years of cigarette smoke. Outside on the terrace—ah, a terrace—is a rattan table with two chairs where I can take my breakfast at whatever time I choose to serve myself.

I have a kitchen; I have a bath with a tub and an instant on-demand hot water heater. Mrs. József Cseka, who greeted me last evening as I arrived, gave me a brief tour of the place and told me in Hungarian spiced with a little English where I might find a market for supplies just down the hill. Meantime: "Here's tea and coffee," she showed me more than told me. And "*Jó éjszakát*," slightly bowing as she bid me good evening and handed me the keys. Simpatico.

What I especially love about this room of my own, besides my secreted bed and my bathtub with its on-demand hot water, is the fifties wrought iron record rack next to the daybed and beneath the lace-clad windows. No records, no record player, but that record rack with its close-together slots where I imagine LPs by Perry Como or Dean Martin or Jo Stafford or some big-band Benny Goodman my father loves might await their turn on the hi-fi. Or a Hungarian rhapsody that Mr. And Mrs. Cseka might have danced to on some long-ago evening years past.

Gesztenyés (will I ever be able to pronounce the Hungarian words?) Street takes me gently down the hill, the passing buses filled with schoolchildren. Then a stroll along the Danube on a wide pedestrian promenade called Széchenyi rakpart—another name I play with in my mind—before it changes to Belgrade, which I can say.

The weather is warm, the sun glazing the still-green leaves on maple and black locust trees. I stroll then find a place to sit along the parkway and watch people. A woman passes who swings her arm with each step and I am reminded of my oldest sister. I see her walking to high school one morning, gray skirt, green sweater, arm swinging. Did I know she was pregnant then? Did she? Pregnant and soon to be married, leave school, and live in the housing provided for navy families—a seventeen-year-old girl with a baby and an empty apartment and a man who was not good to her. Now neither of us is young anymore and she still wants the same thing: a man to love her and take care of her and sleep with her; a man to make everything alright. Take it from me, sister, it doesn't always work out that way.

Without plans or direction, I wander into an exhibit at the National Museum, which displays a bone from the hand of Saint Stephen I, Hungary's first king. Press a button and the bone is illuminated for three minutes. I gaze for three minutes at the bone of a king from 150 years ago, contemplating death and what is preserved. Tom—ashes to ashes, sown on a hillside and witnessed by a sightless grove of avocado trees.

All along Váci Utca Romanians line both sides of the broad avenue holding handmade goods for sale. Block after block of men and head-scarved women displaying embroidered tablecloths and napkins, lacy and brightly hued, along with blouses, skirts, and shawls. The handiwork is beautifully intricate. I don't stop for a closer look and I don't buy anything. So many things I gave away, sold, or just tossed out when I left. The first releasing when I moved from Jamul, the house Tom built—that strange, oddly shaped house on a hill. After he died it was simply too large, too far out in the country, too much for me to care for. And anyway I know this: I'm not a country girl. I moved with Tom to the country because he loved open spaces and possibilities and I loved him, but to be out there alone? Who's going to take care of all of this? I asked the hillsides, the orchard, the house with all its memories.

I love the smell of bookstores and breathe deep as I enter the international bookstore on Váci. New books have the scent of fresh paper—virgin except for the impressions of the press—and a chemical odor of ink imprinted onto paper. A used bookstore has its own scents—dust and must that create an itchy tickle in my throat and can make me sneeze. Walking into a bookstore provokes an excited urge deep in my body, an almost sexual excitement coupled with a kid-at-a-carnival giddiness in my chest. So many books. So many stories.

This was Tom going into a Home Depot or handyman store. Tools. Building things. Possibilities. And much like Tom, who couldn't pass a yard sale that displayed tools for a bargain price, I can't pass a used bookstore without going in. Likely I will lose myself for an hour, often more. Likely I will take home more than I'll ever read, but there's always hope. I live immersed in possibility.

On this midweek afternoon in early September the air is still warm but not heavy, and the sun sends honeyed hues into the store through dusty plate glass windows. The international bookstore's shelves hold a generous selection of titles in English, a welcome sight to a single-language-speaker such as myself. Books left behind by other travelers and students: romances, mysteries, thrillers, popular fiction, classics.

How long since I've read *The Great Gatsby*? Years. And there's Faulkner's *As I Lay Dying*, which I can't remember if I've read or not. I am choosing books, holding many options in my hands, forgetting I'm on foot with only my small daypack already heavy with belongings. I'm not home where I can just add another bookshelf or add to the stack of unread books beside my chair in the corner by the window. Among all those books I don't recall there's no chair with a stack of books; I don't have a home.

I wander dusty aisles with well-worn floors amid the aroma of used books, page through yellowed paper once touched by another's hands, maybe held under a bedside lamp.

This is part of the pleasure of buying used books. The idea that you are not alone on this journey; someone has gone before and the book holds the memory of them, while you, in your own midnight bed under the glow of your own lamp, can fit your fingers exactly in the place others' fingers have been. Someone else who couldn't remember the last time she read *The Great Gatsby*; she, too, turned the pages, just one more chapter, one more page, before she placed the book on her bedside table, turned out the lamp, and turned to sleep, images of Jay and Daisy and gala parties and longing filling her dreams.

Matthias Church on Castle Hill offers refuge, as have other churches, when the tourist crowds, the sounds and smells of the city—the wailing European police sirens, the bus exhaust, all those moto engines, not the deep and body-vibrating growl of a Harley but the higher-pitch whine of scooters and motorbikes that hit a different place in the brain—become too much. Sometimes with all that input I get dizzy, nauseous, headachy, and need to sit. Quiet. Still. Away from the sun. I need shadows.

This is how great churches save me. The whispered presence of centuries of prayers offered, candles lit, a place of human suffering and hope and sometimes celebration, and for weary travelers like me, a place of peace and solace.

Here in Matthias Church—a grand Gothic church with a gold-tiled roof—I find a pew where I can sit alone in the middle of the day and forget all that is outside, escape from the cacophony. Here, the tiled floor is intricate with colorful designs that reveal more of an Eastern influence than other churches in which I sought refuge in London, Cologne, and Salzburg. During the Turkish occupation of Budapest, the church was converted into a mosque. Now it has once more found its Catholic roots and mass is held regularly. The stained glass windows tell their Bible stories. I close my eyes long enough to let darkness cover my lids, erasing the light. Then, after a time, I open them to the surprise of sun shining through the glass—all those jewel tones, all that color.

Here, under the church's high ceilings and in shadowy corners, I can simply be present. I buy a candle, rove among the small chapels along the perimeter of the nave until I come to a saint whose blessing I need that day. I light my candle from the mother candle and say my prayers—always a prayer for peace and a wish to be with Amy and Chris, and Camille and other friends, and always a prayer for Tom who wouldn't care if I prayed for him or not. Well, he would *say* he didn't care, but I know that tender heart. And he would know my whisper.

I do all this—the candle, the prayers—even though I don't believe in the intercession of saints. I don't believe in the God that is represented by these great cathedrals. I am a make-believer. I believe in lighting candles and saying prayers though they may go no further than my whispered words held forever in this holy place. Because of all the candles lit, all the centuries of fire and prayers offered, because others do believe, this is a holy place. So here on this early September afternoon, the sun shining and the leaves not yet turned, I come to rest and to call forth my own holy self.

I wake up still tasting the dream of a dark, thin man. He was strong, persistent, not cruel but determined in his kisses. I don't remember that we actually had sex, but I can still feel his kisses and his lean body against me.

It rained last night and the morning came slate-colored and cool. I'm reluctant to leave my hideaway bed in the carpeted corner of my room. Remnants of the dream stay with me as I draw my bath. The tub is narrow but long enough to accommodate my length. The narrowness gives me comfort. A snug fit. Warm water reassures my body. I notice that I have lost weight in my hips, my stomach, my thighs. My legs are taut from the miles of daily walking. The water cools but still I stay in the wet cocoon, lingering with dream images for that much longer.

Breakfast is bread and honey and ripe peaches slightly bruised from their trip home in my pack. I read my morning meditation book about giving love and love will be returned. Words about growing into wholeness. I'm reading Liv Ullmann's *Changing*. She also writes about giving love and being whole. I need these words of encouragement from others; they comfort me and remind me that though I may believe I am alone in this, I am not unique. I am merely human.

I dress and ride the bus across the river, thread my way through the crowds on Váci Utca and take the metro to Opera station where I walk a block under the broad-leafed maples that line Andrássy Avenue. At the train reservation office I write my request on Smurf notepaper (where did that come from?) then fill out the form. Since Yugoslavia doesn't honor my Eurail Pass, I count out the forints for my ticket. A few more days in Budapest, then on to the next cities—Split, Dubrovnik. Always on to the next.

On my return trip to Váci, where I'll take my notebook to Café Gerbeaud, a handsome young man boards the metro at the stop after mine. Broad-shouldered and blond, he is blessed with lips that suggest all manner of erotic possibilities. He glances at me and I consider offering him money to come home with me and then, refreshing my thoughts with surreptitious glances, spend the rest of the short journey fantasizing him in my bed hidden behind the draped curtains, his sweet, strong body over me.

I don't know what my fantasies were when I left home those few months ago, packing a year's supply of condoms (what did I imagine a year's supply would be?) and a small, finger-sized vibrator. But with the exception of that celibate night with Marty in Room 24 at the Bali Hotel in The Hague, I haven't even approached the idea of sleeping with anyone except through these imaginings that come via surreptitious glances at handsome men on the metro or dreams that arrive unbidden.

NOVEMBER 1986
Toronto

One afternoon on that last trip Tom and I made together, we were in a friend's apartment on King Street. I don't remember where his friend Dave had gone, but Tom and I were alone. The two of us on a daybed. I remember a yellow quilt, the only bright thing in the otherwise dim room. Both of us dressed warm against the November chill. Jeans, sweaters, heavy socks. Tom's clothes loose on his body. Mine too. Tom wasn't the only one losing weight. Living with someone who's dying can cause that.

Side by side in the lamplight touching along points of our bodies, holding hands—those long-fingered hands of his. He could do so much with those hands—fix almost anything; plant trees; hoe a garden; hold a pen, a cigarette; type elegant sentences on a page; hold my face; touch my thigh, my breast.

"Why don't you want to make love with me anymore?" he asked. That deep, resonant voice.

Our fingers intertwined. His body so thin.

"I'm afraid I'll hurt you," I said, and I was. Afraid the weight of my body would crush him, that my arms holding him against me would break his fragile bones.

"Please," he said.

I turned to him, put my leg over his, then posed astride him, holding my weight on my knees—one leg on either side—and opened his sweater, unbuttoned his shirt. His chest pale. Bones prominent. A spare line of dark hair. Beneath that thin layer of skin and under those fragile bones, the place on his chest where the cancer started.

A mass, they called it when they saw it on the X-rays.

"See, right there," he'd said that June day just four months before when he told me, pointing to the place.

Now I touched him there with my fingertips. "I'm sorry," I said.

He pulled my sweater up. I helped him take it off. My shirt under that, then my bra. I leaned in to him. Skin touching skin, warm.

I dared lower my weight onto him, to lean close, my face, wet with tears against his neck and kissed him there. Where our chests pressed together his heart beat against mine, a strong beat. The heartbeat of a man alive. A man wanting me.

We kissed. How long had it been since we'd kissed like that? Kissing like lovers.

And soon, belts loosened, zippers undone. One leg struggling out of jeans, never mind the other. Never mind the rest of our clothes. Just the wanting. Lovers wanting. Blindly finding each other. No thought of pain or crushing or fragility. No thoughts, just bodies. For just that long.

And then the careful undoing, careful sliding off. Side by side but touching all along our bodies, his arm embracing me.

I gathered the yellow quilt around us, pulled it close around his shoulders and leaned my head on his chest. His heart beat against my cheek, slower and slower still, but still strong.

∽

An American Express office is like a church on those days I receive a package from home. I say *home* because that's what we call the place we're from, the place that, if we're away, we intend to return to. But I don't really know what I mean when I say *home*. I don't know exactly what I mean when I say *church* either, but the days I go to an American Express office and there is a package for me, it's as though I have been welcomed, blessed, and forgiven.

This morning I ride down the hill on the bus and cross the river to Pest to find the local American Express office. I ask the young woman at the counter if there's a package for me, then wait in the muffled sunlight that comes through the window while she goes into a room I can't see. I stand waiting in the huaraches I have been wearing and wearing out, an aqua T-shirt and black cotton skirt, pack slung over one shoulder—I stand in my hope and anticipation.

"Sorry," she says, businesslike. "Nothing for you."

Disappointed, I say my name again.

"Sorry," she says. Her voice carries sympathy; she really is sorry.

"How long for a package from the US?" I ask.

"About a week," she tells me, and I count the days, trying to remember what day it is and what date. Except that I write the date in my journal every day, I wouldn't know; it's hard to keep track when I have no place to be, no one to see.

I give the woman my next forwarding address: General Delivery, American Express, Dubrovnik. Who knows where or when it might find me: If not in Dubrovnik, where next? Greece? What about Turkey? I'm still considering Istanbul. And Egypt.

"Dubrovnik," I say. "American Express, Dubrovnik."

Back out onto Váci, I pass through the gauntlet of peddlers with their fancy tablecloths and pictures and hand-knitted baby things to Café Gerbeaud, where I order a cappuccino and take a table by the window.

These cafés are like churches too. Small chapels along the road like way stations for lonely travelers on pilgrimages. I settle in and open my journal.

In a session a few weeks after Tom died my therapist, Charlie, wanted me to give words to the emotions I was experiencing. "Sad," I know I said. *Lonely* would have been a word. *Confused. Afraid.* He kept pushing me for more words to illustrate, I guess, the layered complexity of mourning, of living on after the death of someone so integral to a day-in and day-out life. "Missing," I finally said, after searching for a word that could possibly capture the entanglement of my emotions. You couldn't say, *I am missing,* as you would say, *I am sad,* or *I am lonely,* or *I am scared.* But to suddenly be alone in a world where so recently someone was with you, someone so dear and necessary and family, is to be struck with a great sense of missing.

This morning alone at my table in Café Gerbeaud, where all around me are people living in a different language and an unfamiliar world, I am overcome with a great sense of missing. The waning September sun comes through the café's window and stains a dim square on my hand as I write. My hands, both right and left, are bare of any jewelry. I left my wedding ring, a plain gold band, in a jewelry box in a storage unit along with Tom's, taken from his finger that January afternoon he died; the ring loose on his thin fingers.

A chair scrapes against the floor and I become aware of subdued conversations. The pair of older women at the next table with thick arms and sweaters over dresses, lined faces so like the faces of my own aunts. We come on my mother's side from eastern European heritage. More Polish than Hungarian, but what difference when you go back far enough? Borders change, names of countries change. Today as I travel my next destination, at least in my loose plans, will be Yugoslavia, once part of the Ottoman Empire.

Classical music plays quietly. I sense echoes of those who have come before—who sat at this same table and played out the drama of their own lives. The love affairs, the confessions, the gossip and exchange of secrets, news of the day, quotidian details of lives lived.

I met Kati Mati at an AA meeting on Kiss János, but she is more like the Stranger at the Crossroads, that figure in fairy tales and folk stories who sees us from the outside but knows us on the inside, the one who can be a trickster but can also foretell the future. Strangers at the Crossroads are given to riddles and cryptic questions.

She invites me to dinner at her apartment one evening. I take the bus across the river and follow her directions along old streets, past stone buildings grimed with age and, here and there, bullet holes in the crumbling concrete, evidence of wounds inflicted on the glittering, elegant city.

Kati Mati (I want to say her whole name each time) has wild hair that haloes her face. Her skin is young with few wrinkles, though she is a confessed sixty-one. We sit in her apartment as afternoon fades and evening comes on. It's comfortable here, a room overstuffed with art and color and Kati Mati's stories.

"Let me tell first," she says. "Gemini rising has to go first. Libras have more patience." (One of the first things she asked was my zodiac sign.)

She talks and talks and talks in her exotic Hungarian accent, her lipstick a little smeared. Stories of living in New York, in Palm Beach, of men she's known, artists, her Hungarian past, of the revolution and why she left Budapest for America (the bullet holes) and why she came back. "Home is home," she says.

She serves sparkling water and almonds and after more stories goes into her small, comfortably messy kitchen and makes our dinner, continuing to talk as she works. Pork chops, boiled potatoes, and fresh tomatoes from her sister's garden, tomatoes red like tomatoes are supposed to be, not that faded pale red of supermarket tomatoes. These tomatoes have the passion of Kati Mati herself.

She tells me I'm not eating right.

"You need someone to take care of you. You don't care enough for your body." She serves more food. A dessert of something crusty with honey. Everything smells delicious and tastes like memory.

She's right about caring for my body. I don't cook for myself; I drink coffee for breakfast, while lunch and dinner are haphazard—dinner back home was sometimes popcorn and M&M's. This isn't how I was raised.

My mother's Midwestern meals always included meat and potatoes, vegetables and salad. She rolled her own noodles for chicken and noodles and boiled ham hocks and lima beans that tasted even better the second day. She made pork chops baked in the oven and served over scalloped potatoes. Oh, those pork chops. With those pork chops, I was a bone-chewer. This Thursday night at Kati Mati's I want to chew the last remnants of meat from these pork chop bones. This is how hungry I am for life—I want to chew its bones, get to the marrow.

Kati Mati knows about living that way. With her exuberance, her grand gestures, Kati Mati is a bone-chewer. She pulls at her yellow-gray hair as she talks, gesturing extensively to make her point. Hands open, arms outspread then crushed against her chest, then waving in the air.

Those elegant hands remade fine, old, precious tapestries at her gallery in New York: a brownstone on East Sixty-Second Street. She was expert at her work, she tells me, and I believe her as I stand to examine more closely a small indigo and gold and lilac weaving on her wall.

"You'll marry again by the time you're fifty," she says.

"Do you really think so?" I resettle myself in the worn armchair that faces her matching one.

"Oh yes," Kati Mati says. "You're a Libra." As if that explained everything.

My forty-eighth birthday is just a month away. After Tom, I can't imagine ever marrying again.

Once, a few days after our day-after-Christmas lunch that extended into nights and days when Tom had moved his clothes from his car into my closet, we stood against the rail of the deck at my house in Cardiff-by-the-Sea gazing down the hill toward the ocean, mesmerized by the forever blue of the Pacific.

"Marry me," he said.

"I don't believe in marriage," I replied, neither of us looking at the other.

"If you say no, I'll never ask you again."

"Never is a long time," I said.

"I'm a long-time man," he said.

We stayed that way for another few minutes, both of us leaning on our elbows on the railing, both of us looking out to the merging horizon of water and sky.

Kati Mati doesn't want love for herself, she says, not romantic, sexual love with a partner; she is in love with what she is doing. She tells me she rises every day at six and writes.

"Everything I did, I did for my mother," she says, taking us into a new world of memory and story. "Every day I waited for her to turn to me and say, 'Yes, I love you.'"

Like me, like so many of us, searching always for that perfect mother-love we believe she possesses. The ultimate approval. The heaven of love, which is impossible. But we never know that and wouldn't accept it anyhow; this need is infantile, desire without words, without understanding. Our greatest need—*my* greatest need—is to be enough. To finally be able to bestow that perfect love upon myself.

It's late now. We have tea and continue our stories. Kati tells me she cried every night for seven years after her divorce.

"Crying to God, 'Just give me a hand to hold,'" she says. "And the answer came. 'You have two hands. Grasp your own hand.'"

I remember the kaleidoscope mirrors at the sensory circus in Salzburg creating a circle with myself, holding my own hands again and again. My self reflected six times six times six, ad infinitum. And the boulder above me as I lay beneath it, skin and bones and a barely beating heart.

"Explain yourself, Judy," Kati Mati says, like a command. "Why do you travel around the world by yourself?"

I'm glad for the tea: taking a sip offers a moment to consider her question. I've answered this question from curious others in the last few months, usually with an offhand response about finally having the time and the opportunity, or "I'm sort of between things," or "You know, just seeing what's there." But I know I can't be glib or offhand with Kati Mati.

"God knows I've asked myself this same question often enough on this journey," I begin. "I think it has to do with finding myself."

"But can you not do that at home? Must you go away to find yourself?" I'm pretty sure Kati Mati already has the answer to this question, but still she presses, "Are you not the same at home?"

"It has to do with taking away the familiar so I can't lean upon props. Go through life without consciously making choices. It has to do with risking," I say, making it up as I go, testing ideas, searching her face for reaction. The light in the room is soft from the floor lamps near us but shadowy in the far reaches.

"Risking my safety. Not my physical safety but the psychological safety of knowing the way. Of knowing how it's done. The risk of saying, 'I don't know how to do this.'" I pause, try to order my thoughts. "It has to do with the experience of the thing. Seeing the world and myself from a broader view than 'home.' Recognizing that San Diego or San Francisco or even America is not the center of the universe.

"Honestly," I say, "there's also what I wanted to leave. The pressure of time and requests and giving—and sometimes resenting the giving. Knowing I need space and open time." It's a kind of confession to reveal these things about myself. A relief that's layered with a veil of vulnerability.

Then Kati reveals that between her tenth and eleventh year of sobriety—exactly where I am in my own recovery—some outside/inside irresistible urge pushed her to go. Like me back in San Diego, at that time she was sponsoring several women in Los Angeles, deeply involved in their lives, busy and always getting requests to talk, to meet, to take time for another phone call.

"So I got a garden on the hillside near Sepulveda and Pico. The government gives you the land." Those graceful, well-worn hands wave in the air as if conducting an inaudible orchestra. "I dedicated myself to that garden," she says, telling me she spent her days there giving it the same addictive attention she had given her work with the gallery in New York. "I built a meditation place, benches in the sun," she says. "For a year I let go of all the women I sponsored and went only to a single meeting a week. In that garden, I withdrew into myself and I was renewed."

That's the word she used—*renewed*. Fulfilled within herself. Changed. She sold her condo, moved to Florida, and began living between Miami Beach and Budapest.

"This is the last chapter," she says then, gesturing toward the room and all it contained. "I know it. I can feel it. This is finally what I do."

In the warm lamplight of Kati Mati's art-cluttered apartment, the leftover aroma of the dinner she cooked still in the air, I wonder what it would be that I would finally do and when I would know it.

SEPTEMBER 11, 1990
Budapest to Split

I board the night train for Split. My companion for the eighteen-hour journey is a Hungarian woman, older than me, also traveling alone. We sit silently across from each other and smile in that way you do with fellow passengers on a train. I have my book and my journal; she has her knitting.

We pass Lake Balaton. I get up to stand by the aisle window and she joins me. We don't speak: my English, her Hungarian, either way we don't understand each other except in our quiet standing together, gazing out the windows as we travel.

Vacation cottages line the shore. Tall pine trees stand in yards with lawns still green, flowers still blooming in jaunty window boxes, though now in mid-September the houses appear vacant; most summer residents have gone back to their homes elsewhere, their holidays over for another summer.

In the afternoon light the big shallow lake is green-gray, the color of my sister's eyes. A few windsurfers skate the lake's surface but no boats, no swimmers. Fall is coming, cold weather creeping in on its coattails.

A sudden, sad loneliness grabs me in the chest with a physical grip; my stomach tightens. This is how memory comes: the sensory cue, the body's response, the emotion that accompanies the actual memory—the cottages around Lake Balaton remind me of the cottages in Orangeville, near Toronto where Tom and I stayed with his parents. Peg in one cottage and Big Joe in another, each with their new life partners, and Tom fishing off the dock of one lake or another. I always thought we would have a place together on the coast of British Columbia—the Sunshine Coast, perhaps Garden Bay where he loved to fish.

God doesn't count the time on earth a man spends fishing.

We pass and pass and pass by Lake Balaton, the largest lake in central Europe, and I stand at the window remembering us. Picturing the dream that can never be, my eyes fill, my body wants to cry, but I consider my compartment-mate. I have my emotional shield up. I'm being "Nice Judy" today. Nice, companionable Judy for this long overnight journey to Split.

I stand at the window, silent with my sadness.

We puff along across the Yugoslav border. Passports are checked and rechecked. After a few hours Stephan, the car attendant—who is attractive in a dangerous sort of way and who began as friendly and courteous and became too friendly—brings drinks my compartment-mate and I didn't ask for or want, some sweet-smelling Hungarian brandy. She rolls her eyes at me but drank anyhow, because to do otherwise would be rude. No longer Nice Judy, I am rude. She and I pass food back and forth—I share bread and cheese; she, tomatoes. Those incredibly red, ripe Hungarian tomatoes.

Later in the quiet rhythm of the train's movement I read *The Ballad of the Sad Café* by Carson McCullers and am moved by the story. Is it the mood even the title suggests, those first paragraphs that describe the town and the people there that affect me so? Is it Miss Amelia's loneliness or remnants from my own heartbroken moodiness?

McCullers was only twenty-three when she wrote her first book, *The Heart Is a Lonely Hunter*, another affective title. Born the same year as my mother, she died at only fifty.

Through the bug-littered window, the passing landscape appears gilded in the afternoon sunset and I consider that I am nearing that age myself and have yet to claim myself as a writer, what I always knew I would be—and yet am not. Picturing that little girl with her paper and pencil, writing sentences and thrilling to the magic of it, I want to say, like Kati Mati, "This is finally what I do."

SEPTEMBER 12, 1990
Split

Five thirty. The train stops. No one wakes us and there is no announcement. No sign at the railway station says the name of the place, but I am fairly sure I have arrived in Split. On the train everything is locked. The WC emits odors so foul I don't want to enter even if I could.

The station is small and dirty and closed. A few men stand around outside the stone building. The inevitable backpackers roost in their sleeping bags in a dimly lit corner. Opposite the station is the harbor, the sea inky dark. I roll my pack around the station a few times. A young man opens the door.

"Do you speak English?" Always my first question. I learn the station and money exchange open at six and decide to set off in the still-dark morning down a cobbled street in the direction the helpful young man pointed. I pass the tourist office, closed, but then finally, blessedly, a public WC.

"One mark," the woman says. I haven't changed money yet. In Hungary *money* is *forint*; in Yugoslavia it is *dinar*. I don't know what a *mark* is. I dig in my bag of change and come up with something, hold my open palm out. "Go ahead," she says, taking pity on me.

After, I rest on a wall facing the harbor. The sun rises on the other side of the hill, washing the sky in a sweetly pink blush, and a slight wind picks up. The harbor is filled with ferryboats that carry passengers to the surrounding islands, down to Dubrovnik, north to Rijeka, and across the sea to Corfu. Fishing boats and sailboats litter the dark water. The fresh scent of sea is nothing like the earthy river smell that accompanied my time in Budapest.

A young couple passes by, their toddler linking them together hand in hand in hand while his baby steps clumsily attempt to keep pace. Memory gives me a snapshot of my mother posed on the grass in some long-ago front yard, three blond daughters clamoring all over her. Her expression is a little annoyed, but mostly I read fear. I don't imagine we are what she wanted for her life—three daughters in just over three years. I wonder what she did want for her life before us, before my father. I wonder if she had a plan, a dream, some wild fantasy that took her away from her everyday life.

Who can say who falls in love with whom, and who is to judge? Did my mother fall in love with my father, or did he persuade her to open her legs and she did—out of need or passion—and she became pregnant, and there they are fifty-plus years later. Did she give up her dreams, folding them away as she folded each diaper from each new baby? We never spoke of this.

Somewhere along the way I picked up *Her Mother's Daughter* by Marilyn French. I read French's first novel, *The Women's Room*, in those glorious, riotous years of our consciousness-raising and connected the many ways French's telling of the lives of women in the forties and fifties echoed my mother's life, that is, in the expectations of women's roles and how they were "supposed" to live their lives and conduct themselves. Details I was carefully taught and attempted to emulate—marry early, have children, tend home and hearth (*Take typing so you'll have something to fall back on*)—even though these teachings went against the grain of my wanting more, my need for some semblance of independence, and my dreams of becoming a writer. My mother more than once referred to herself as "just a housewife," demeaning her role, her life, her very self and never hinting that she was chafing against its restraints or had dreams beyond the life she led. Still I want to imagine that she did take imaginary flights into another kind of existence where she didn't describe herself as "just" anything. Those times I watched from my tree house while she hung our laundry on the clothesline stretched from tree to pole in the backyard, I wonder if she didn't gaze beyond the wet flapping sheets and towels and girls' school dresses she'd have to iron and daydream herself another place, another life, one without laundry and daughters spying down from tree houses, a place with no daughters at all.

In my adult life—with my first husband and my second—I lived a life different from what I dreamed until finally an overpowering restlessness wouldn't allow me to stay and divorce followed. Those jobs I had in those early years involved writing, yes, for newspapers, radio, television, advertising, PR; but what of the stories that filled my head, what of that daydreaming young girl, high up in her tree house with her notebook and pencil; the angst-filled adolescent, writing rhyming poetry and one-act plays for class assignments. What of her?

I can't help but wonder about falling in love or lust and giving yourself away, sacrificing some kind of authenticity or destiny or gift given. I want to be the kind of woman who can fall in love again, who can be with another and not give her deepest self away but still claim herself as sovereign and keep her dreams worthy of pursuing.

The bus ride from Split takes four and a half hours along the Dalmatian coast. Outside my window, rock-pebbled islands rise from a sea of startlingly clear blue-green water. Next to me is a blond, good-looking Yugoslavian man who speaks some English. We make small talk—the kind you exchange when neither has the language to go beyond small. His thumb and top portions of his first and second finger are missing. I admire his thick mustache, which rides above his generous lower lip, but I don't have the words to tell him.

SEPTEMBER 13–18, 1990
Dubrovnik

The paving stones in Dubrovnik have been worn smooth and shiny and reflect the light as well as the shoes of strollers and the occasional bicycle. There are no cars inside the ancient walls; the passageways don't allow for them, nor does the tourism bureau. Stone buildings rise three and four stories and are topped by terra-cotta roofs. Taller still are the church towers, one here, one there, their blue-tiled domes arched against a darkening sky. Just at sundown bats fly overhead and squeal. I want to stride the ancient wall around the city the same way guards paced that very wall on the lookout for who might approach, who might invade.

I take a room for six nights in a pension across the main square and up a series of steep stone steps. Once inside there are more stairs to climb, then a double bed with an orange spread, couch, dresser, and separate bath. The smiling woman who rents to me says she'll also do my laundry for a few dinar extra. I don't have a plan. But for now I have a bed, a table, and a lamp to write by.

The walls that encircle the city were built in the eighth century. I walk atop them, my feet falling on footpaths made nearly 1,200 years ago. I wonder what it might have been like to be a woman in this ancient city. Lugging buckets of water home from the fountain in the square, hanging clothes out fourth-story windows with no screens to keep the bats at bay. I wonder how the people who lived here maneuvered their heavy furniture—thick-legged tables, carved bedsteads—up the narrow passageways that angle away from the central Placa. I could barely heft my pack up the steep stone stairs that lead to my pension. And what of plumbing? A sudden gratitude comes over me for my toilet and sink and deep bathtub and for the kind lady who offered to do my laundry.

At Kavana Troubador near the harbor, the music is guitar—mellow and sweet, Chet Atkins. Earlier I went to the American Express office outside the city walls to book a tour for Sveti Stefan and get information about the ferry to Corfu, my next destination. Probably. The desk person mentioned an express package from the US. Finally, the long-awaited package from Camille that didn't arrive in Budapest is here.

I sip my cappuccino and tear open the package, impatient like a teenager in her prom dress awaiting her date. Inside, the letter Camille composed with a few whimsical graphic touches on her new Macintosh computer is juicy with news of her life. Her hot new love interest, plus a swimming and camping and bicycling weekend with a friend. I get a shot of jealousy—or fear?—that in my time away I might be replaced as best friend. It doesn't last, that schoolgirl twinge of human pettiness before some reasoning part of me steps in to say, That's the risk you take when you up and leave. Others' lives don't stop because you're not there.

Inside are actually two letters—the one composed on the computer and another one handwritten in Camille's generous loopy handwriting and two books. I am wealthy in books. The Carson McCullers and a Sylvia Plath from the international bookstore in Budapest, and now these two from Camille. I scan the covers. One—*A Country Year*, about a widow who buys a farm in Missouri and keeps bees. The second—*The Widows' Adventures*. Two elderly sisters set off on a cross-country drive. One sister can't drive, and one is blind. The blind sister drives while the other gives directions. Delicious.

At sunset, after passing through the Pile Gate, I amble along a magnificent park overlooking the Adriatic along the gravel footpath, meaning to go down some stairs to the sea when I spot a man farther along the way—naked. Just as I enter the stairs he takes hold of his large, rather stiff cock and begins to masturbate. This is strange. Not the sight of the man and what he's doing, but my response, which surprises me. Another time I might have been shocked, embarrassed, even frightened. But this evening it's almost as if I have come upon an animal doing what animals do with no mind to the world around them, like the time out near a muddy pond when I witnessed turtles, one atop the other, mating in the open air. I don't mean to compare the man to an animal, but really, what are we after all?

I turn around, climb the stairs behind us, and proceed to the higher path above him.

Farther down the way I find a bench facing the sea. The sun sets slowly, resplendent, hanging in the sky, first amber then apricot then the orange of the tangerines that clustered the tree at the edge of our property in Jamul. How long it stayed there, round and perfect in the western sky above a green sea turned molten. *How can this be?* I wonder, the sun setting again and again, perfect every time.

On a tour with a group to the Bay of Kotor, I'm traveling among a couple dozen strangers—tourists, all of us—an unusual experience for me on this journey, yet here I am this Tuesday morning in Montenegro stopping at a café outside a museum for my first cappuccino of the day. Nearby are remarkably preserved Roman mosaics from the second century, which all of us traipsed off the bus to view.

Beside the still, glassy water of the bay, we gaze across to see the Island of Saint George with its monastery and, next to it, the man-made island of Our Lady of the Rocks.

The legend goes like this: Two sailors, one without the use of his leg, setting out on a voyage, come upon an icon of the Madonna and Child painted on a rock in the sea. Reaching the end of a successful journey, they take the icon ashore with them, only to discover the next morning it has disappeared. But, miracle of miracles, overnight the crippled sailor had regained the use of his leg. Months pass and the two sailors—brothers, it's told—set out on another journey. Once more they come upon the icon in the sea. Convinced the symbol had been responsible for the healing of his leg, the sailor told the miracle to the local priest and it was decided a church dedicated to Our Lady would be built upon the rock. From then on sailors, voyage after voyage, year after year, before setting out—superstitious and always in search of blessings for their perilous journeys—placed rock upon stone upon crag in the bay until the islet grew large enough for a church to be built and dedicated to Our Lady of the Rocks.

The Bay of Kotor is in the Republic of Montenegro—I learn that Montenegro was named Black Mountain not because the mountains are naturally black but because, after the Turks invaded and enacted an especially bloody crusade, the region's widows took to their black mourning clothes. It's said the mountains, too, became black with mourning.

I have just read in the *Herald Tribune*: the United Kingdom and France announced the deployment of troops to Saudi Arabia.

Invasions—ancient and forever.

After purchasing a few postcards at a tourist shop and a purple-and-teal bikini that I intend to make great use of, I cross the Placa, daypack slung across my shoulder. A few housewives with their shopping bags are, like me, gathering supplies for dinner. I purchase bread, cheese, water, and grapes. It's harvesttime and the pears look juicy and delicious; I buy a couple of those, too, and continue along.

A man catches up to me from behind and begins walking alongside me. He's tall—my head comes to his shoulder—and long-legged. He bends down and begins humming in my ear, "Lara's Theme" from the film *Doctor Zhivago*.

"Remember this song?" he asks, his English heavily accented.

"Yes, 'Lara's Theme,'" I say. "Pretty."

He hums more. We walk side by side, he leans in to my ear, our arms brush each other's.

"Where are you going?" he asks.

I'm reminded of a man in Rome a few years ago when I visited with Amy, crossing a piazza near the Spanish Steps. As the man passed he bent toward me. "Remember me from twenty years ago?" he'd asked and continued on by as if he wasn't expecting a response.

I appreciate these two approaches as unique, different from the usual, *Where are you from?* or worse: *Hey, baby.*

Once Tom and I went to LA because he had an audition at some studio. Later that afternoon as we drove along a quiet neighborhood neither of us knew—palm trees, wide streets, no traffic—Tom pulled over to the curb, stopped the car, and asked me to get out and walk along the sidewalk. I didn't know what he had in mind, but I knew for sure he wouldn't drive off and leave me like those old high school pranks we called *ditching,* a senior-class initiation where kids, mostly girls, got "kidnapped" and driven out to the country, where they were left to find their way home.

I get out and begin my stroll. He drives slowly beside me for a few moments, then he rolls down the window and leans across the seat. "How much?" he asks.

So this is the game we're playing.

"Everything you've got," I say and get in the car beside him.

I don't answer the humming man in the Placa. He is polite and lets my nonanswer be the no I intend. I'm grateful he doesn't press it.

Back in my room I make a picnic on my orange-covered bed and read *The Bell Jar,* another discovery at the Budapest bookstore. Careful not to get the pear juice dripping down my arm onto the pages, I come upon an odd recipe: *melt grape jelly and French dressing together in a saucepan and fill an avocado half.*

Here's Tom, standing in our kitchen in his red-checked shirt and boots still smelling of the orchard. He's holding a halved avocado just harvested from one of his trees on the hill, digging in with a spoon— loving it as much for its buttery flavor as the fact that it came from a tree he planted, laid water to, fed. He probably wouldn't like the grape jelly and French dressing mix; he liked his fruit ungarnished, straight off the tree.

After seven weeks traveling alone, I am familiar with many aspects of solitude—at least the way I do solitude. Reading, writing, simply being alone and quiet at the edge of the Danube, in a park in Oslo, on a mountain overlooking the ancient city of Dubrovnik. At times like these I can just be, present and complete.

I'm familiar with the parts of being alone I don't like, too—eating alone, choosing a place to stay, facing a day that is empty of anticipation. I'm familiar with myself: I like to have a to-do list, some kind of plan even if it's only doing my laundry, making a train reservation, or finding a way to oil my Swiss Army knife. And I have lately discovered these, as a result of so much time alone:

- That I'm not as naturally gregarious as I thought I was.

- That given the choice my body seems to like staying up late and sleeping late.

- That I like music to accompany me, whatever I'm doing or not doing.

- That I often project and live in the future rather than being present in the now.

- That I don't care all that much about museums or historic sites and such, but I like visual delights and jaw-dropping vistas; I don't make a good tourist, but I love the journey.

- That when I'm on a budget I get stingy and become preoccupied with the cost of things.

- That I'm becoming less self-conscious the longer I travel and have taken on an attitude of instinctively doing as I want rather than watching to see what others are doing—unconcerned about the "right" way to do it (whatever *it* is).

- That I am becoming more assertive in getting what I want, less accepting of that which isn't comfortable for me.

- That I'd rather be alone than with someone with whom I simply make boring small talk.

- That I can put up a fairly impenetrable wall and keep people at a distance.

For reasons I don't know, I crave solitude. After living alone and now traveling alone, moving from place to place, I find myself lonelier than I've ever been in my life. Still I am content. Something lives in the solitude that I want, or more, that I need.

Question: Is traveling alone better than seeing a therapist? Perhaps, except that the therapist asks questions, nudges, listens; a travel journal merely offers a blank page.

On a damp afternoon at Brasserie Lora just down the passageway from my pension, I make notes on just such a blank page, scratching some remembered quote from Camus about the fear of finally being with ourselves as we are "without the protective defense of the factory or the office or whatever to give us reason for being."

I'm Judy Reeves and I . . .

In Dubrovnik I can't distract myself with an AA meeting (no meetings are listed in the international directory for Yugoslavia), and most other English-speakers I've met are Brits on package holidays, which is fine until I run out of small talk. I find refuge in places like Brasserie Lora with its tiny lamps on tiny tables, its walls of red tapestry, ceiling painted black, where Barbra Streisand sings "Woman in Love." I order a second cappuccino and fill blank pages with a kind of euphoric recall of my familiar, safe life in California, then write about wanting to experience more of this mystery of myself, this individual, independent self I'm discovering or inventing or simply imagining.

Another evening in my room, on my bed, this time eating a pear and chocolate- and raspberry-topped cookie, I read more of Sylvia Plath and identify with Esther, both of us judging ourselves inadequate in ways that we've never realized before. Here we are, Esther and me, decades apart—her, a teenaged fictional character living in New York in 1953, the year the Rosenbergs were executed; me, a forty-eight-year-old real-life character traveling in 1990, in a world that appears to be preparing for yet another war—both of us searching for our identities.

I take off my watch and earrings, change into my nightshirt, and settle into my upstairs room in this ancient house with the windows open and the draping plants on the wrought iron sill outside, the everyday sounds of a neighborhood quieting.

I read from *The Bell Jar*, "I took a deep breath and listened to the old brag of my heart: I am, I am, I am."

Sylvia Plath's haunting writing, like Carson McCullers's before her, sets up an ache inside to express my own voice, to give words to the stories I long to tell. If writing is what I always come back to, where I always find myself going toward, if this is the place that disturbs me yet also gives me solace, the thing that seduces me and at the same time eludes me, then this may be where I will find the way into the authentic self I know exists.

SEPTEMBER 19–23, 1990
Cavtat

The noon ferry brings me to Cavtat, roughly nine miles south of Dubrovnik on the Adriatic coast. Whitecaps froth the sea as I look back toward the walled city, which I can just make out. Small boats dance in the harbor as if conducted by some wind aria, and farther out a yacht, white and majestic, gracefully dips in the waves. Across the harbor palms line the promenade and restaurants wave their umbrellas as if inviting me to come sit in the shade and drink it all in. Magenta bougainvillea climbs white stone buildings with roofs of red and orange tiles and the spire of a church—Our Lady of the Snow—rises above it all. Behind the town the brown-gray mountains of coastal Yugoslavia stand rugged and uninviting.

Soon I'll go out into the world, but for now I like the luxury of sitting on my protected balcony at the Macedonia Hotel where I've taken a single room for a couple of nights. The wind hums through the pine trees on the hillside, the same familiar sound as in Vancouver, Oslo, San Diego. And the rhythm of sea pulsing against the rocks speaks the same language all over the world.

For a few months after I moved from our big house with the orchard in Jamul and before I bought the condo at the estuary, I rented a furnished apartment very near the ocean and very far from the home Tom and I shared. It was a short-term rental and I was a short-term woman, unsure of the next—whatever.

I'd been seeing Rex, the on-again, off-again man, for a while, but he was true to his untrustworthy reputation—which I'd been warned about by friends—I became the next in a long line of fickle relationships. All the deep grief I'd yet to express over Tom's death, all the emotions I'd left unfelt as I took up with Rex in some kind of romantic escape, came to the surface. Living as I had during those few months so close to the ocean, my grief over losing Tom came in on tide swells and ninth waves. I could not stop crying. The apartment became synonymous with that sorrow and the physical expression of it. I named it *the crying house.*

Midafternoon. I stretch out on a lounge down a set of stairs created from rocks on the sheltered man-made beach at Hotel Macedonia. These rocks, brown and sharp-edged, cracked and creviced, are not like the smooth gray boulders that litter the hillsides east of San Diego. An hour on my back, eating a cheese and tomato sandwich; an hour on my belly, daydreaming. A dip in the cool green Adriatic, shower it all off and back to the lounge, face to the sun.

This is what I do—turn over and turn over again, all the while thinking about what I've been thinking about. I want to see the future—to know how this is going to turn out: this journey, this life. I'm unsure how what I'm doing today—lying on the beach in a small tourist town on the coast of Yugoslavia—will affect me and the choices I make in the future. Will I look back three years from now, six years after Tom's death, and see how it all fits together? By then I'll be staring fifty right in its face.

In *A Country Year*, the book that came in that fat package Camille sent, Sue Hubbell writes about older women. We are numerous enough to be a class, she says. "Because our culture has assigned us no real role, we can make up our own. It is a good time to be a grown-up woman with individuality. . . . Social rules are so flexible today that nothing we do is shocking. . . . Provided we stay healthy and can support ourselves, we can do anything, have anything and spend our talents any way that we please."

I remember what Kati Mati said that evening in her art-filled apartment in Budapest when we talked about becoming "self-actualized."

"You're almost there, Jude." And coming from her, that wild-haired, fascinating Hungarian Stranger at the Crossroads, it sounded like a promise.

Near sunset I pause at a rocky point just up the path from town, looking due west. If I set sail in that direction I would wash up onto another shore—Italy.

I am joined by an elderly British couple. We chat about places to go, places they've been, as we look out to the sea.

The land slants down toward the water, and below us a man stands on a rock. He's naked, facing the sea. Long and lean and seen only from the back, he gracefully dives in. The shore is not far down, several yards, and easy enough for us to keep him in view. As he swims below, the British woman wonders aloud if he is, in fact, nude. Apparently she hadn't seen him before he dove in. She watches him intently, stretching forward on our bench so that her husband and I have to lean back and look around her to continue our conversation. While she keeps an eye on the swimming man, her husband and I talk of nude beaches. He tells me how Yugoslavia has always had a penchant for nude beaches (they've been coming here for twenty years), and they don't have them in Britain.

"We have one in San Diego," I tell him, "Black's Beach. I once ran into an old junior high classmate as I emerged naked from the surf." We laugh; I'm a bit embarrassed at the memory. Meantime his wife is concentrating her gaze on the man in the water.

After a while they leave, shuffling down the precarious path toward town for an early dinner. I stay behind on the bench as the sun begins to paint colors in the sky, brassing the water. Soon the man emerges from his swim, drying but not dressing and looking up at me as he finds a cigarette in his set-aside clothes. He stands, legs slightly apart, penis semi-erect. I watch him briefly, cast a glance toward the path that leads away, then turn back to him. He's posed at the edge of the small cliff smoking and gazing at me. The sun is behind him, outlining him in silhouette, but still I see him clearly, even his face, which has a serious demeanor.

Not a chill but a kind of fear drapes its shadow over me. It's not that I'm afraid he's going to come up the cliff toward me, but something about him—his studied stance, the deliberate manner in which he smokes his cigarette—is too blatantly sexual. The way he stands as if he's a performer and I'm his audience and this act is more for his pleasure than mine suggests I am merely being used.

I get up, turn my back, and walk away. I don't realize how quickly I am moving until minutes later I overtake the British couple.

SEPTEMBER 23, 1990
Dubrovnik to Corfu

Even though we're weeks past peak season, the upper deck on the ferry between Dubrovnik and Corfu is crowded with passengers as we watch the sun set over our starboard side. The few young travelers, already drunk and rowdy, will probably stay up all night, revel into the wee hours, and eventually find places to sleep on the open deck, while below I'll try to sleep in whatever cabin I've been assigned.

Down, down, down a series of stairways that turn and turn. The cabins are located deep below the water. The air is cool; the light dim; the passageways narrow, empty, and echoey. My berth is in a dimly lit cabin with four beds: two up, two down. I'm relieved to be the only occupant and glad for the quiet.

Soon the quiet is too quiet. I try to find sleep on the hard and uncomfortable lower berth, but my worried mind offers fantastic visions of ferries that leak oil, overturn and spill helpless passengers into the cold green water, or catch fire below deck with no exit for those of us this deep in the belly of the ship.

A long-ago friend once told me that when she was a young girl she believed everyone but her could turn their mind on and off, so that when they wanted to sleep or when they didn't want the thoughts they were having, they could just flip a switch. Of course she learned that simply wasn't true. No one is born with the magic on/off switch; we must study, we must be patient, we must practice if we are ever to learn to turn off our minds at will and become enlightened. I don't know if my friend ever attained enlightenment, but clearly I have not.

SEPTEMBER 24–26, 1990
Corfu

We arrive in Corfu during two of Greece's frequent strikes—this time garbage and electricity. This means piles of trash are stacked along dirty streets where overflowing bins lean against every building. Walking near the harbor, I make wide circles around heaped-up, thrown-together mounds of trash and hold my breath as I maneuver the unevenly paved streets.

The electrical strike means power will be available only for certain times every day. I learn it's wise to try to get this information first thing in the morning so you can plan your meals, phone calls, or whatever you need electricity for. But just because the times of the daily blackouts are posted doesn't mean that is when they would occur.

Like many travelers who have only been to Greece in their dreams, I expected iconic whitewashed, blue-domed buildings, houses with blue-painted doors, and views out to turquoise seas, not these European-style buildings, wrought iron sconces, and castles. I am not disappointed, only surprised. This surprise is not my first of the journey and I know it won't be my last. For now I plan to stay just a few days in Corfu; my real destination in Greece is Athens, and then . . . and then . . . who knows what additional surprises might intervene.

The Corfu Liston Restaurant and Café is posed at the edge of the old town bordering a park. Big trees whose names I don't know shade the street, which is closed to traffic and lined with restaurants. The historic establishment rests under a colonnaded extrusion that spreads the length of the block. The esplanade is modeled after Rue de Rivoli in Paris, I read in my travel guide. "Behind are the shuttered alleyways of an ersatz Venice. . . . Throughout the town the smell of steaming lobster and veal mingles with the wafting stench of raw sewage gurgling up through the street grates."

Marv and Joanie, a couple coincidently also from San Diego whom I met on the ferry, invited me on a minibike tour of the island, but I'm not interested in touring the massive hilltop castles the guidebook brags about. I'm in Greece, I don't want any more European castles. I want . . . I want . . . I want . . .

Judge me or not, when this kind of unidentified desire descends upon me I go shopping. No longer the curious wanderer with her notebook and her solitude but a tourist like any other going shop to shop, longing hovering around her like an aura, unable to identify what might quell it.

I wend my way along the promenade, and there, in a shop window bright with colorful clothing and classic handbags, I'm drawn to a gorgeous blue coat. Blue the color of domes on whitewashed churches, doors on stuccoed walls, and painted tables at seaside cafés. Blue that will always say, *Remember that time in Greece.*

Even though the weather is changing and it's not sticky hot; even though I am still dreaming white-sand beaches, turquoise waters; still visualizing sunny Greek islands and music and *Opa!*; still I am drawn to that knockout coat.

"May I try it on?" I ask the elegant saleswoman with her burnished earrings and polished smile, who is obviously glad to see me, the only shopper in the glittering and well-appointed shop.

The coat is warm, a loopy weave of wool intricately embroidered with the summer-bright colors of flowers that drape hanging baskets and window boxes. I slide my arms inside the sleeves, the satin lining smooth on my skin. It fits perfectly.

"It was made for you, madam." The saleswoman holds the matching scarf in one hand and steps over to a glass counter that displays a dazzling array of costume jewelry. I gaze at myself in the full-length mirror and believe that, yes, this coat was made for me.

She returns with a gaudy brooch of bright azure glass held in a filigreed setting.

"Turn this way," she orders.

She takes me by the shoulders, faces me away from the mirror, and studies me with the intensity of an artist appraising a half-finished work. Next she wraps the scarf around my head with a flourish and secures it with the flamboyant brooch. Then she whoops the Greek equivalent of *voilà!* and with a triumphant expression turns me back to the mirror.

I almost laugh aloud. I look ridiculous. Like I would never look in real life. I am costumed. All I need are false eyelashes and bright red lipstick, and I'd be ready for my close-up.

But I love the coat—it was made for me—and I love the saleswoman's enthusiasm and her expensive earrings, and I love that she believes I could carry off the entire getup.

"I'll take it," I say with no idea how I'll fit the bulky coat and matching scarf in my backpack. "I'll take the brooch too."

Of course she knew I'd take it. She did her job well. I might never wear the pin but I can't turn it—or her—down.

I carry the bulky package away with me. I'll find a way to get the coat home or send it on to the next place. No doubt I'll need it in Helsinki in November, where I begin the only other confirmed event on my yearlong agenda.

In the old Corfu harbor ships with names like *Theologos* and *BiBH* and *DimosP* and big car ferries from other islands dock each night at sunset. A large plaza adjoins the embarcadero, its olive and eucalyptus trees filled with birds all achatter as they settle in for the night, sounding like teenage girls at a slumber party. I write in my journal on a harborside bench; it grows darker. No electricity yet this evening. Will there be power or not?

A slender man in a cotton shirt, with a dark shadow of beard and eyes the color of deep woods, attempts to coax me for a stroll on the beach or to have a drink later at another place. But he's given to monologues and not really interested in anything I have to say. He has his line, his stories, and his charm all packaged up and offered to a single woman at a solitary bench.

"No thanks," I say. I didn't say I prefer my own company, but that's the truth. Still I make notes about his approach. To be a writer, I've been told, is to make notes of everything. And so I do. This man, even with his dark eyes, isn't as charming as the one in Dubrovnik who hummed "Lara's Theme" in my ear. The ships, the birds, the Greek man and his approach—all of it material for who knows what or when.

SEPTEMBER 26, 1990
Corfu to Patras

I'm confused by geography and the names of seas we cross on our nine-hour journey from Corfu to Patras on the west side of mainland Greece. The Adriatic Sea from Dubrovnik to Corfu, where at some point we entered the waters of the Ionian Sea, which, as we ferry south, becomes the Mediterranean? Somewhere over there is the Aegean. No wonder it took Odysseus ten years to return home. (And how long will it take me? And again the question: Where is *home*?)

I'm traveling with Marv and Joanie again. Our ferry flies the Italian flag and comes from Brindisi. I change some drachmas to liras and buy a delicious Italian frappé. Joanie talks of their travel, of work, of people and places in San Diego we might have in common. I tell of places I'm going and outline or make up some of my options for when I return to California. I talk about living in Hawaii for a while and muse about staying in Bali; I always thought I'd return there. We speculate about people making a life for themselves in Baja California, living in trailers in an enclave by the sea. Easy talk on an easy cruise from one Greek island to another.

It's become too hot on the top deck and I leave Joanie and Marv and take refuge on the shady side of the ship, where I lean against a storage compartment for life jackets. Beyond the indigo sea are islands, barren mostly, that remind me of the hills of Southern California near the Mexican border not far from where Tom and I lived. The islands are dry, gray-green, and not inviting from this far off, but distance can be misleading. I remember the hills on our property in Jamul, how green they became in Tom's vision of an abundant, mature avocado orchard.

SEPTEMBER 27–30, 1990
Athens

Before I left San Diego, a friend recommended the Acropolis House in the Pláka, the old historical neighborhood that clusters around the northeastern slopes of the Acropolis where the streets are labyrinthine, the architecture neoclassical, and the atmosphere tantalizing. Pale yellow and pink buildings crested with fancy plaster wreaths line the narrow cobbled lanes, and olive trees spread their shade along the sidewalks. Delicious aromas tempt from tavernas, and shops say, "Come in, come in, see what I offer."

I'm not seeing the blue of my coat yet, nor the whitewashed walls so present in travel photos and tourist postcards. I explore the cacophonous streets outside the Pláka, taking in the *nefos*—the smog that is Athens's own, a combination of woodsmoke overlaid with exhaust from buses especially but also cars and motos. After just a ten- or fifteen-minute outing along the busier streets around Omonoia Square, I have a headache and stop at a pharmacy for aspirin and throat lozenges.

Still there's something about Athens that fills me with a sense of anticipation and curiosity, a kind of hunger.

In other places—Budapest, Dubrovnik, Salzburg, a few others—I visited historic sites and notable buildings. Those were interesting, often fascinating, usually beautiful or scenic, and I learned, I experienced, I saw, I responded. I wrote, made notes, took photos, and sent postcards, all because I wanted to take in what I was experiencing. But I never felt the same layering of emotions as I have since I began my stay in Greece. It is as though a sixth sense has lit up inside me and I can almost smell the burning.

I am at a loss to wrap language—a specific, solid thing—around whatever this yearning is. Words are so concrete. Maybe there is no language for this unspecific desire. The best I can do to set down my own astonishments, as Annie Dillard instructed, is to try one word and if not that one, another, and follow that with another: *This* is the color of the building, *this* is the shade and density of the light, *this* is the sound of footsteps on the cobbled street. Also the unevenness of cobbles beneath sandaled feet, the rancid smell from the continuing strike that leaves garbage in heaps on stained back walls and alleyways. And in the distance, music—that familiar American song on someone's radio serenading me through an open window.

I want to believe in something greater than myself—a *higher power*, as I have learned to express it through my years in twelve-step programs. But I love the myths and mysteries, the legends and stories born from cultures other than my own. Here in Greece the poet in me, the theatrical dramatic actor-self, aches to trace the steps of the gods and goddesses. To go deep into stories and legends and myths, right here in the places they originated.

It's clear that my search for meaning and connection has brought me to Greece not on a quest but an undertaking quieter than the adventure suggested by that word. Nor is it a pilgrimage; I don't know enough to have that kind of dedicated direction. This Grecian journey is an exploration, I want to say, into the Self. But more than that, it is a search for connection to something both higher and deeper. A spiritual seeking that assures me that I am not alone.

Today I go to the Acropolis. Climbing the hills, I take the wrong, or at least a different, approach than directed by the manager at my hotel and wind up among private homes, climbing narrow steps between whitewashed walls until I finally join the general path that other pilgrims follow.

Vendors in booths along both sides of the cobbled street offer their trinkets, their postcards, their snacks, and cold drinks. My feet have become accustomed to the uneven pitch and cracks. The vendors are mostly dark-haired, smiling Greek women. This is different than when I traipsed the Váci Utca in Budapest, where a sense of sadness tinged with desperate boredom emanated from the Romanians who lined the wide boulevard. Here, along this winding road where no cars are allowed, the impression is more lighthearted.

I stop for a cold drink at one of the booths. The day is not particularly hot but the climb up the long pull of hill is tiring, and though I have only my daypack, I'm aware of the drag of it on one T-shirted shoulder.

The woman in the booth offers a friendly greeting, *kaló proí* and offers a many-petalled flower along with my drink. The blossom is pink and pretty though not fragrant. She smiles, says something I don't understand, but the exchange feels personal; I feel seen and acknowledged as an individual.

These small moments warm me—the strong and assured Greek woman with her gift of a single flower; the man at the traveler's desk at Keleti train station in Budapest who said, "Simpatico"; Kati Mati and the meal she prepared. These and myriad other kindnesses mean so much as I travel solo; I'm grateful for being seen and recognized as a fellow human being.

I continue to the temple ruins, climbing stairs worn smooth and glossy from ancients and tourists alike. Worship has been practiced here for five thousand years. The site as it stands today was dedicated to Poseidon, god of the sea, and Athena, goddess of the life-sustaining olive tree among other domains. Today the Parthenon is masked by scaffolding and roped off to keep us from clamoring through its ancient walls.

Wandering about the site brings more layering of emotions. Some sadness but also gratitude at being there and something unnamable but familiar. As if some ancient understanding or knowledge has been awakened and is stirring. Through my tears I lift my camera to take photos of the graceful columns that glitter blazingly white against the Greek-blue sky, hoping to capture on film some evidence of whatever mystical essence remains here.

OCTOBER 1–9, 1990
The Cyclades

The island cruise is a two-week tour of the Cyclades that will include Andros, Tinos, Ios, Kea, Mykonos, Naxos, and Santorini. *Cyclades* roughly translates to "circle," and the islands in this grouping form a loose ring around Delos, the sacred birthplace of Artemis and her twin, Apollo. According to mythology Poseidon, god of the sea, furious with the Cyclades nymphs, turned them into islands by slamming his trident into a mountainside. Myth doesn't tell us why Poseidon was so angry with the nymphs, but who knows what can set off a god?

I wander along the seaworn, sun-bleached docks of Zea Marina, the ocean scents tainted by diesel, fish, and waterlogged wood. Ever-present gulls overhead make their pronouncements, boats *knock-knock* on moorings, ropes and ties clank against masts. The motors of small skiffs murmur softly as they turn and head out to sea.

We're scheduled to leave early from Piraeus, and this October morning is still gray as I search for our boat. My sense of adventure is bright—the part of me my father awakened all those years ago, the part that gives life but scares me sometimes with its wild need to go, to leave, to *adventure*. The part of me that is insecure and a little frightened I continue to trace to my mother. Formed in pre-cognition, this worrying voice often whispers in the ear of the free spirit. "*Shh*—not now," I tell it, still searching but not finding the boat.

Grappling with Greek, English, and animated gesturing, the harbor policeman tells me my boat isn't here yet but may be by eight. "No," I insist and show him my reservation confirmation from the tour company. We roam the wooden docks until finally we find her—the *Aegeana Kima*, a sleek yacht with a capacity for sixteen in several tiny staterooms with stacked bunks and an open deck. Onboard she is nothing at all like that dark and shadowy ferry of my middle-of-the-night crossing from Dubrovnik to Corfu. Even below, the *Aegeana Kima* is light and airy.

Our captain, who so far as I know does not have a name beyond Captain, is a dark, brooding Greek with a face that wants a mustache. A man not given to stories of sea voyages or Greek myths, which I so wanted to hear. We'll get no archeology or geography; he sails his boat and communicates to us through the first mate, Tony, the younger of the two men. Tony is friendlier and, in his heavily accented English, gives us details about the boat—where to sleep, where to store our belongings, how to use the shower and flush the toilet. "Pumpa, pumpa," he says, illustrating how we must push the pedal beside the john in the tiny room that also holds the shower. "Don't shower often," Tony warns.

The boat is rustic; "simple" is how the brochure described it. No hot shower. Shared facilities. But there are many places to be—inside, outside, up top above the cabins, in front where it's windier and shaded by a canvas awning. In the rear where noise from the motor is loudest but the wind is less and the sun hotter.

We are eight for the island cruise: Dorte, a barely-beyond-college-age German girl from Frankfurt, dark-haired and pretty, with fresh skin and cornflower eyes; Eva, from Holland, also young, also pretty, also, like Dorte, single; Ruud and Anna Marie, a very young honeymooning couple from Amsterdam—he wears studious glasses, she's bright-eyed; Phillipe, a thin thirtysomething Frenchman, self-conscious and shy; Gabriella, an Italian who works for the defense ministry—friendly and a bit round; and Martha, a Canadian from Vancouver, a few years older than me. Tall and thin, she is a plainspoken journalist.

Martha and I are the only two who are signed up for the entire two-week cruise.

All speak some English except Gabriella; she speaks some French. Phillipe's English is as basic as my French, which is to say *inexistanté*. Martha also speaks French, which is the Canadian way ("*Quelle heure est-il?*" Tom used to occasionally ask). Eva, Dorte, and the honeymooners speak impeccable English, as well as their native languages. Everyone except me and including Tony, the first mate, drinks wine, ouzo, and beer. It's a holiday. There will be drinking.

Kea, the first of the islands we visit is small, not well-known, and hardly touristed. Across the water on the cliff's edge stands a cube of white building—typical Greek island construction. Church? Lighthouse? Too far for my camera to capture, though a stunning picture forms as a tall-masted ship sails by. Four of our group have gone exploring, four of us stay at our campsite on the beach.

The Aegean seawater is as fresh and clean and invigorating as travel brochures promise, so clear that even as I stand immersed up to my shoulders, I can see details of my feet, toe by toe, stirring up sand, prying up a shell. Above the cliff a honeyed halo forms as the sun continues its journey, in the distance mountains of the mainland ascend deep gray and purple, a strip of plum before the blue. I know the darker colors are caused by the noxious *nefos*, but that doesn't diminish the beauty.

As the sun sets, the air cools, and the colors disappear from the sky and the water I return, still dripping, to my place on the sand next to Martha. The honeymooners keep their own company a little farther down the shore.

"Do you think about remarrying?" I ask Martha, who is also a widow; her husband died of cancer nine years before. I ask because Kati Mati made her pronouncement that I would marry again by my fiftieth year. Before she suggested the idea, marriage wasn't something I imagined as a natural or assumed part of my future life. Three years into my own widowhood and the on-and-off relationship, which is currently off, marriage isn't something I'm even considering.

I've gone by four last names now, why would I ever want to take another one? Changing identities another time could only serve to confuse me further. Is Judy Reeves the same person as Judy Gray, I mean, besides the changes that come with aging—a little wiser, one hopes, certainly more experienced in the ways of the world. I say my original family name to myself; it sits unfamiliar in my mind. Who was she, that young girl with her dreams of travel and writing, who despite her need for independence gave it away again and again?

"I'd like to find someone to travel with," Martha tells me. "More of a companion." She takes her gaze from the sea to four men just down the beach who are playing wiffle ball, observes them for a moment. "That one is really hung," she says. I actually guffaw, a most unladylike sound, grateful to be relieved of my heavy thoughts.

Twilight comes and along with it mosquitoes. I want to go back to the boat and change and get ready for dinner, but the others haven't returned from their walk and I said I would stay with their things. These are the drawbacks about traveling with a group—your freedom of choice gets sacrificed to commitments and consensus.

From Kea we sail to Evia, a fishing port and home to our captain. After a night of not much sleep I watch the sunrise from the deck as we set out for what will be a five-hour crossing for Tinos. Time on the open sea can be rough. Anna Marie got sick last night, Phillipe isn't feeling well either, and Eva looks a little green under her enviable tan. I am fine but practicing preventive measures—no writing and no reading as we sail. I remember Tom telling me on one of our first fishing outings, *Keep your eyes on the horizon. Eat something.*

We arrive on Tinos in time for lunch at a pretty outdoor restaurant with red tablecloths and awnings to match, ladder-back chairs, and a view out a greenery-shaded patio to the sea. After fresh fish, tzatziki, pita bread, olives, and ripe tomatoes, we hike the hill to the Church of the Evangelistria, a holy place famed for its miracles, which the faithful sometimes crawl on their knees from the port to reach.

These pilgrimages and shrines cause me to wish again that I, too, had the absolute faith of the true believer. To find solace in myths and miracles that are passed down and reenacted, held sacred and celebrated without question and with devotion, and to follow familiar paths as you wander among columns and light candles at scented altars. What great comfort it must be to know the way and follow the path.

The wind has come up and we must stay in Tinos for a few days. Four members of the captain's family from Evia join us, all of them up early, talking rapidly and loudly. Mornings on the boat are not peaceful—breakfast is ready before we arise, the Captain bellows down the hall in his loud voice, Tony goes through the cabins knocking on doors to wake us; then comes the *pumpa pumpa* of the toilet, the group chattering in all our different languages.

Even when we're not on the boat, we're still together—for meals, the beach, or excursions en masse to see what there is to see. This is so different after months of being alone, lodging myself in places to settle in, linger, and write—cafés, park benches, my single rooms in two-star hotels or pensions.

In a way, though, traveling with a group is easier—I don't have to make all the decisions. In fact, I don't have to make any decisions. The group decides when and where to eat, miraculously reaching some kind of multilingual consensus. The boat goes where it goes—or doesn't go. Sometimes our pace is slow as conversation gets translated—Dutch to German to French to Italian to English or some mix-and-match of all the languages. Gabriella, who speaks Italian and French, is very funny and laughs easily. Anna Marie does terrific imitations of Phillipe and we all laugh except poor, thin, shy Phillipe, who drinks more wine. Dorte doesn't make jokes; instead, she fends off advances from Tony, who gets angry at the rebuff and also drinks more wine.

The toilet is our greatest source of humor—the pumping, the acrobatics of using it on the rough seas, the line in the mornings. Martha hates the toilet and tells us so. She is intimidated by it and the necessity to *pumpa pumpa*, and she hates the shower, such as it is. I agree, it isn't much.

The weather on Tinos is still bad. Strong winds blow in and clouds eclipse the sky; even darker clouds hang behind the hills like bogeymen. The Meltemi Wind, I learn, is an annual wind that blows from the north and is strongest in summer but often lasts into the fall. The Souva Café offers iced Nescafé and a place to sit with my journal, but even with nothing to do except be here and write, I'm not relaxed— wind does that to me. Southern California's Santa Ana winds always set me on edge, but when I was alone in our too-big house after Tom died, they felt especially menacing coming accompanied by the threat of wildfires, as they often do.

Martha and Dorte have taken colds. Martha has talked of jumping ship in Naxos on Saturday and not continuing next week. These long, windy days on Tinos, I consider what's next for me. Abandon the plan of the next six days on the boat, sacrifice the money, and take a ferry to Mykonos for a few days, then on to Santorini by myself? I'm as uncertain as the weather.

Finally, the fifth day of our cruise, we sail for Mykonos. It's late afternoon nearing sunset and we'll be there before dark, in time for dinner. The winds are fair, the air warm, and we have each stowed away in our favorite places on the boat. I lean against the cabin in the shade and watch the moonrise.

When I was a little girl I believed the sun and the moon were one entity: sun side in the daytime, moon side at night. Then one afternoon as I stood on the sidewalk in front of our house, rising high above the houses and trees in a sky still bright with summer sun—the moon! Full and round and clear as I'd ever seen it. A day moon.

This was a discovery. Something I thought I knew disassembled by the physical facts right there in the sky above me: sun over there, moon up there. Two separate bodies.

I didn't go running to my mother to tell of my discovery. I

held it to myself, some precious, private information I needed to consider.

That day may have been when I became something of a lunatic—moon-mad and still to this day in love with the moon. I believe in its influences, those proven by scientific fact and those deeper mysteries that draw me to my window at night and fill me with longing.

I rest against the cabin wall of our small craft in the middle of the Aegean Sea. To the west the Greek sun is setting, coloring the sky in molten magic; to the east a full moon rises, her face shaded flaxen. The sun and the moon. One at each end of the Earth and us in the middle, floating along her watery skin on a boat with wings.

Island of the Winds is the name for Mykonos, and its iconic windmills rise above scruffy hills, blue domes, and whitewashed buildings.

Mykonos is fabled. Formed from the petrified bones of giants killed by Hercules goes one story; formed in anger from a sea nymph by Poseidon goes another; named for Apollo's grandson, the first ruler of the island. Mykonos is the quintessential Greek-island fantasy for those of us who have romantic myths of our own. Those windmills, those white, white buildings surrounded by a blue that can only be imagined until you see it with your own eyes.

Martha and I jump ship in Mykonos, both weary of the tight quarters, the forced company, the captain's whims. We were both especially weary of the *pumpa-pumpa* bathroom with its tiny, hand-held, seldom-functioning cold-water shower. We were ready to sleep in a real bed and not bunks stacked one atop the other and to bathe in a full-body shower where you can let the water run as hot as you can stand it and leave it running as long as you want.

Truth is neither of us is a sailor, and frankly I was a little bored since I couldn't read or write during the long hours we sailed island to island. I've never dreamt of sailing around the world. An afternoon on the bay, yes. But when it comes to journeys I'm a solid-ground girl, a road trip woman.

We found a small hotel tucked in one of the narrow stone streets in the town of Chora. It's good to be off the boat, to open my pack and air out my few clothes, to have a bed I can sit up in and not hit my head. I like having windows that open to the radiant day through dancing curtains.

We share a room at the Zorzis Hotel for a few days, wander the streets, search cafés for afternoon coffees and early dinners. Mornings and evenings we sit on the flowered and shrub-planted hotel patio.

Being on this lovely island, I sense myself opening. The image is of a bud that has been tightly closed and is now slowly loosening its outer protective leaves. I can't stop stretching my arms high over my head and wide out from my sides. I stand tall in our room in the morning when I get out of bed, shower as long as I like, and take long-legged steps to the patio for morning coffee and breakfast. It's as if I've been living in a box and not a very big one. Even on Mykonos's narrow streets I take long strides and like the brush of my skirt skimming my bare tanned legs.

The proprietor of our hotel, Jonathon, a gregarious Greek about my age, is a bit round for my taste, but attentive and generous to Martha and me. And talkative. He's a storyteller and kind of amusing. He's like the sort of movie you want to go to after a hard day. A distraction, a comedy that doesn't even pretend to have any deeper meaning. That's how Jonathon strikes me—a diversion.

One morning, as Martha and I were finishing breakfast on the patio, he invited me to come to his house for drinks one evening.

"Sure," I say, "but I don't drink."

"We'll have cokes," he says. "I don't drink either."

So, just for diversion, I agree to go. Martha shakes her head as if to say, *What are you thinking?*

He gives me the address; it's not far from the hotel, a few blocks. "Turn left at the building with the red door and left again where the blue railing on that building's stairs is missing a few slats."

After a day of wandering shops and cafés and visiting the dock, I follow Jonathan's directions, and with none of my usual wrong turns, I arrive and knock on the door.

"Come in, it's open." Muffled from inside.

I enter.

The lamps are low, giving the place—its brocaded wallpaper and over-stuffed furniture—a shadowy dimness. And there is Jonathon sitting on a gold sofa, naked except for a quilt wrapped around his lower torso.

"The cokes are in the refrigerator," he says, nodding toward another room.

This could continue to be a lighthearted romp or turn into some kind of a horror movie. Or a movie you don't want to see at all.

"Oh," I must have said. Or something equally expressive. Sometimes *oh* covers everything—the acknowledgment of the present situation, the recollection of your friend's dubious head-shaking, the surprise. This undressed man, his hairless chest with drooping breasts, a round belly that is better disguised beneath the loose-hanging shirts he wears at the hotel, with only that quilt around his lower half, one naked leg protruding from under it. The overstuffed sofa, the over-done wallpaper, the dim light—fringe on the lampshade, for God's sake—the whole scene ridiculous and a little creepy.

"Oh." I know I say it this time. "No thanks. I can't stay." I mumble something not too rude but also barely articulate and back out the door.

Martha is lounging on the patio smoking when I arrive at the hotel.

"I told you," she says, flicking ashes into a glass ashtray.

Martha leaves a few days later. Her cold wasn't any better and her cough was getting worse. She catches a ferry back to Athens and then plans to fly home to Canada a few days later. We'll keep in touch, we promise. I'll remain on Mykonos a while longer, finding another pension. Zorzis Hotel and its proprietor are no longer comfortable nor amusing. I want to spend more time on Mykonos's beaches, and I want to go to Delos, the most sacred of all the Cyclades and myth-rich with antiquity. I'll decide where next after that.

Sunday morning I'm up and out early. The light is lovely as I lazily stroll to the harbor. Here fishermen hawk their bountiful catch, laden carts flaunt fresh produce, and Petros the Pelican rules the roost. This Petros isn't the original mascot; the first came to the island in 1958 after being saved by a local fisherman. That Petros lived a long, healthy, and celebrated life until he was hit by a car in 1985. Today's Petros is doing his best to fill the webbed feet of the original—certainly the tourists adore him; I took a photo too. I wanted to pose Travel Girl beside the pelican but had been warned not to get too close. Apparently Petros doesn't like to share the spotlight.

The winding, narrow streets are quiet this morning, brightly painted shutters still closed. But the cats—the cats of Mykonos are everywhere, some talking to me as I pass, some ignoring me as only cats can. I stop by the church—Panagia Paraportiani, the famous landmark that graces guidebooks, maps, postcards, and calendars. A woman sketches; I take photos—the church's gently sloping walls are ashimmer in the early-morning sun. One wall is veiled with bougain-villea; light and shadow form angles and shapes.

I hesitate to photograph a graceful blue-shuttered window draped in lace curtains on one home I come upon, as if my camera is an intrusion into someone's life. Instead I close my eyes and attempt to capture the image in memory, a moment of time and place that exists only here and only now.

After lunch at the Anchor Bar I find my way to a beach near town and spread the woven mat I purchased at a local shop. The afternoon has become long-shadowed as I attempt to read but for some reason can't. Tears slide silently down my cheeks. The rhythm of small waves *shush-shushing* against the sand lulls me into reverie, recalling our honeymoon on Fiji. How white the sand there, how clear the water. I find myself wondering if I'll be on another beach somewhere else in the world six months from now, sitting alone on another long-shadowed afternoon, crying from an unnamed sadness. The farther inside I explore the deeper it seems to go, this melancholy. Deeper, deeper still, and there is ever more sadness, more to grieve, to mourn. Not just Tom—his terrible sickness and death—this sorrow isn't personal or unique to me. More simply a condition of being human, of living on the earth, being conscious of our tender hearts. This is not a bad thing, this deep sadness. One of the many books that I left behind in San Diego is a well-worn copy of *The Rubáiyát of Omar Khayyám*, which, among many other paradoxes, addresses both joy and sorrow.

> *Then a woman said, Speak to us of joy and sorrow.*
>
> *. . . When you are joyous, look deep into your heart and you shall find it is only that which has given you sorrow that is giving you joy.*
>
> *When you are sorrowful look again in your heart, and you shall see that in truth you are weeping for that which has been your delight.*

I wipe away the tears with the back of my hand and glance around to see who might have noticed my crying. Few of us remain on the beach as clouds rise from the northeast and a slight breeze picks up. Across the Aegean, Tinos rises smoky and blue-gray in the distance. A ferry comes into sight, small and far away. Closer up, the barren hillside of Mykonos where stone fences crowned with whitewash lead to cubed buildings marked with cobalt doors and shutters. A few scrappy bushes, magenta bougainvillea. The island's iconic windmills, squat and solid atop the hillside.

Mykonos is blue, blue like the ink from my pen, and deeper. Rich, royal blue and deeper yet. Deep navy of the deepest waters of the Aegean. Indigo and then lighter. And white—bright, clean white with no shades of yellow, not a hint of gray. Sugar-cube houses, stacked cube upon cube, climb the mountainsides, cleaving to the angles of hills that echo the rounded mounds atop churches whose domes are sometimes stained lapis, sometimes bloodred, sometimes left white to gleam pure and bright in the island sun.

Mykonos is narrow passageways between whitewashed buildings and stones drifting in a confusing, convoluted maze that leaves the traveler either frustrated at her inability to find her desired destination or sighing open-mouthed at yet another postcard scene before her.

Mykonos. Singing birds in cages that hang from balconies and eaves. Saffron-yellow birds caroling complicated arias made louder by echoing off white walls. The *putt-putt* of three-wheeled carts that ferry supplies through town, hauling luggage from cruise ships and airport as more and more of us arrive hour after hour, day after day.

Mykonos. The slapping of squid and octopus on rocks as fishermen tender their catch to sell to restaurants, tavernas, and stands. Gentle wavelets that tiptoe in rather than crash and overpower the sand. Can I say wavelets that kiss the sand?

Greeks yelling. Sometimes in anger, other times because that's the way here. Yelling at each other, yelling at their guests, their customers, their families. I am learning not to take it personally. It's not me, I think—a new twist on the old breakup line—it's *you*.

Light changes the face of white buildings and barren hills. Early-morning sun bright on red geraniums and Greek-blue doors and sweet yellow kittens lying on whitewashed stones. Late-afternoon gold on scarlet bougainvillea.

Mykonos. Sensuous and sensual. And for a reason I cannot name, sad.

Poor Leto. Pregnant by Zeus and banished by his jealous wife, Hera, to wander, unable to find a place to bear her children, twins who would be the gods Apollo and Artemis. Everywhere Leto went she was turned away by those afraid of Hera's rage. Finally Zeus makes Delos appear, a floating island surrounded by swans. It's here Leto is able to find a birthing place. Artemis is the first of the twins born; an easy birth, it's said. But Apollo's birth took nine days and nights. Difficult because Hera—upon discovering Leto laboring on Delos—kidnapped Eileithyia, goddess of childbirth, forcing Artemis to help her mother deliver the infant.

I love the myths and their conflicting details—triumphs and tragedies, murders and betrayals and transformations. Leto herself, upon learning some disapproving townspeople had poisoned a well from which she drank, turned the populace into frogs.

My Midwestern upbringing doesn't contain any myths. Stories are repeated, of course, a family legend or two handed down, one involving Jesse James, or at least his mother or his brother. Another features Johnny Appleseed, and I'm told Daniel Boone is a distant ancestor. But I long for something more. I want to come from people who experienced a mysterious or even mythological backstory. This is why I was attracted to the Catholic Church, beguiled for a time by stories and rituals, but eventually disenchanted by rules and dictates. This desire for the mystical is why I consult the tarot, believe in moon magic, try to translate messages written in the stars. Wondering why I've come to Greece and why I'm on a ferry sailing from Mykonos to Delos on this fine mid-October afternoon.

Delos is like a battlefield strewn with the remains of a civilization at war with the elements. Can it be that this place was once the reigning jewel of the Cyclades, the holy place that gave birth to Artemis and Apollo? At another time of year, in spring when the poppies bloom, then one might see this barren, windswept place as a cradle of life.

The now-dry sacred lake holds a single palm that rises like a promise or a memory. I wander among the ruins where Leto gave birth, where city-states ruled, where Artemis was worshipped. I spot another woman walking with the same reverent step. She also opens her palm on the remarkably cool columns and gazes with searching eyes over the once-holy place. She, too, may be searching for her roots, her connection with the spiritual, the beginning of herself. We don't speak, this woman and I, only nod as we pass.

Quietly touching the white stone, stroking its rough, sparkling surface with an open palm, I wait for the awareness that I belong here or once did, the sense of connection that makes itself known in hot salty tears and long sighs from a place deep inside, which speaks of both mystery and knowing. I wait, but only awe comes as, hand against stone, I witness the remnants of a people who lived eons, millennia, before my time here.

Away from the ruins rises a steep and rocky hillside. At the crest, tired after my trudge up, I find a large flat stone, crawl up on it, and lay back, letting its strength cradle me. The ages-old Aegean wind whispers over my body and dries the sweat of my efforts. The warmth of the granite stone spreads along my spine and arms and across the back of my thighs. The light breeze brings the soft sound of the ocean as it brushes the shore. I am alone here, though remnants of other tourists and seekers remain—empty plastic water bottles, discarded film boxes. Eyes closed against their blasphemy, my lids tint red by the afternoon sun. I wear a bright yellow Hawaiian shirt I found at the flea market in Athens, the fabric warm from my granite cradle and the sun on my chest and stomach. I want to take it off and lie naked atop the stone, but I don't. I sigh once and once again, deep audible sighs that carry on the wind and out over the sea.

OCTOBER 9, 1990
Mykonos to Santorini

Aboard the Mykonos-to-Santorini ferry I notice a young man leaning against the ship's rail: dark-haired, his arms muscular in a fitted white T-shirt. I stare openly at him, and maybe he gazes back at me. He's wearing mirrored sunglasses, so though it appears he's seeing me, he could be looking past me into the far horizon toward our destination.

OCTOBER 9–14, 1990
Santorini

The Loucas Hotel in Fira features a series of rooms with dimly lit sloping walls that penetrate into the hillside. These cave hotels, as they're known, are common structures on Santorini, built onto the cliffs to take advantage of the view—which is, in a word, jaw-dropping. On the terrace I gaze west toward islands formed by a volcanic explosion 3,600 years ago. Far below, ships loll in the calm waters of the caldera and the setting sun gilds the steep cliffs as if confirming Santorini's reputation as the most beautiful of all the Greek islands.

My bedroom, with its low ceiling and two single beds, leads to an empty room that opens to the bath and a handheld, open-walled shower. The curved walls of the empty room display replicas of iconic Minoan murals—young women bearing bunches of crocuses in their outstretched arms and long-legged antelopes drawn in simple, graceful lines in volcanic black and a deep red the color of dried blood.

Something ancient in me is stirred by the frescoes. I want to sink into the mysteries of Santorini. *Devil's Island*, some call it. Maybe because of the fiery volcanic explosion centuries ago. Some historians have aligned the timing of the eruption with stories in the Bible—three days of darkness and the parting of the Red Sea. A more popular legend links Santorini to the lost city of Atlantis since archaeologists continue to unearth ruins from the ancient civilization of the Minoans with their advanced water systems and mills and many-storied city structures. I remember reading about vampires on this island and wonder at the tale's origin. As a young girl I was fascinated and a little afraid watching early vampire films—Dracula's filmy black cape, the sensuous woman asleep in her satin nightgown—the whole thing in shadowy black and white, underscored with minor notes from an unseen orchestra.

Alone on my balcony at the Loucas Hotel as evening comes, my thoughts turn sensuous. The physical beauty of the island, the sweet breeze, the generous curve of whitewashed domes silhouetted in twilight, boats lifting and dropping with the motion of the sea. I want to be held and touched. I want to kiss someone and have his hands on my body, my breasts tanned from topless sunbathing. I want to be caressed and murmured over. I want sighing breaths in my hair, lips on my neck, strong arms around me. This is what I take to bed with me as I slip naked into one of the two single beds in my slope-walled room.

The T-shirted man with the mirrored sunglasses and good arms I noticed on the ferry from Mykonos arrived at Loucas Hotel this morning as I enjoyed toast and fresh fruit and the view from the terrace. Afterward he stopped in at Canava, where I went for my second coffee. Later as I board the bus for Kamari Beach, he is there again.

Considering these seeming coincidences as we ride down the hill to the black-sand beach, I recall the ease with which I used to go for quick pickups and one-night stands. The casual sex and easy rationale—actually there was no rationale; it was totally hedonistic. It was the seventies. And alcohol was involved. Always.

That young woman was looking for love in all the wrong places, as the song goes. Looking for approval, for acceptance, a sign that she was okay in the world. The sexual energy that drove her wasn't the kind of pure sexual energy I experienced with Tom but a misplaced, misidentified need. Of course the drinking didn't help, or the drugs, which only added to the general madness of the times and gave me— gave all of us—permission to break the rules, to be wild. Mine was a rebellion against the sexual repression I was raised with, that Midwest Methodist puritanism of secrecy bred with shame that resulted in all manner of dysfunction. My mother once told me, *Everything bad that's happened in my life has been on account of sex.* I never asked her what that *everything* was, but I do know being a curious, sexual young woman was a threat to any sort of contained order.

It's time to forgive that young woman who gave herself away so easily.

Lying topless on a rented chaise at the black-sand beach, the erotic energy I experience today isn't tainted with shame but born of the sensuality of my nearly naked body, warm sun on my skin, a cool breeze that makes my nipples erect, and fantasies of the young man who seemed to be all the places I was.

Enjoy it, I tell the woman I am now, *for what it is.* A reminder from your body of the fullness this life has to offer and the richness of your imagination. Who knows what stories might be forming there, awaiting their time to be released.

Each evening on Santorini I join the crowd at Franco's Bar for the ritual witnessing of the sunset. This time, my last night here, as I gaze into the tranquil sapphire waters of the caldera, I attempt to capture the beauty, the colors, the light, in my journal. But such magic can never be captured in words. It isn't just the painting of color by light, it's the emotional response to witnessing such beauty, taking it in not only through sight but in the scent of the sea and the sounds on the patio—voices of people from all over the world who've been called to this mystical place. There is also the call of seabirds as they circle low over the azure water, the clinking of donkey bells, and the breath of breeze on my skin as I savor this good cappuccino served in a gleaming white cup.

An opera plays from hidden speakers, and as the resplendent sun dips into the sea the aria rises in a great arc. This is sunset as total-body sensory immersion. This is holy. This is a prayer, an amen to the day. We are held in thrall for long moments almost as if we are not breathing or are breathing as one.

And then it's over.

We commence back into our dialogues, our importances. But

surely we must be somehow changed, having experienced a phenomenon that none of us could divine nor replicate, try as we might through painting or poetry or the artifice of photography. There is a reason beyond reason that we gather at Franco's Bar and places such as this the world over every afternoon at sunset; I know of no one who is indifferent to it, no one who can turn away in the presence of such beauty. The experience is something we need no matter who we are or what we believe. I am not alone in my reverence and my desire to be blessed.

OCTOBER 14, 1990
Santorini to Piraeus

The beauty and tranquility of my time on Santorini carries over until it is ruptured when our six-bed all-female cabin on the ferry to Athens is invaded in the night by a man. His wife or girlfriend is with him—it must have been she who was assigned the bunk beneath mine which they both, somehow, occupy. He reeks of booze and its stink permeates the whole cabin, along with his pervasive man-smell of basements, laundry hampers, and last week's gym clothes. And he snores. When he gets up to use the sink that stands in the narrow aisle between the rows of bunks, he is inches from my face.

This man's privilege, not to mention his odoriferous, hulking presence, sets up an anger I know is not mine alone but arises in response to a millennia of invasions by men into women's private, intimate spaces. An ages-old smoldering has taken up residence in my body, where it looms like that ancient Santorini volcano. I turn my head, turn my whole body toward the wall and pull tight into myself. There will be no deep sleep the rest of the night and no more sensuous dreams.

We dock in the middle of the night. Groggy from scant sleep, I gather myself, join the lineup to exit the ferry, and, once ashore, find a taxi.

"Acropolis House," I tell the driver. "The Pláka."

We drive the darkened streets into the old part of Athens where the road seems to be some sort of Minoan labyrinth. The driver turns this way then that looking for my hotel. His mutterings and snorts relay his building frustration.

Finally after another turn, another street, and no hotel, he stops his cab and orders me out. I don't understand the words he uses, but his tone is one an angry husband might use with his wife, as if I had burned his dinner or ruined his favorite shirt in the laundry. He gets out of the driver's seat, opens the back door, and says, "No!"

That I understand.

"Acropolis House?" I ask. "Kodrou?" saying the name of the street.

He mutters something I don't understand and points down the darkened street.

I get out with my pack. He slams the door after me, gets behind the wheel, and takes off. His taillights blink then disappear as he squirrels around another turn.

Dark. Empty street. Alone. I have no idea where I am, what time it is, or where my hotel is. I wish for some of the anger I held in my body in the night on the ferry, but what I get instead are tears. Dammit.

It's quiet of course. Even noisy Athens, one of the loudest cities in Europe if not the world, is quiet this time of the morning. This is before the birds, before the first hint of dawn, before any lamps come on in any bedroom or kitchen. So you choose—right or left. Up the hill or down.

I choose down and set forth, my pack bumping along behind me. Down and down, around the next curve, and there in the distance, a soft glow on the darkened sidewalk. Following some natural human instinct, I go toward the light.

The beacon is coming from a small café. Inside, a woman behind the counter wears an apron and the face of someone who is used to being up at this time of the morning, a weary droop of eyelids and a determined set to her lips.

A couple of stools line up along the counter; a small table rests by the window. The aroma is of coffee and something good baking. I take a seat at one of the stools. I want to be near the woman. I want to hear her say *kaliméra*. I want to see her smile.

"*Kaliméra*," I say. "Coffee, *sas parakaloúme*," mangling the pronunciation.

OCTOBER 15–16, 1990
Athens

October 15, Monday—my forty-eighth birthday. After I pick up a thick envelope of mail at the American Express office I take myself up the hill to Totristato, my "home" café in Athens and am delighted that the young woman at the counter hasn't forgotten me in the two weeks I've been away. She smiles her pretty dimpled smile and says hello in English.

"Cappuccino?" she asks, as much a reassurance as a question, like she's welcoming me back. The people at the Acropolis House offered the same warmth when I checked in after finding my way along the dawn-lit streets.

Balancing the cup in one hand, fresh croissant on a tiny plate in the other, and with the fat package under my arm, I settle in at a table by the window and open this generous birthday present. Inside:

- Amy catches me up on her doings—waiting tables at a place that's attached to a popular nightclub and doing comedy where and when she can.

- Camille writes that she wants to open a café in San Francisco. I want to call her and tell her, "Wait for me!"

- My son, Chris, who stayed with me for a few months in Jamul right after Tom's death, writes a brief hello, an *I'm fine* note.

- Davinia, a longtime AA friend, asks why I don't settle down in one place and make some friends, a comment that comes across as more scold than curiosity. I want to write back and say, "I'm still trying to figure that one out."

- Jill, a friend of a friend I met in London, encloses pages of her stories in her newsy letter, keeping me up on her writing progress.

- Loren, an American I met at the international bookstore in Budapest, sends a postcard with a gorgeous photo of a sunset and suggests I join him in Istanbul. Which I won't do but consider while I bite into the delicious almond croissant.

- Al JaCoby, my old boss at the *San Diego Union* and my first mentor, invites me to write travel pieces, which he says he'll attempt to place. He lures me with compliments on my writing and the suggestion that I could earn a little money. I'm giddy and want to share the invitation with someone but there's no one to share with, so I just grin into my cappuccino.

- And finally in that thick packet a birthday card and letter from my mom and dad. Though the card and enclosed letter are signed from both, my dad wrote it. His handwriting reminds me of my grandmother Gray's, his mother, the same spiky slant that addressed the birthday cards she used to send when I was a girl. Daddy's letter tells me he loves me and he's proud of me for taking this journey by myself. He doesn't say so, but I know it's a journey he would have loved to set off on. I'm touched by what he wrote, and coupled with the memory of my grandmother, with whom I always felt deeply connected, I can't stop the tears.

My grandmother's death was the first I experienced as an adult—my other grandparents all died when I was young, and what did I know of death then, or what loss forever even meant, or how grief would one day affect me. No single death can prepare us for another; each loss brings its own unique dimensions and colors. I don't know how to compare the absence of my grandmother with the absence of Tom.

My grandmother hasn't been a part of my life for many years, and even before her death we weren't close, at least not physically. Not in our daily lives. Now when I experience an intimation of her absence, as with the reminder of her handwriting on birthday cards, it's accompanied by a sweet memory—a photo of her grinning in anticipation as we ready to board a helicopter, something she said she'd always wanted to do. I touch the soft underside of my own arm and feel the softness of her arm around me as we sat side by side on the couch, and I hear the sound of her voice reading to me.

Tom's voice, which I have often heard in these few years since his death—on audio recordings of commercials or material we produced together—comes not with sweet memories of him but the painful reminder of his absence.

Knowing from the loss of my grandmother that with time the absence of someone we loved and lost becomes more familiar than their presence, I believe, hope, trust this will be true for Tom too.

But not yet. Not yet.

What a freight train of emotions carried in one bulging package.

Happy birthday to me.

JUNE 1986
Jamul

The first terrible hints that something was wrong came in June just after Tom's forty-fourth birthday. I awoke to him sitting at the edge of our bed, his back to me, hunched over, his back curved so the knuckles of his spine showed.

"Are you using a different detergent or something?" he asked.

"What do you mean?" I sat up, leaned toward him.

"My chest—some kind of an itch or irritation. Only inside."

I touched his bare shoulder, his skin still warm from sleep. "What?"

"I don't know." The timbre of his voice held curiosity but also a trace of something else: concern, gravity?

He got up then and disappeared into the bathroom. We didn't speak of it again until some weeks later.

Summer in the backcountry starts early and stays late, and I was already hot. Changing the sheets on our bed one morning, I noticed some small scuffs along its redwood base. I bent down and ran my finger along them, skimming the indentations when Tom came into the room. I glanced up to where he stood just past the doorway.

"A mass—" he said, then stopped speaking and put his open hand on his chest near his heart.

"What?" I straightened up, went to him. "What do you mean?"

"In the X-rays; he called it a mass."

"Who?"

"Jim."

Our friend who lived down the road and had a small chiropractic practice connected to his house.

"I asked him to take an X-ray," Tom said. "He told me I should see someone."

His voice, that beautiful voice that was the reason for our meeting all those years ago, that voice cracked and he couldn't say more. He didn't need to.

We stood together in our bedroom on that hot country morning and held each other.

"It's not going to go away," he said finally.

∾

OCTOBER 17–18, 1990
Delphi

In the morning I will take the tour bus for Delphi, one hundred miles from Athens and high above the Gulf of Corinth in the shadow of Mount Parnassus. I will stay overnight and return to Athens late the next day.

As with the Cyclades, many myths surround Delphi and its origins as a sacred place. This is one:

Delphi was believed to be the center of the Earth—the navel of the world. The place the two eagles released by Zeus met—one flew east and one west. Here Zeus set down omphalos, the sacred stone, to mark the place and the Delphic oracle was born.

Pythia, the oracle, purified herself in the water of the Castalian Spring. Next she breathed the fumes of burning laurel leaves that sent her into a state of ecstasy, from which she uttered incoherent words. These utterances were then composed into verses by the priest and the interpreters attempted to render meaning from the prophecy.

In the first reenactments of the sacred ceremony the Pythia were chosen from among the young women of Delphi. However, as time went on, to be certain of their virtue, the priests selected priestesses from among women who'd passed their fiftieth year.

This recognition of and reverence for women beginning their crone years is one of the reasons I've come to Dephi. The other is because I believe in oracles. I look for signs and signals; I'm enthralled by synchronicities, by clairvoyance. This fascination with the occult began in my adolescent years when I consulted the Magic 8 Ball, a globe the size of a grapefruit, black and shiny and heavy in the hands of an eleven-year-old girl.

"Close your eyes and think of a question," my best friend Betty tells me. We're in her bedroom for another sleepover, where we'll climb up on her high bed and gaze out the picture window through the elms and sycamores and dream our futures.

"A yes-or-no question," Betty says.

I hold the Magic 8 Ball in both hands, hefting its weight—which surely indicates its gravitas—and try to think of a yes-or-no question. So many things I wondered at that age in our old farmhouse of a home, my dad the butcher at a small-town market just outside St. Joseph, my mother at home, Monday laundry, Tuesday ironing, and so it goes. I dreamed of an extravagant life different from that of my parents. Of movie stars and swimming pools; being on a stage, singing into a silver microphone, wearing a slinky dress with a flower behind my ear. Being Brenda Starr, reporter, traveling the world on adventures in search of the story. I dreamed another me entirely and the Magic 8 Ball held my future.

The Magic 8 Ball's answers were positive: *It is certain, Without a doubt, Outlook good.* Or negative: *Don't count on it, My sources say no, Very doubtful.* But there were also those that teased with uncertainty: *Reply hazy, try later; Better not tell you now; Concentrate and ask again.*

After the Magic 8 Ball came the Ouija board, sitting knee-to-knee with other seekers intrigued by the possibility of knowing the future, our fingers resting on either side of the planchette as it moved across the board, spelling out cryptic messages word by slowly revealed word formed from the alphabet printed around the board's perimeter in gothic letters.

Every day I read my horoscope in the newspaper—Libra, September 23–October 22. *People born under the sign of the scales are peaceful and fair; lovers of beauty and harmony; the sign of partnership. Libras seek out others as much as they seek balance.*

These early searches were precursors, or rather indicators, of a lifelong seeking, not for clear yes-or-no answers—only wouldn't that be simple, a clean and final end to the search that has been a defining aspect of my life, one that consumes me even to this bright fall day where I find myself in Delphi in the shade of Mount Parnassus before another oracle.

After a visit to the Archeological Museum and the Sanctuary of Apollo, I seek refuge in the Sanctuary of Athena, another ancient site excavated and preserved in Delphi. To get there I follow a road for a short distance from Apollo's Sanctuary, down a hill, then down a path, and down and down into a tree-shaded site much smaller than the one I'd just explored with its theater encircled by five thousand stone seats and the nearby vast field where the Pythian games were held, and where stone seats for seven thousand still rise on the hillside above the green.

Here in Athena's Sanctuary all is still except for the birds in the many olive trees and the soft breeze high above, which causes the leaves to reveal their silver-gray shadings. Few other visitors wander the site.

Two women from Spain and I share a stone bench where we speak softly, honoring the holiness of the place. The Temple of Athena in the Parthenon in Athens is a holy place too. But in this sun-dappled sanctuary I am more aware of sacredness, though I can't say what I am worshipping. I am sanctified, at peace. There are only our voices, the birdsong, and the dry green smell of the olive trees.

After a few moments I separate myself from the others and slip silently among the ruins, placing my palm against the columns as if taking their pulse, a physical connection of two living beings. I do this: palm to tree trunks; palm to wooden doors and beams and tables, against the curve of clay pots; palm against the earth, against the stirring skin of the ocean, lakes, ponds; palm against paper as my other hand travels across the page, chasing language. And yes, palms against necks and faces and lips.

"You will experience many heartbreaks," a long-ago palmist intones, holding my hand in her two and skimming her finger along the Heart line. "Your Heart line is broken in many places," she says, shaking her head, uttering a sigh.

My right hand, the one I write with, was tattooed decades ago when, after sharpening my pencil on the hand-crank sharpener adhered to the wall of my sixth-grade classroom, I accidentally stabbed myself in the palm just above the Heart line. A residue of lead dust stained the small puncture and is still there today, faint and barely visible but present. Though I had been writing my stories and poems and plays for a few years already, I believe I marked myself there and then as Writer.

As I've confessed, I am a superstitious woman, always searching for signs and omens. I give significance to flights of birds, try to read the hieroglyphics of fallen rose petals, and attempt to translate hidden messages in the words of a book left open on a table.

In Athena's Sanctuary shadows grow long and the sun glows golden against Mount Parnassus—home to the Muses—as it sets below the rocky walls of the Phaedriades. The afternoon cools as I ascend the hill back up along the path that will take me past the ruins of Apollo's Sanctuary, the theater, the field, those three iconic columns, back into Delphi itself and my hotel.

Alone, I follow the path high above the sloping hill of olive trees and come upon a bench where I stop and gaze into the valley and far, far below where the silver ribbon of the Pleistos curves sensuously. The sheen on the olive trees gilds the gray leaves. No wind bothers the leaves. All is quiet and serene.

A tabby cat wanders up and winds himself around the legs of the bench then against my legs, bare beneath the length of my skirt. I bend to pet him. "Hello kitty, kitty," I croon and scritch behind his willing ears; his tail curls next to my calf. "Kitty, kitty," I say again. He talks back, a soft meow. I pat the bench beside me, inviting him up. At first he doesn't respond. "Kitty, kitty," I say in that high voice we sometimes use with cats, patting the bench again. This time he joins me and we sit, kitty and I, at rest. My hand lightly on his head rubbing his soft gray ears.

Then there is a man behind me. He may have come along the path and I didn't see him because I was leaning over attending to the cat.

"You are the queen of all this," the man says and sweeps his arm to take in all that is below us—the steep hillside, the silver-and-gold olive trees, the gleaming Pleistos.

He wears workingman's clothes, hair the color of coal and eyes appreciative of the vista; he's short and broad-shouldered. He smiles. Sincere. I smile. He sweeps his arm again. "All of this."

He stands there for a moment, then moves on. The cat jumps down and ambles away, too, sauntering nonchalantly as cats do.

I survey all that is before me—this magnificent view. I want to be fully present in this moment as the sun is at that precise angle, as the trees are that exact turn of color, as the river flows in just that way. I put my palm against the wood of the bench, still warm in the late afternoon; our pulses beat together. This is all it takes to be Queen of All—to simply be here and be present.

OCTOBER 19–29, 1990
Athens

The package from Corfu has arrived. My Greek-blue coat the woman at the shop promised to send. The date stamp says the package has been at the parcel post for days and I'm grateful to the two women at the post office on Omonoia Square for their persistence in helping me locate it. I wish to be able to tell them about the saleswoman, how she said in her charmingly accented English, gold earrings gleaming, "It is made for you, madam."

Another morning of coffee and the *International Herald Tribune* at the Every Day Café. French President Mitterrand says war is inevitable and I don't want to believe him, though now there are 200,000 American, 15,000 British, and 11,000 French troops stationed in the Gulf region.

I've come upstairs because of the crowd below and now sit among teenage girls on a tour. I watch as they interact with each other. The popular ones, the girls who bounce from table to table, gossip, and giggle. I notice how they touch each other, how they're dressed, in outfits so carefully chosen as they show off for one another. And I watch the others. The left-out girls. The chubby one in the wrong color purple; the little one, smaller than the others with no makeup and no smile, no sign of animation on her sweet face; the single Black girl among the gaggle of white girls, so obviously wanting to be a part of, to be included. She calls out to a table of the popular girls and is snubbed by all of them. As she turns away our eyes meet, and I can tell she knows I have seen her slight. I look away from her shame. I know about being left out, not being good enough, of being somehow *less than*. My high school experience wasn't all that different from many others, but when it's happening, when it's your present life, the pain and shame overshadow everything else. I want to make notes about these girls in my journal but hesitate, knowing they'd really be notes about myself, about all of us forever on the outside. It's not exactly a prayer I say, but I wish for these girls, for all of us who were too exuberant, too curious, too rough-edged, too whatever we were that made us different, I want us to know we are enough; we have always been enough.

My friend Linda is in Athens for a few weeks before she and I head off together to join our group for the journey to the Soviet Union. She's traded homes with a Greek couple and is staying in an apartment a few kilometers on the other side of Stadiou Street, which serves as a boundary for the historic neighborhood of the Pláka. Linda's younger sister, Karin, is visiting, too, and the three of us have planned a dinner in a typical Greek restaurant where we'll eat dolmas and moussaka and spanakopita, lots of just-warmed pita bread with bowls of tzatziki, probably some messy and dangerously sweet baklava for dessert paired with strong Greek coffee.

We set out toward the Pláka for an evening of dinner and dancing—*Zorba the Greek* dancing with white handkerchiefs, our arms around one another's shoulders. Bouzoukis and tambourines and *Opa!* We're ready for the lively gaiety of it, the energy and fun and probably looking ridiculous as we attempt the complicated steps of the Greek dances. The restaurant we've chosen, a touristy place in the old town, promises all this.

It's a bit of a distance from Linda's apartment and already dark when we set out. After crossing Stadiou Street and entering the Pláka, we come to a short, narrow bridge with a small stone wall along each side, large cypress trees guarding it. Midpoint on the bridge, a group of young men has gathered, five or six of them, lounging in a cluster. They smoke and laugh in that casual way young men have.

When I was a girl, having to pass groups of boys ganged up like the young men on the bridge was to endure exposure. To be the object of evaluation and appraisal. I'd become self-conscious and not know what to do with my arms, which felt clumsy and out of place on my body. I'd squeeze the muscles in my stomach and butt tight and stare straight ahead, hardly breathing until I got to the other side of what felt like some kind of a test.

Older men were worse. As if they felt more entitled or in some way obligated to make comments, often just loud enough for you to hear, other times even louder, especially if they thought they were being clever, trying to get a laugh from their cohort.

Athens is a noisy place, especially in parts of the city where cars, motorbikes, and delivery trucks all compete for the limited space on narrow streets. And there's something about the shouting—always it seems the shouting. This evening is no different: the night is clamorous with traffic and odors that accompany the noise, exhaust and trash and cooking and people, people, people—locals and tourists alike. The streetlights offer only shadowy light.

At the bridge we are forced to cross single file because of its width and also the cluster of young men. Linda goes first. She lives in San Francisco and travels the world. She's confident, experienced. She sets forth striding and I follow, getting my stride on too. We both cross the bridge, and actually I don't give the men much thought—I'm not that girl anymore. I know how I look. We catch up on the other side of the bridge, but Karin isn't right behind us.

Back on the bridge I hear the men's voices, their laughter. We turn and she's there, midpoint in the crossing, her arms around herself, huddled in protection or hiding. A couple of the guys have stepped toward her, one is touching her arm, others are saying things. They speak Greek of course, but every woman knows exactly what their words are.

Linda and I both dash toward them calling Karin's name. Head down, she comes toward us as if she's suddenly been released from captivity. She's shaking and near tears. The guys are laughing, that awful sound that sparks so many memories and, with the memories, shades of long-ago shame.

It takes a while to calm Karin. Linda and I alternate soothing her and swearing at those men—at all men.

"Assholes!"

"Sons of bitches!"

We speak in English, but they know what we're saying. We each have our favorite expressions. I imagine we look fierce. The men move away, their nervous laughter echoing as they slink into the shadows.

After some minutes of huddling together—"Are you alright?" "You okay?"—the three of us continue on to the restaurant.

The food, the music, the dancing, all these things happen, but the evening carries a pall. The gaiety and liveliness goes on around us, but our participation is forced and we don't stay long.

The trip from Athens to Hydra is less than two hours by ferry, and I want to see one more island before Linda and I leave for Helsinki. I don't know much about Hydra—it doesn't hold the magic or mystery of some other places I've visited in Greece, but it is where, in the sixties, Leonard Cohen wrote some of his most iconic songs.

It's late October and weeks past peak season as I wander around the fairly deserted town near the port on a rainy, chilly day. My shoes get wet and my feet are cold. Still this is a charming place as I walk the narrow stone streets, peeking behind half-opened doors to flower-filled courtyards and beyond. The light is soft compared to the bright sun of Mykonos and the changing tints of Santorini. The views are lovely, shrouded in mist, which shades the gray rocks of the island even more gray. The occasional touch of scarlet bougainvillea gives color to the scene.

And there are cats. Cats everywhere, even some baby kittens this late in the fall. I spot a mother tabby bringing a fish home to her brood. She fights off other bigger cats then drops the fish whole before one of her litter, the shiny creature almost as big as the half-grown kitten. Then the mother begins licking the ears of another smaller kitten. A mother's work, never done.

Both the gallery and a boutique I wanted to explore are closed and I decide not to visit the archeological museum—it's too chilly and wet. Instead I return to my room at the Amalissa Hotel to read. My current book is Paul Theroux's *My Secret History*, and I get lost in the story, believing I'm in Africa. At a chapter break a strange sensation comes: I look up out my window, and for a moment I'm not sure where I am. I nestle down under the blanket to nap but notice a pubic hair, black and curling, caught in the weave. Clearly it's time to go back to Athens; I came too late to Hydra.

That night I dreamed I was setting out on my own to travel across the US. I was going to buy a Mustang convertible and drive. A man was there—Tom or the on-and-off boyfriend, though the mustached man in the dream looked like neither of them—and a young couple. They all wanted to go with me. I had no trouble deciding I didn't want to travel with the young couple, but the lover connection was more difficult; he held me and pleaded with me to let him go. It seemed clear that if I said yes I'd no longer be going on the journey I'd determined but on his journey. It might seem like a joint decision, but it would really be his. If not outright then a series of compromises. He would want to drive the car.

Making the choice in the dream was painful. I was almost ready to give in, to say, "Yes, come with me," but something stopped me. I would be giving myself away. "No," I said to the man in my dream. "I must go by myself."

And I do. I go back to Athens for another few days before I leave for the next place.

OCTOBER 29, 1990
Patras to Florence

Linda and I will board the same ferry I took from Corfu to Patras a month ago, now en route from Patras to Brindisi. This is the first of what will be multiple hops by ferry and train from Greece through Italy, Germany, Sweden, and finally Helsinki where, after forty hours of traveling, we'll connect with our group bound for the Soviet Union.

We haul our bags via bus and trolley to the train station then from the train to the ferry office, to port police and customs. Fortunately I can roll my big backpack along on its wheels, but Linda doesn't have any such contraption and must shoulder her bag. She's also carrying a kilo of fresh carrots she bought at the street market before we left Athens, their tops bright green and fernlike.

"You never know," she says when I ask the obvious.

Linda is a friend from San Francisco I met through Camille. Months ago when I began planning my trip, which would include the group visit to the Soviet Union, Linda suggested we meet in Athens and make the long journey north together. She's a world traveler and arranges for house trades far and wide as a way of exploring new places. I like her confidence, her dark hair and freckles.

Our ferry arrives in Brindisi at five—I'm groggy, with a body sore from lugging my luggage; Linda's bright and enthusiastic.

Another train ride and many hours later we're in Florence, where we'll stay overnight. We have left behind the myths and legends and antiquities of ancient Greece. The worn stones and crumbling pillars, the spectacular statues with their broken arms and broken faces. The sea, the music, the indecipherable-to-me alphabet.

Had I not been committed to the Soviet trip I'd have stayed longer in Greece.

In Florence I can marvel at the art—who wouldn't? The magnificence of the paintings, sculptures, and mosaics I have only seen in books, in films, and on postcard reproductions and every other surface from umbrellas to handbags to coasters and shot glasses. Now I'll see the actual works, which will no doubt bedazzle and stun. Still something is gone, something I can't hold in word or thought.

I know at some time I'll make a return trip to Greece. It will be different, of course; I will be different. I remind myself that I am a romantic and we romantics must beware of our inclination to hold memories too dear.

OCTOBER 30–31, 1990
Florence

Today we witness Michelangelo's *David* in the Galleria dell'Accademia. You can't say *see* because that implies a passive state. One *experiences* Michelangelo's *David*.

The pedestal upon which the statue poses is nearly as tall as I am and the statue itself stands seventeen feet taller still, rising majestically, godlike, to the center dome of the room. The light is soft and filters through the translucent skylight, casting a pearly tint that creates the aura of a holy place. I wander around and around the huge, muscled sculpture, veins and lines distinct; life fairly pulses in the marble and I am transfixed. A little dizzy, I pause in my slow circling, and from this spot my gaze falls on an ankle sculpted in graceful curves, an equally well-balanced arch, and finely carved toenails, embellishments on what is the most magnificent foot I have ever seen.

Unless, except.

Some years ago, awaiting an appointment at a medical office, a dark-haired woman sits opposite me holding a tiny baby to her breast, the newborn swaddled in a soft yellow blanket adorned with sleeping lambs. Peeking from one corner of the blanket is a tiny pink ankle and foot. This wee foot, the only part of the baby exposed, is delicate and beguiling. I long to touch it. Sliding my thumb against the soft skin of my middle finger, something deep and old and tender rises in me.

Here in this softly lit atrium I am in the presence of this indescribable, massive sculpture, the foot of the statue larger than an entire swaddled baby and at the same time in memory's long-ago vision appears that tiny infant's foot. One centuries old, carved of marble—not indestructible but nearly so. And the other, fragile and precious and perfectly, tragically, human.

From the breathtaking top of the Duomo we look out over red-tiled rooftops and church spires and point out sites seen that day, places we'd been in addition to the Galleria dell'Accademia. The Uffizi— rooms and rooms of paintings where we stand before masterpieces for just this long, and then on to the next, until one has blurred into the next; Santa Croce Basilica where we pay homage at the tombs of Michelangelo, Dante, Machiavelli, Galileo, and many others.

Now, weary tourist that I am, I settle in at a café and order a rich frappé while Linda, the much better tourist, is off for one more museum. In my journal I list names of artworks but no descriptions, no emotion, no reflection or response. It's all too much to take in for this Libran. I have reached sensory overload and don't recall the many and rich details of the day except for the images of the two feet: *David*'s sculpted marble and the infant's skin and fragile bones and toenails tinier than the petal of a miniature rose.

NOVEMBER 1–2, 1990
Florence to Helsinki

There's something about a good German train—it's no wonder words to describe them like *clean* and *efficient* and *predictable* have become cliché. Still those are the words I use as Linda and I travel on just such a train from Florence to Munich to Hamburg. We travel from one city to another and I'm not sure where I am or when we get to the next place and when we leave again. On this clean, efficient, and predictable German train we glide smoothly past farmland, still green in the late fall. On hillsides trees show orange and russet as we pass lovely small towns where church spires point straight up into a gray sky that occasionally clears to blue. All is neat and orderly in contrast to the colorful disorder that was Greece. Here small garden allotments are lined up next to the tracks, each plot housed with different structures—lean-tos, small sheds, and what look like miniature homes. I am in voyeur mode, gazing out the window and imagining who stays in those small structures, who works the ground and harvests the crops. Here I see myself in dirt-caked jeans with sunburned cheeks looking up from my hoe and waving as the trains pass by.

Halfway up the hill to our home in Jamul, a curve of our driveway created a spread of flat, open land where Tom and I planted gardens our first few springs there. A couple of migrant workers helped ready the soil and Tom brought home pickup truckloads of acrid-smelling fertilizer from a chicken farm nearby. The first year we overplanted zucchini—every amateur gardener's mistake—bright green worms the size of my little finger infested the sweet corn, and rabbits made quick work of our tender lettuce sprouts. The second year we let the juice of tomatoes still warm from the sun dribble down from our eagerly grinning mouths as we stood between the furrows and harvested possibly the finest cantaloupe I've ever tasted. But by year three we'd both pretty much lost interest in the constant demands of gardening and staked only a few token tomato plants and, I can't say why, some pole beans that crawled up makeshift bamboo tepees but failed to give much fruit. By year four the garden was but a memory as Tom's interest had turned to the next thing—he'd discovered computers and became captivated by, as he said, "The first new thing I've learned in years." I was relieved to get back to mornings on the deck with coffee and afternoons at my desk with my old-school portable typewriter.

Scant years later, by the time I sold most everything and launched myself into this journey, the typewriter had become a computer of my own, now stored away with a few other things, including Tom's ancient Underwood, on which he once two-finger-typed a love letter and signed it:

From the man who wants to marry you . . .
because you are my everything . . .
and more.

Winter approaches as our good German train continues northward. On the platforms at the small stations where we stop, travelers wear heavy coats and hats. I finish my current read, a novel about a woman choosing between lives: one as homemaker with children and one in a career. An interesting exercise—poised in the place I am now, a crossroads, will I choose this or that? And what exactly do I mean when I write *this* and *that*? My choices aren't those of the character—early on I chose career, and anyway my children are adults with independent lives of their own. Still I must at some point make choices—return to San Diego, take on a new role in San Francisco, go back to Greece and create a life there. That last option is more fantasy than anything else, but then why *not* fantasize? Now is the time to imagine myself choosing this or that—fantasy or otherwise.

Linda snoozes in our seat and I pack myself up and move to the café car for coffee and a solid surface to support my journal as I write sketchy and tenuous imagined visions of myself.

What if: San Diego. Find a place at the beach. Take up with the journaling group. Take more writing classes, maybe enroll full-time in school. Explore the new while staying within the safety of the old. A place where you know the names of streets and where to shop for what you need. Family is there. That on-again, off-again man you were seeing. Or not.

What if: San Francisco. You've always imagined living there. An apartment on one of those hills rising up from the bay, maybe a peek-view of the Golden Gate Bridge. Or North Beach where it always smells so good. Consider plans with Camille for the café you've talked about. No need for a car and you could hang out at those great bookstores. You can take classes there too. Great writers have always lived in San Francisco.

What if: Greece. Find an island home somewhere in the Cyclades—some sweet whitewashed house with a garden. So many places you didn't even visit. Or live in Athens where there's good English-speaking AA, which makes for a ready-made community of expats. You could learn to speak enough of the language to get by, study the ancient myths, imagine yourself blessed by the Muses, become a poet. In Greece no one knows you. You can make yourself up from an imagined past into an imagined future.

The rocking of the train brings me back from fantasy and I close my journal and glance out the window. As we pass more orderly German countryside, an oft-repeated AA saying comes to mind. A saying reiterated by older, wiser sponsors to those who think taking themselves someplace else to "start over" will solve their problems: "Wherever you go, there you are."

So, for me, it's not about returning to San Diego or relocating to San Francisco—cool though that might be—or even living the fantasy that is Greece. Wherever I choose to go, there I'll be. Will I still need to say, "I'm Judy Reeves and I . . ." or will I finally be able to say, "I'm Judy Reeves," and have that be enough?

The ferny green tops of Linda's few remaining carrots have wilted by the time we arrive in Stockholm, where we'll spend most of a day before our ferry to Helsinki. We disembark into the cold day, and I wear my blue Greek coat for the first time, snuggling into its loopy wool. It snows the kind of snow that doesn't stick but melts to liquid when it lands upon anything solid—my face, my hair, my coat.

"Café Gråmunken," I say to Linda and tell her of the savory deliciousness of last summer's cappuccino as we aim ourselves toward the old town. The city is different this late in the fall. The leaves have gone from the trees, no jaunty flowers brighten window boxes, no outdoor cafés beckon. The streets are crowded with people dressed in heavy coats, long pants, boots, hats, and gloves. We stop at a small shop and I buy lavender mittens to pair with my coat. I wonder what the saleswoman at the boutique in Corfu would say in response to my choice.

NOVEMBER 2–3, 1990
Helsinki

Dinner in our Helsinki hotel is some kind of potato casserole that reminds me of one of those Hamburger Helper single-dish wonders I used to whip up for family dinner on school nights. I hand-wash my pants and attempt to dry them with the hair dryer, but it disturbs the TV. Linda is watching *The Streets of San Francisco*. She might be a little homesick. I understand.

Tomorrow morning we'll rendezvous with two dozen other members of our group to begin our journey to the Soviet Union where we will spend two weeks traveling under the auspices of Creating a Sober World (CASW), a project of the nonprofit US-USSR Initiative. The project's mission is to bring information about alcoholism and AA's message of recovery to places it doesn't exist.

A few years ago Camille went on a CASW trip. She was so impressed with the organization and their work that she took a job with them. Shortly after Tom died I helped move her to San Francisco where the group is headquartered, smuggling her cat Spunky into her third-floor walk-up apartment in the Marina District. I visited them often, driving up the Pacific coast and staying for days at a time. Each visit included enthusiastic stories of Camille's trips to various cities in the Soviet Union and CASW's important work. So naturally as I made plans for my around-the-world journey, it didn't take much convincing for me to join this November trip.

Camille and the CASW staff arranged for our group to meet with people in Moscow, Sochi, Odessa, and Leningrad. Ours will be the eighteenth such visit the organization has sponsored in the Soviet

Union. Traveling with us will be a doctor specializing in addiction treatment, counselors, members of Al-Anon, and recovering alcoholics. Twenty-four men and women of all ages from all over the US, some with many years of recovery and others newer in their sobriety, but all of us committed to sharing our experience, strength, and hope.

I had no idea of what kind of physical or psychological condition I'd be in when Camille and I would see each other again, but the anticipated reunion has been a grounding pole to which I have often found myself clinging. We counted down months and weeks in our many letter exchanges; finally the time has arrived.

I've gone from the warm and generous sunshine of Greece to what will be a winterish November in the Soviet Union. I'll go from three months of virtual solitude to two weeks of virtual immersion with two dozen others, all strangers except Camille and Linda. From my unscheduled, spontaneous life to days and nights planned, organized, and communal.

At least for the next two weeks we'll have a translator for an incomprehensible language—no small relief—and a guide for the unknown places we'll explore. I'll be with my dearest friend, encircled within the warmth and welcoming friendship of AA. And laughter. Laughter is a hallmark of our fellowship. "We are not a glum lot," our literature says. Attend any AA meeting or the informal gatherings before or after and you'll hear the most raucous, joyous, from-the-belly laughter you've ever heard. Laughter and tears and love—these are the touchstones of my experience in Alcoholics Anonymous.

It's a paradox: to want to be welcomed into a group where acceptance is almost guaranteed and authenticity not only encouraged but well-nigh demanded, and yet to miss the safety of being alone, where it's easy to hide. There is no hiding in AA. This has always been the scariest part for me. Exposure. Vulnerability. Being seen as I am beneath the constructed persona.

One evening when I was a girl, my mother and I were side by side on the same scratchy brown couch where I explored the world atlas with my dad. I'd just learned about adoption and was curious about it.

"Am I your real girl or am I adopted?" I asked my mother.

"Of course you're our real girl," she said. "Who else would have you?"

All my life I have tried to believe she meant her comment as a joke. *Ha ha.* In my mind I know she did but oh, the fragility of little girls. All my life since that evening some part of me, some vulnerable little-girl part of me, still believes, *Who else would have you?* If my mother believed that, then certainly it must be true.

Camille brought a suitcase I'd prepacked with warmer clothes before I left San Diego, though I expect what serves as winter clothes in San Diego might not pass muster in the late fall in the Soviet Union. Still I'm grateful for the sweaters and leather boots, the jeans and the mukluks I got on a trip to Canada.

Camille breaks away from greeting the others in our group, some she knows from previous trips, some from CASW and San Francisco. She's coleader of this trip and will have other people and business to attend to, details to go over, agendas to make, remake, and reconfirm. But for right now we have found each other.

We hug tightly and for a long time, and I'm crying and don't want to let go. How long since I have been welcomed into an embrace by someone who really knows me and has been through it all with me? Someone who knew Tom when he was alive and well and as he got sick and was with me in the confusing and complicated aftermath of his death. Someone who has heard my confessions and knows my fears and loves me anyway. Someone who encourages my dreams, is patient with my indecisions, and forgives my transgressions. Who else can make me laugh like she does? I'm braver when I'm with Camille. I may be more of who I am with her than I am with anyone.

She is strong and sturdy and seventeen years younger than me. She has a head of big hair, curly and dark, and eyes sometimes the color of emeralds and sometimes like the sea at its deepest green. She's smart and well-read and articulate and is not afraid to take on any project. A capable woman, she is also creative. She names her cars and bicycles and makes up nicknames for herself and me. She writes entertaining letters in loopy, artful handwriting. She is my best friend and I am beyond joyful to finally be in her company.

NOVEMBER 4–8, 1990
Moscow

The first of what I expect will be two weeks of early "up and at 'em" routines begins at six as our group meets for breakfast, then boards the bus bound for the Helsinki airport and our hour-and-twenty-five-minute direct flight to Moscow.

Flying over, it's impossible to see through the fog cloud—which is, in a way, how I see this next portion of my journey. Or rather how I don't see it. Though we've been given an itinerary—four cities over two weeks—what will happen and how and with whom . . . all of it is a misty fog.

At the Moscow airport we descend into the chilly afternoon, straggle across the blacktop, and gather in a line for a long wait to go through customs.

Members of the group, nine men and fifteen women, get to know one another as we wait. And wait. Linda and I have paired up next to each other in line. In front of me is Bruce, a friendly man with wire-rim glasses, and next to him Jan, who is familiar though I haven't met her before. Despite the airport's dim lighting and gloomy surroundings—all bare walls and high-ceilinged echoes, spirits are high even though some of us yawn from our early morning and lingering jet lag. Finally we're all checked, inspected, stamped, welcomed in an official manner that's lacking warmth, and gather for our bus ride into Moscow itself.

We line up again. I expect there will be much lining up over the next few weeks. As we board the bus, we're welcomed, warmly this time, by our Intourist guide, Armani. With the floppy lock of hair that grazes his pale forehead and his Russian-accented English, he reminds me of Vladimir, whom I met in The Hague, and that reminds me of Marty and the Bali Hotel, and I can't help but smile at the memory. More stories to tell Camille when we're alone.

Throughout our time together, our group will rotate assignments for various duties: AA leader of our daily meetings, which is my assignment for the day; WOD (Worrier of the Day, who counts us as we board and reboard various transportation); SOD (Scribe of the Day, who keeps the "official" journal each day, making notes and recording events); and HOD (Hugger of the Day. AA is known for its ubiquitous hugging).

This organizing is friendly and certainly necessary. Who could require more corralling than two dozen independent-minded, naturally rebellious individuals who, though sober, are still alcoholics? As they say, you can eliminate the alcohol, but you've still got the -ism. It's all lighthearted, even playful, with the faux officiousness of the titles and the mock seriousness with which we accept our assignments. Still, traveling in a large group is as foreign to me as the Cyrillic letters posted throughout the airport.

Our hotel is in the center of town across the street from the Arbat, a historic and inviting kilometer-long pedestrian avenue of shops and street artists.

Some of our group are going sightseeing, but due to my assignment as AA leader for the day I won't join them; instead I'll unpack at the hotel and settle in. This evening we'll take the metro to an AA meeting that was started during a visit by a previous CASW group.

On the agenda for our second day: a tour of the Armory and the Kremlin and an AA meeting at Hospital 17, a treatment center for alcoholics.

First the Armory. Floor after floor, room after room, display after display of religious icons, plus the jewels and crowns and clothes and carriages of the czars and empresses and aristocracy—the Armory glitters with incredible displays of wealth. Our guide rattles off names and facts and figures and points out different techniques and styles and methods of working with the gems and gold and silver while we elbow each other and mutter such profundities as *wow!* and *look at that* and *holy shit.*

Furs and capes, statues, crystals, glass, delicate cloisonné figurines, ten iconic Fabergé eggs that open to reveal miniature coaches and castles and scenes of forests with bejeweled birds and brightly painted serpents. In another room the miniatures inside the eggs are echoed by life-sized coaches. Tapestries. Paintings. Crowns and orbs and scepters of gold, all encrusted with kilos of stones. Rubies as big as my thumb, emeralds the size of a robin's egg. Diamonds and pearls and topaz, cases and cases of them displayed in expansive rooms with gorgeous ceilings and chandeliers and walls of gilt.

Finally the tour ends and it's a relief to be outside. The air is chilled and not quite so rarified. Real life again with people like me plodding along, cheeks ruddy from the chill, fists stuffed in pockets. I need toothpaste, which seems such a practical thing after the excesses of the Armory. Camille and I separate from the others and head off to a small market on our way back to the hotel. Compared to what has just overwhelmed us, these shelves are skimpy with goods: one of these, three of those, an empty space or two, then another lonely item. No glitter, no gilt, no legacies of czars or czarinas. The contrast between these two places—the Armory with its riches beyond comprehension, and the shops with a scarcity of the most common of daily needs: toothpaste, laundry soap, baby bottles—could not be more dispiriting.

This afternoon Yeltsin and Gorbachev give speeches in celebration of the seventy-third anniversary of the October Revolution in Red Square. A parade is scheduled, too, which many of our group will attend. But I go with five others to Hospital 17, with its 6,500 beds for alcoholics, where we'll speak to staff about inpatient treatment, particularly from the perspective of alcoholism as a family disease. I participated in a family program when my father was in treatment, so I could share from personal experience. But more helpful to the staff was what I learned in the business Tom and I developed that provided marketing plans and communications materials to treatment centers across the US.

It was largely Tom's business and his marketing genius and production talents that made it unique and effective. Though I continued running the company for a few years after he died and absolutely believed in the message and the work itself, I knew in my heart it was not my work. I didn't know what my true work was, but I did know what it wasn't.

After I moved out of the Jamul house and to the beach I began exploring other interests. I'd been leading seminars on journal writing for treatment centers for several years and as a lifelong journal keeper myself, knew the process to be an effective tool for self-discovery and memory excavation. So I dipped a curious toe into organizing and leading private journaling groups in a nonrecovery setting. I invited six or eight women for weekly gatherings of writing and reading our work aloud, not for critique but to share our stories. I loved writing in community, something I hadn't done since my best friend Betty and I would climb up into my tree house and write stories in our schoolgirl notebooks. I'd also taken a screenwriting class at the University of California, San Diego, and a short-story class at a local community college, studying the craft and developing work for possible publication. These explorations into writing were exciting and stimulating in a way the business wasn't and woke up some old remembered alive part of me. The thrill I got from expressing my own voice in my own words and the rush that came from creating stories that seemed to arise from some mysterious somewhere was something I wanted more of.

Camille, who'd gone to the parade in Red Square while I was at Hospital 17, told me that there was some evidence of, not revolt and not exactly protest, but something. A few people made signs and dared to speak out. The tight grip of the Soviet Republic was loosening with three Baltic states—Estonia, Latvia, and Lithuania—declaring independence from the laws of the USSR.

My worldview during these last months of 1990 is not political. While I am aware of events taking place in the Middle East, primarily because of US involvement, monumental shifts are taking place elsewhere. But my perspective remains personal.

It's our last day in Moscow and a holiday in the ongoing celebration of the Revolution. While others of our group are off on another tour or another AA meeting or meeting with officials, Camille and I are on our way to Red Square, where we'll meet Camille's friend Brian, a New Yorker currently living in Moscow, and Vladimir, whom I met at the summer conference in the Netherlands. AA has a way of making it a small world.

A sprinkling of snow, powdered sugar atop the wet black streets of Moscow, disappears as quickly as fairy dust. I'm wearing my Canadian mukluks, my blue Greek coat, and my new lavender Swedish mittens. My ears are brittle with cold and the wind carries our words away.

All along the Arbat, like Váci Utca in Budapest, shops offer an array of goods from souvenirs and sweets to beauty supplies and bread. Once the main entrance into Moscow, the Arbat is frequented by busking musicians and street artists who stand beside paintings hung on wrought iron fences that remind me of the fence surrounding Luxembourg Gardens in Paris. Small displays are set up on makeshift tables hung with brightly colored scarves. Cafés along the way look warm and inviting and we both inhale deeply as we pass but we don't stop. A line in front of an ice cream store stretches down the street and coming out the door are two lovely Soviet girls, arm-in-arm, licking their ice cream cones as though it were a fine spring day.

Farther down we wander past the block-long peace wall. Last year, Carolyna Marks was invited by the Center for Creative Initiative and the Vocational Schools in Moscow to work with Soviet youth to build the wall, a vibrant and colorful collection of tiles painted by seven thousand children, each with their independent visions of peace. Bright suns and birds, flowers, and many kinds of trees decorate the colorful tiles that even on this cold gray day glow with the brilliance of idealized hope.

Almost a year ago to the day, the Berlin Wall came down following monthslong protests that blossomed into revolutions in several Eastern Bloc countries, including Poland and Hungary and now in the Soviet Union. It's the time of *Peristroika*, a reformation within the Communist Party.

I want to linger to take in the individual tiles but time, time, time, a factor I haven't experienced for months, pushes us on.

Our aim is to get to the ceremony of the changing of the guard at Lenin's Tomb. We don't have tickets to go inside the actual mausoleum, which is fine with me. I imagine his displayed corpse as frozen as the ground we stride on. At the hourly tolling of the chimes of Spasskaya Tower, an officer leads two guards of identical height, each with a rifle balanced in one hand, to replace the two who stand on either side of the door. There, for the next hour the guards will pose motionless and then the ritual is enacted again and again, hour after hour, no matter the weather or temperature. We stand in the cold, our breath foggy as we watch the enactment of the ceremony, and then on to the next stop, tourists once more.

NOVEMBER 8–11, 1990
Sochi

Stalin built his summer dacha in Sochi, this resort town on the Black Sea where he came for his rheumatism and political plottings and where he hid out behind thick walls and bulletproof sofas. Originally constructed in 1937, the fortress is now a museum. We don't go on the tour, but we're told that behind the desk in his former office sits a wax figure of the dictator. Imagine: Lenin frozen in his mausoleum in Moscow, and Stalin a wax figure posed stiffly at his desk in Sochi. I can't help but picture the bones from that long-ago king's hand on display at the history museum in Budapest—complete with push-button illumination.

And then remember on a citrus- and avocado-studded hillside in Jamul, Tom's ashes long gone into the ground.

One sunny and warmish afternoon Camille and I stroll along the seashore on a wide promenade lined with palm trees. After the cold and snow of Moscow, the sea and the palms are welcome and familiar. How often have I walked or jogged or ridden my bike along the boardwalk that runs several miles from the south end of San Diego's Mission Beach to the far reaches of Pacific Beach—beaches I have been going to, living beside, and playing on since I was thirteen years old. Saving my money and taking the 8 bus to Belmont Park where I squander quarter after babysitting quarter to ride the Giant Dipper; daring my first bikini and slathering my teenage body with coconut oil to lie on the hot sand and listen to Elvis, the Everly Brothers, and

Sam Cooke on a cool turquoise transistor radio, every song meant especially for me.

How good to be near the sea, the air heavy and laden with salt and memories. As we stroll along we tell stories of our lives since we last saw each other in San Francisco, details that got left out of our many letter exchanges, and we talk of our future—a café we'll open when I return to the US. "We'll call it Café Britska," we decide. *Britska*, a word originated during a long-ago game of Dictionary, defined by one of the players as a treat of coffee and cheese and for some reason made us laugh to tears. Such silliness often happens whenever we're together, Camille and I; we can't help ourselves. It's what I miss and what I haven't done in too long. Left alone I take myself way too seriously.

Along the promenade we come upon a man selling coffee from a makeshift café. There's no actual building, no tables, no chairs. There is just the stout, friendly man with his modest fire and his small Turkish pot.

We each order a cup and watch as he adds finely ground coffee to the pot, then water, then sugar—lots of sugar—and then heats the dulled metal pot over his fire. After a few moments it boils and he tends to it. A few moments more and he pours the mixture into two tiny cups, which he hands us with a smile. He's missing a tooth.

The cups are so tiny it's as though we're playing house, having tea with dollies set around a child's table. But we're not at a table. We're posed on the seawall, the *shush-shush* of waves against the sand, the palms witnessing the ritual.

"Careful of the grounds," Camille warns, too late, as they coat my tongue and fill the spaces between my teeth like silt.

We sip. Hot. Strong. Sweet. I'm not sure I like the taste. But I like drinking it. I like being on the promenade beside the Black Sea on a mild November day with my best friend. I like the man with his generosity of smile and offering of coffee so ceremoniously brewed. I like the impromptu café of seawall, tiny cups, the strongest coffee I have ever tasted. Even the grounds in the bottom of my tiny cup, fine as sand, finer, are a delight.

"We should make this in Café Britska," I say, my tongue plying the grit that lines my gums.

Near the old sanatorium built in the thirties, the period Stalin oversaw the construction of all the grand buildings in Sochi, are hot springs where odiferous water pours from caves in the rocks. A cloud of sulfuric steam rises from the dark openings. I'm reminded of the cave in Delphi where the oracle underwent her trance and received messages from the gods. Here, the shaded grove is dense with trees and shrubs festooned with streamers of colored ribbon and old handkerchiefs. "Wishing ribbons," we're told by our guide and translator Sergi, a short, slender young man who's friendly enough, though he still holds himself at a formal distance as is the way of these Intourist hosts.

An old woman sits on a wrought iron bench, a large woven basket in her generous lap. Dressed in layers of sweaters, thick ankles crossed, knuckles knobby with age, she reminds me of a character in a Russian folktale. Her gnarled hand holds out a bouquet of bright ribbons from her basket.

"You have only one wish," she says, Sergi interpreting her words, "but it will come true."

I choose a yellow one, frayed at the ends, and take it to a garlanded tree, where I find a branch just high enough to require tiptoes to reach. Breath held, I knot my yellow ribbon to the branch, then close my eyes as I release it, my wish and ribbon flung into a canopy of green.

My wish is not for world peace; I leave that to others who believe such miracles are possible. I wish for something more personal. Peace within my own heart, an answer to my persistent, unabated longing. And a wish for Tom, wherever he might be.

"When you're dead, you're dead," he'd said to our friend Terry, who'd once asked him if he believed in life after death. This was after Tom's diagnosis when he knew his cancer was terminal. Terry knew it too. "Ashes to ashes and all that."

And what do I believe in? The heaven I learned about in Sunday school? The new-age teaching that we're made of everlasting energy and will merge again—energy to energy—after our current life on this plane? And if Tom and I didn't believe the same thing, did that mean that those few years we had together were all we'd ever get, for all Eternity?

Saturday morning, like every morning, we begin at 7:30 a.m. with an AA meeting of our group, sometimes in someone's room, other times in a meeting room in whatever hotel we're currently lodged. Later this afternoon an open AA meeting is scheduled—the first ever held in Sochi—but before that Linda, Susan, and I go shopping. We barter for shawls from a sidewalk seller and buy small eucalyptus branches whose fragrance takes me home to San Diego. I can't stop lifting mine to my nose and inhaling deeply. We search through collections of postcards and sets of illustrated stories at a bookstore. I purchase a package of fairy tales, charmingly drawn. It doesn't matter that I can't read the writing, the illustrations tell the familiar stories. I buy a Soviet calendar for 1991, anticipating the new year, anticipating a return home even though I'm not sure where home will be. The calendar, oversized and printed on slick rollable paper, features a haloed Saint George astride his white stallion, his mighty lance piercing a dangerously fanged serpent. Both saint and dragon soar Chagall-like in a golden sky above the rooftops and minarets of Moscow.

The shop offers tourist memorabilia, too, including an entire shelf of brightly colored matryoshka dolls, the iconic little stacking figures with one doll tucked inside the other, inside the other. This is how I envision my story. The outward story is this journey, and inside this story is the story of Tom and Judy, and inside that the journey we took the last months of his life, and inside that other journeys, and inside those, other stories, each one represented by another doll until finally the littlest doll is revealed—me. There is no opening up this little girl, she just stands there in her bright dress, alone and alone. All the other stories are cracked open and the final story is the littlest girl alone with nothing inside.

First memory: French doors lead to Mommy and Daddy's bedroom; sheer curtains cover the door's windows. The little girl stretches up to reach the crystal doorknob. She wants inside. She stands on tiptoes in scuffed white shoes, her fingers touch the knob but she can't grasp it. Her hand is too small and the latch is out of reach.

Does she cry? Does she yell? Does she keep trying to reach that crystal knob, stretching and stretching? Does she give up and collapse on the floor, or does she give up and walk away? The first memory gives me none of this, only the girl stretching to reach the crystal knob.

The closed door. The gauzy curtains. The crystal knob. The little girl. This is the stuff of fairy tales. Of metaphor. Of myth and legend. Symbols whose meaning is left to the listener of the tale to interpret.

Sharing in an AA meeting through an interpreter is difficult, adapting to a rhythm of speaking that allows sentences to be deconstructed and reconstructed and watching the faces of those receiving the translated words for their reaction while at the same time trying to remember what I wanted to say. At AA meetings I am more of a stream-of-consciousness talker than a thoughtful speaker, sometimes circling around to discover what I want to say, trusting the meander will ultimately find its way to a conclusion that makes sense. No wonder I often see furrowed brows on some of the listeners as the interpreter tries to find the way through the thicket of language. *Listen*, I want to say, *I understand. Sometimes I have trouble finding what I'm trying to say too. You should read my journals.*

The sun shone brightly again this morning, our last in Sochi, buttery-yellow as the fall leaves caught and reflected the light. The ash trees are bountiful and still fully leafed in that perfect moment of autumn before it surrenders to winter. Camille and I and Galena, a woman from the Sochi fellowship, have been invited to the psychiatric hospital for a talk with two Soviet women.

Upon entering the hospital I'm struck by the odor. I can't identify it—antiseptic, yes, but something layered beneath or atop. It's the same smell as at the men's treatment center in Moscow where I had to breathe shallowly to avoid nausea—an old mold and damp basement odor overlaid with the distinct stink of something dead or dying. The floor here is the same as the other place, too, soft under the stained red linoleum. In the meeting room at the men's hospital a single dim fixture clung to the ceiling, and from its center a spider dangled from a thin web. Here the doors to the doctor's office are padded and covered in vinyl that echoes the dingy red of the floor. They remind me of doors in some tacky bar I used to drink in; an appropriate reminder as we push through. A table has been set for us with tea and cookies, and two anxious-appearing women sit at the table. Galena begins to share with us in Russian and so another meeting commences.

I leave the meeting, as with all the meetings, knowing this is good work, sharing the message however we do. "This is my story," we say. "This is my experience." It's through the telling of these stories, each and every one, that we connect as human beings. I believe this is true not just "in the rooms," as we say in AA, but inside and outside all the rooms in all the countries in all the world. It's in this connection that we are no longer "other" but a part of something larger, which serves to help us know we're not alone. It's possible that through our stories—told and listened to, exchanged one to another to another—we can ultimately create some kind of world peace.

NOVEMBER 11–14, 1990
Odessa

On our first night in Odessa we're treated to a floor show of sorts that features scantily clad female dancers and well-muscled men. A magician performs sleight of hand to tinny recorded music under a purple spotlight that shows the wear in his baggy tuxedo. The performance is not for us—an audience is present closer to the stage; we watch from the back of our hotel's ballroom as our late dinner is served.

Fall in Odessa, an elegant city of old European-style buildings, wide streets, and leafy boulevards. The tattered and worn beauty speaks of a once-grand past now in disrepair. Here, leaves that had just turned bronze in Sochi have gone gorgeously scarlet, a sensuous, deep, almost throbbing red, as if Mother Nature is reminding us of what we hold inside. "Winter is coming," she tells us, "and it may be long and hard and cold, but you are also the lustiness of spring, the passions of summer."

In the park rosy-cheeked children zipped up in colorful snowsuits gather leaf bouquets in mittened hands, and memory takes me back to fall in Missouri. We sisters collected russet and gold leaves still tinted with shades of green and ironed them between squares of waxed paper to be clothespinned in windows, mimicking stained glass. We dove into mounds of dried leaves raked in the side yard where Daddy scolded us for making a mess of what he'd made order of. But his scolding wasn't to be taken seriously; I imagine had the piles been higher, denser, thicker, he would have dove into them himself. The smell of burning leaves, smoke rising into the stone-washed Midwestern sky, and Daddy standing guard with his rake to keep the small fires under control. For days after, black circles scorched the still-green grass and the smell of burning leaves lingered in the fall air.

How easy to become nostalgic with just a few teasing sensory images; how the past always wants to be a part of the present.

Today's AA meeting is held at the Seafarer's Club, a grand old building that at one time housed the stock brokerage and now shares the space with the civic philharmonic and opera company. An opera is in progress when we arrive. We wait until the performance ends and the singers change out of their costumes to find our meeting place. I recall all the meetings I've been to in damp, linoleum-floored church basements and metal-folding-chaired community centers and consider this: We're participating in a meeting of Alcoholics Anonymous staged in a sumptuous performance hall where the soprano's voice still echoes her last stirring high note and the final chords of the orchestra still resonate against elegantly carved walls. Here we are with our own tragic stories and our own unshakable hope.

Odessa is a favorite city for many of our group but not for me. All the cold, wet traveling after months of sun, touring with the group and sharing meals, meetings morning and night, presentations to strangers through interpreters, the constant push of energy for one who has been solitary for so long—all this has caught up to me in Odessa and laid me low.

The outward focus of our mission doesn't allow time for the kind of introspection and reflection I've experienced for the previous three months. My journal writing is sketchy; I skip complete days, even two and three at a time, when I used to write every day and often several times a day. As I read through recent pages I see very little inward focus and no recording except after the events—sometimes days after—and by then even the facts are hardly facts anymore; instead

I write reconstructed notes that are dubious recollections shaded by time's passage.

Impressions and observations are spoken rather than written. Talking with others in our group, and at meetings the focus is on the disease, the program, its twelve steps, and how they relate to our lives and our recovery. Talking, talking, talking. My throat is sore and my mind fuzzy.

Rilke comes to mind: "Your solitude will be a support and a home for you, even in the midst of very unfamiliar circumstances, and from it you will find all your paths."

I am homesick for solitude.

We wait for our bus to the airport in the hotel lobby where men in brown coats and hats smoke cigarettes in brown shadows under the stairs. My mind says spies, though what do I know of that world except from books and movies?

The bus arrives and we load in with our suitcases, our mementos, the things we carry. Bruce, Hugger of the Day, stands with arms outstretched, dispensing hugs as we board, and Stephen, Worrier of the Day, counts us.

On the bus Camille makes announcements concerning our arrival in Leningrad. There is a promise of hearing John's completed extravaganza of twelve-stepping among the steppes or "I'll meet you at the samovar, Vladimir." Camille looks gorgeous as she stands before us, her bottle-green scarf serving as backdrop for the red rose she holds, given to her by the messengers who came to see us off. I am assigned Scribe of the Day and receive the well-handled daily journal from Susan.

NOVEMBER 14–16, 1990
Leningrad

From my window seat on the plane I look below to the geometry of fields—flat as Kansas but with asymmetrical plots that defy my remembered Midwestern farm-logic. The colors: beige of winter, yellow of harvested crops, brown ditches dusted with snow, an occasional touch of green. Trees: pines, evergreens, and always birches, now bare of leaves. A frosting of ice slicks the tarmac as we walk from our plane to our new bus.

Nona is our Intourist guide for Leningrad and she rattles off impressive lists of facts and colorful history as we ride through straight, flat streets of the newest end of the city, crossing through what used to be the "hot fields," where refuse was burned in Peter the Great's time. We pass hothouses where tomatoes and mushrooms are grown and by factories and huge conglomerates of buildings. Even the industrial area of the city promises beauty as we cross first one canal, then another, and then turn onto the main thoroughfare. At first I took copious notes of Nona's facts and figures as part of my Scribe duties, but as we continue into Leningrad the grace of the city captures me and I surrender to it. No more notes.

Spires of the skyline gleam in the last rays of the setting sun and soon buildings become silhouettes. Our hotel is the Pribaltiskaya, which rises at the edge of the Baltic Sea. We're told there is a sea view, but darkness shrouds it from our eager eyes.

From the bus we descend, find our bags, and trudge through a labyrinth to our rooms. Then—delight! A luxury we haven't known since the Klaus K Hotel in Helsinki ten days before: bathtubs.

—

Leningrad is magnificent—broad avenues and grand buildings built by Peter the Great in the European style and named Saint Petersburg after him. Islands. Rivers. Bridges. Green, open, and empty parks. Trees leafless in the cold. The first day we go sightseeing: Saint Isaac's, the square where artists share their work, and the Hermitage—the Winter Palace of the czars.

I don't do museums well. Quickly overstimulated, I can't hold all the beauty. Often I find myself moving along with the crowd, one piece to the next until I'm exhausted with sensory overload. Consequently I don't recall the individual pieces we saw at the Hermitage in its countless exhibits. There were gold-leafed domed ceilings, baroque rooms, and rooms and rooms of priceless art.

This afternoon we're entranced by another magnificent sunset as we stand near a bridge over the Neva river looking back over Saint Isaac's Cathedral; the sun's last honeyed streaks catch the spire of the Admiralty.

I silently promise I will return to Leningrad in a few years—some spring when the broad-leafed trees along the river are full and green and the lilac blooming. But now it is November. We're told rationing will begin soon for meat and other foods. Already there are ration cards for alcohol and cigarettes.

Thursday evening after the AA meeting a small group of us take the metro to a private home—Mark and Irina are friends Camille met on a previous CASW trip to Leningrad. We gather around a table and dream with them, dreams of an outpatient program with trained alcohol-addiction counselors, something that doesn't yet exist in Leningrad. All this is conveyed in Russian, translated into English, and our replies translated back from English to Russian. Lots of smiles as we listen to our words, one language to the other and back again.

Across the table from me Volodya and Gayla's tiny baby daughter rests against Camille's shoulder. I relax within the warmth of this gathering of recovering alcoholics and consider the effects of our trip and the seventeen previous trips and the groups that will come after. Certainly these seeds we are planting would take root, and who knows how many lives could be changed, how many alcoholics would find recovery, how many families would be reunited.

Later Mark drives us back to our hotel through the snowy streets of the city. Bruce and Shasha are in the front seat, Camille, Peter, and Linda in the back with me spread out across their laps. How our laughter rings out into the frozen Leningrad night. I silently wish for it to echo through this long and difficult winter.

It's a frozen day when we go to the Piskaryovskoye Memorial Cemetery to witness the mass graves of those who died during the Nazi's nine-hundred-day siege of Leningrad. Half a million bodies are buried here, mostly people killed by starvation or illness, some by violence. Acres and acres of graves with a single marker at the head of each row noting the year—1941. 1942. 1943.

Flowers lay stiffly atop the markers. Cardinal carnations and ice-tipped amber mums captured in full bloom. A bride and groom are here when we arrive, her white dress brilliant against the bright cerulean sky. We watch silently as she places her bridal bouquet upon the raised marble square that surrounds the eternal flame. She and her new husband stand for a moment, heads bowed. This is the custom—each newlywed couple makes a pilgrimage to the cemetery between the wedding and the reception—a ritual to memorialize and honor those who did not survive those dark nine hundred days.

A simple display of black-and-white photographs captures the reality of the time and place. Among them are these images:

A starving girl looks into the camera, her long hair frames her gaunt face.

Bodies borne on stretchers carried by gray men in gray clothes.

A still life of the daily ration of bread—twenty-three grams, made of one-half rye flour and who knows the other half.

Tanya Savicheva kept an accounting of members of her family as they died, writing the dates of their deaths in a simple schoolgirl's notebook. Her picture is displayed next to the sheets listing their names and deaths. The last line reads: "The Savichevas have died. They all died. Tanya is left alone."

Funeral music plays over loudspeakers. At the far end of the cemetery, away from the buildings, a granite wall is engraved with a poem written by Olga Bergholz: *Nobody is forgotten. Nothing is forgotten.*

Above the wall poses a statue of Mother Russia, her arms outstretched to encompass all the graves, all the souls, all of us who come to witness the sorrow and the suffering.

I stand at the end of one of the rows of mass graves, at its edge a bronze marker—1942, the year I was born, the year Tom was born. There are others, row upon row upon row of graves—all from 1942. October 1942. *How many that month?* I wonder. October 15. How many died the day I was born?

I am crying for them—the ones who died the day I was born— and for all of us as I tread the frigid earth, sobbing in messy snorts of snot and tears, steam rising from the alive animal of my body.

My deep and wet anguish is not simply the mass graves but being alive amid the stark reality of all that death. I imagine bones beneath the frozen earth. People—men and women and children, babies, not buried each and each in private and holy caskets but en masse. Bodies and bodies and bodies together. Were they placed, gently, carefully, wrapped in shrouds? Or—oh, the words: *tossed, dumped, thrown*— one atop the other or pushed together, their still-giving flesh squeezed in side by side. I can't stop myself from thinking these awful thoughts, but I can't bear them either.

I come upon one of our group members—Stephen, a tall, sweet man—among all that death, and I stumble into his arms. We stand together, holding each other for how long I can't say. Until I am emptied.

How much of my despair is what I have not yet expressed for Tom, I can't say. How do you separate private and personal grief from grief we must experience as human beings, one for another—for all of us, for what life does to us, and for what we do to each other?

The others are already aboard when Stephen and I return to our bus. I don't speak to anyone as I board, and though their eyes ask questions, I drop my gaze to the floor. Stephen takes one seat and I another to sit alone in an empty row, where I stare out the dirty window, seeing nothing as we ride back to our hotel.

NOVEMBER 16–21, 1990
Helsinki

Our last flight aboard Aeroflot takes us from resplendent, tragic Leningrad to Helsinki. We bus to the Klaus K Hotel—all of Helsinki so far as I have experienced is bright and clean and modern, a return to luxury. Or so it seems after the dark and dingy hotels in the Soviet Union, though those were certainly not the darkest or dingiest places I have ever stayed. There have been motels along some of the blue highways in America, fishing camps in Canada with Tom, stops along the Tahuamanu River in Bolivia, even a place or two in Greece, and, oh, Mexico.

I will admit to being a spoiled American woman. Just give me a polished sink and a floor you can walk on barefoot without sticking, crisp sheets, thick towels, a bathtub slick with shine, and hear me sigh; these luxuries may seem only skin-deep but some sensibility in me relaxes. To excuse myself and my selfish ways, I blame celestial influence. "I can't help myself," I explain to nobody, "I'm a Libra."

In a final few days our group unties itself. By ones and twos people leave to return to homes, families, jobs; Linda back to San Francisco. Our last AA meeting overflows with love and gratitude and shared intimacies. We have—all of us—been traveling with open hearts. We have experienced the same from our Soviet counterparts. A universal truth about Alcoholics Anonymous: "We are survivors of the same shipwreck," the saying goes. Our connection with one another when we trust and when we are honest, open, and willing (the "HOW" of our program), there is no stronger bond, no acceptance more generous of our flawed humanity.

Camille and I will stay a few more days in Helsinki with friends we know from AA, Tuula and Rauski. The room they provide is cozy—a thick Scandinavian duvet on a large, soft bed. In the morning white curtains open to a white world. It snowed in the night. Six to eight more inches of snow so airy it catches in the trees and shrubs, big puffs that look like captured clouds.

Tuesday is Ladies' Day at the George Street Baths. It's cold in Helsinki as Camille and I explore the downtown streets and I am grateful again for my coat, mittens, and mukluks. We've stashed oils and lotions and shampoos in our packs. I don't know what to expect at the baths, but I've learned it doesn't much matter what you expect—life will ultimately have its way with you anyhow.

Our Finnish friend Jorma told us about the baths. "Go, go. You will love," he said. And so we go, go, to the George Street Swimming Hall—*Yrjönkatu uimahalli*—the oldest public swimming hall in Finland.

Swimming nude. Sauna nude. Massage nude.

Though I've done some of each, I've never done them all together and never with a group of strangers. I'm both shy and excited for the experience, like making love with someone for the first time.

We enter the hall through great double doors. The air is warm and humid and smells of chlorine, and for an instant I'm taken back to the indoor pool at the YWCA in San Diego where I swam as a girl. We always wore swimsuits at the Y and in those days I'd never even heard of a sauna. Massage was definitely something foreign too; something they did in Sweden.

Inside the baths massive globes glow like full moons above the clear turquoise pool. A balcony perches high above the pool with arched openings guarded by graceful, curved wrought iron. Many closed doors line the hallway along the pool. I don't know where these doors lead and imagine assignations, rendezvous, afternoon delights, a private session with a masseuse. Who knows what pleasures the Finns during their long, dark winters.

Camille and I find our lockers, get out of our clothes, and join the others in the sauna—cedar-scented, dimly lit, dry, and warm. We find our place among the six or eight older women who lounge on tiers of benches that rise two and three high in a rectangle around a charcoal burner where hot coals smolder. We settle in and I go quiet.

"What are you thinking, Jude?" Camille asks. Good friend that she is, she knows when I've disappeared too far into my thoughts. Tom used to just say, *Penny?* to bring me out of my wanderings.

"You know," I answer, and she probably does. She's been on the receiving end of my long and wandering (and wondering) letters of the last four months. Besides, I know anyone can just look at me and see the loss layered underneath it all. Even the woman who cut my hair in Athens looked at me in the mirror and said, "Your eyes, *lypiménos*—so sad."

Scattered around the sauna in twos and threes, the intricately wrinkled and gray-haired Finnish women sit on their small paper squares, casual and comfortable in their bodies. I don't stare; I know the protocol. Still, who doesn't take a surreptitious peek? Seated highest on the tier are two women—one bone-thin, so fragile-looking you imagine she might shatter at a touch, her breasts only a dark hint of nipple low on her chest; the other, round in that fairy-tale grandmother way, like my own grandmother before she died. The same sparse gray hair pulled in a bun, the same arms loose on the underside. And here they are, these two women like the half dozen others in the sauna—the cellulose, the sagging, the softly folding—all with such an open ease about them.

Their quiet influence and the intimate warmth, the muted light of the small space, enables me to relax. My body responds to the hot dry air of the sauna, the cedar smell that wraps around me and enters with each breath. "Let the soft animal of your body love what it loves," the poet Mary Oliver tells us. And mine loves lying naked on the wooden benches, the heat beneath my thighs, my stomach, my breasts. After a while someone senses the air's longing for moisture and tosses a ladleful of water dipped from a copper pot onto the hot coals. A wet sizzle, a billow of steam, and a minute rise of humidity. But it lasts for just that long and soon the air resumes its hot and dry and cedar-scented healing.

Among the women—Camille and me, too—conversations are muted. The mind goes liquid. Tension melts from the body. There is only presence and breathing and an occasional murmured sigh.

And then the body says *enough*. And you listen, because naked in the sauna you can't help but listen to the body.

Just outside the sauna the humid, chlorine-scented air of the pool fills the hall. Ultramarine water ripples under haloed lights. I step down into the blue. I can almost hear a sizzle as the cool water splashes against my body.

I enter slowly, step-by-step, holding my arms out to my side and pulling my stomach muscles tight in anticipation of the chill. I like the incremental entry into the womb of water, the way it gradually assumes my body, slicking the back of my knees and the tender skin inside my thighs, its first wet touch on the soft folds of my labia. After the sauna, entering the pool this way is like foreplay. Or the sauna itself is foreplay and entering the pool is the next sensual experience. I surrender to the buoyant blue, let the water hold me, weightless as I float facedown, arms outstretched, and then, with breath held, dive under, completely immersed in the cool water as much as minutes before I had been immersed in the hot breath of the sauna.

My body is coming alive in a different way, responding to these new sensations. Rather than softly humming, it's singing out loud. I remember this: Tom and me in the shower together after that first night—steam rising like halos off our bodies, touching each other in places we'd discovered the night before as if those places had been transformed. Each touch a confirmation of who we were now, together.

I was told my masseuse would be a masseur, an older man blinded when he was seven by a Molotov cocktail. I have never had a massage from a man before, and I will admit to being a little tense awaiting him in the tiny room, naked on the table except for the soft sheet covering my body. I open my eyes when, after a soft knock, he enters the room. He is older than me by many years. He wears a loose white shirt and trousers. The mottled skin of his face is obvious even in the low light. A gray veil of blindness shades his eyes. He speaks English, though we hardly talk during the massage. I don't ask him about the Molotov cocktail, and he doesn't ask me how long it's been since I've been touched. Neither does he ask why I am crying as, on the massage table in this tiny, shadowed room in the intimate company of this blind man, a deep and familiar loneliness surfaces.

How does this transfer to his hands, I wonder as he reads my body with his touch. I want to ask him, "What does loneliness feel like? What is the texture of grief?"

His strong hands know their work well, and as he continues to find his way through the stories and secrets held by my body, it's as if something essential and physical is released into the scented air and my breath can find its way into places that for months have been covered over or covered up. I am lighter.

After the massage I shower, dress, and go out into the cold bright day to wait for Camille. How clear the sky, as if something essential and physical has been released from it too. How light and delicate the snow resting in the pink of still-blooming heather that lines the sidewalk.

Soon Camille will return to America and I will be on my own again. But these final days of November I just want to be. To rest. For now it's safe to stay in Helsinki. Still I know safe will eventually wear on me, and with that will come the urge to move to the next place. There's no escaping grief, you just have to learn to carry it.

Jorma owns a vegetarian restaurant and health food store where Camille and I meet him and Teemu one afternoon. Health food stores the world over smell the same. The delicious yeasty aroma of fresh-baked bread, spices and oils, candles and incense, and dozens of flavors of herb tea. The walls feature the same posters for yoga and meditation classes, holistic healing seminars, and pictures of the Maharishi.

After a lunch of yummy lentil soup, couscous with fresh green peas, and delicious grainy bread followed by sweet somethings with coffees, we go to a movie—a French film with Finnish subtitles. Jorma translates some but there's no need; it's easy to just be in the darkened theater with friends as black-and-white images flicker on the screen, accompanied by the sort of moody French music that always creates a longing within me. I'm looking forward to my time in Paris, but for now I'm glad to be here.

Our café plans seem real as Camille and I shape the place with our imaginations, including what we love best. Good coffee first of all, and of course. Some light food. Pastries, also of course. An open space of individual tables and chairs, a wood floor, maybe a little scuffed. Nothing too bright or shiny; windows opening onto the street. Art and posters on the wall. An ambiance of community. "We'll host readings," I say.

"And live music," Camille adds. A weekly salon, we agree.

"Will we also have books?"

"Yes, of course, we must have books."

We go on and on as we sit in the cupola at Kappeli's, gazing out at the snow-filled park we tromped through to get here, my feet warm in the mukluks I bought in Canada almost exactly four years earlier. Tom's last trip home.

NOVEMBER 1986
Toronto

Tom's pain has become unbearable. At an emergency room they are able to ease his current suffering, but he is unable to get another prescription for the morphine he must have. His mother's doctor, his father's doctor, his friend Dave's doctor—none could break through restrictions on providing prescriptions to controlled substances. So on American Thanksgiving Day, 1986, we pack up the camper and head south. We'll go back to Charlotte, take refuge with our friends, and make next decisions there.

By now Tom is too weak to drive the rig, so I take the wheel. Toronto to Charlotte—more than 750 miles and at least twelve hours on a route through New York, Pennsylvania, West Virginia, Virginia, and finally, North Carolina.

I'd driven the rig many miles on many trips before, alternating with Tom in that big Ford F-150 diesel pickup with its dual back tires—a *dually*, Tom called it—cab over silver camper and whipping CB antenna that he insisted on. How he loved to exchange trucker talk with cruising big-rig drivers on the road, using his old fishing boat CB handle, "Salmon Catcher," and trading quips in that gorgeous voice of his. We'd pull in to roadside truck stops, sit at sticky counters on spinny stools, drink bad coffee, and inevitably leave the place with a new Willie Nelson or Kris Kristofferson CD.

The rig is not nimble and it's not small and the drive between Toronto and Charlotte passes through some hilly and curve-bedeviled territory. We left at dawn Thanksgiving morning, but in heavy rain the twelve to fifteen hours it will take us to get there promises to be torturous.

We cross the Peace Bridge into the US and for a while the drive is peaceful in spite of the rain. Past Niagara Falls, through Buffalo, we follow the rim of Lake Erie into Pennsylvania. The day continues damp and gray, but the road is good and holiday traffic is fair. We don't talk; what's to be said? Instead we choose CDs and put them on shuffle, letting the rotation surprise us—Willie Nelson followed by the Bee Gees (Tom wrote and produced a Coca-Cola commercial with them in Australia many years before) followed by Linda Ronstadt. But when Kris Kristofferson's haunting recording of "For the Good Times" comes on—*Don't say a word about tomorrow or forever*—I can't bear it and, eyes flooded, push forward, forward, forward until the Bee Gees' glee returns.

Time and the road go on and on. Tom becomes restless, unable to find a comfortable position, and the road, as if tracing his pain, begins to twist and curve its way into the next state.

We stop for gas as we cross into West Virginia. Six-plus hours into our journey and another six-plus to go. Driving the twisting mountain roads, the skeletal trees stark in the flash of my bright lights, I grip the steering wheel as if it were the only thing holding me in this world.

In Virginia at another stop, Tom tells me he's going to ride in the camper for a while. I help him climb his way to the bed that rides over the cab of the truck where he can lie down. As I drive back onto the highway, he's there, riding above me as if he were pressing my foot to the accelerator—go faster. Faster.

Night engulfs us. We're passing through lush green forests and mountains with wild rivers where, at another time, Tom would want to stop and camp and in the dawn's light throw a line in. Now there'll be no stopping. I allow the night and the road to mesmerize me and push thoughts about my body away, though it presses me to stop, to stretch, to pee. Drive. Drive. Drive. This is all that matters.

It's well past midnight when we finally reach Charlotte and find the treatment center where our friends work. I park in the empty lot—only a few lights glow from inside—and, bone-weary, climb into the camper and crawl into bed beside Tom, who is blessedly sleeping.

Dark shadows his face and I don't dare touch him for fear of waking him.

"We're safe, Tommy," I whisper and, exhausted, join him in a dreamless sleep.

The next day Tom is relieved of his pain as much as possible and is outfitted with a full supply of morphine and whatever else might give him ease. We make reservations for a brief stay at a resort in Antigua and get our tickets for the Caribbean a few days later. Tom wants—needs—to be warm. To see the ocean, feel the sun, and to rest as much as he can. So do I.

❧

Our last night in Helsinki, sleeping in the warm white bed in Tuula and Rauski's home, I dream I'm in my own place, delighted with everything around me and how I'd made it comfortable and mine. Then a man comes into the dream—the stranger who is an amalgam of former husbands, including Tom and the on-again, off-again man. This dream man begins to tell me how to arrange things, where to put this and that. In the dream I grow angry and say I will not allow him to tell me how to arrange my life, something I never did in reality. Clearly I don't need an interpreter to translate what my dreamer self is telling my awake self.

The next morning Riita, another of our AA group, takes my laundry home and returns later with fresh-smelling clean clothes and three pizzas. Camille, Tuula, Rauski, and I eat, laugh, cry—this amazing and wonderful fellowship that creates friendships. Later that evening on the way to my ferry Tuula takes us to the Finnish orthodox church where we light candles, each of us planning next steps to wherever our path takes us. Camille tries to convince me to come home now, but I have more journey in me. I don't understand what holds me away, keeps me from returning to begin anew, and I only get more confused when I try to figure it out. My perspective seems rippled, a mirror reflecting back distorted images.

NOVEMBER 21, 1990
Helsinki to Vastradastraat

A note scribbled on an otherwise blank page in my journal: *It snowed grandly in Helsinki.*

I am alone for the first time since October 28, thirty-one days ago, when Linda and I left Greece for our journey to Helsinki and the Soviet Union. Unlike the ferry to Corfu when I was so anxious in the deep belly of that dark metal ship, aboard the *Silja Regina* to Stockholm there are light, warm duvets and a soft bed. My berth is complimented by an adjoining bath, where I shower in hot water, steam filling the small white room. The shower has a removable nozzle I can hold in my hand. And I do, opening the frosted door of the shower to watch myself in the misted mirror, which softens my reflection and makes a shadowy slow dance of my movements.

I don't disembark with the others when we dock in Stockholm. My train/ferry transportation to Copenhagen isn't until later this afternoon. I'll travel forty hours before arriving in the Netherlands. I use my time in port to lounge in the quiet boat, taste my solitude once more, and write in my journal. So many images of the last four weeks—Greece to Italy to Finland to the Soviet Union and back to Finland, always with other people, always with organized plans. Now, once more, I face uncertainty.

How good to be with Sandy again. As when I stayed with her and Bill in Vastradastraat during the early weeks of my journey, their generous home is filled with others—their younger kids, a neighbor, someone's cousin. We talk at the big table in their dining room, picking up where we left off as friends do. I wonder if our friendship will last. I meet people, we spend time together, tell our stories, reveal our secrets. It's the time together that brings us close. Like Julia in Salzburg, Kati Mati in Budapest, and Martha from the boat trip in Greece. Some friends we keep longer, but we can't keep everyone with us forever and ever. One thing I have learned: there is no forever and ever.

Bill and Sandy's second son, also in the military, has gone now with his fellow soldiers to wherever they were ordered. During the weeks in the Soviet Union, we had no news. But now the gathering of troops and the rattling of sabers continues.

NOVEMBER 24, 1990
Brussels to Paris

The day, dark and rainy; my mood, dark and moody. Anthony, an American also going to Paris, sits opposite me in the fourplex of plush burgundy seats. We chat about the kinds of things strangers chat about as their train glides along. Where he's been, where I've been; where we'll be next and why we're going there. The weather. He reaches across the space between us and hands me his card.

"Call me," he says, "when you find out where you are."

The sky lightens as we approach Gare du Nord and to the east a rainbow appears.

This is the stuff of romance novels. A recent widow, traveling alone, meets a handsome man on the train. Though it has been raining, as their train nears the station a rainbow appears. Paris, the City of Light, awaits.

Part of me loves this story. Not the widow part but the rest—the lonely, single woman. Sad, but for another reason; I don't want my story too tragic. The train. The handsome stranger, more handsome in the story than in person. The rainbow. Paris awaiting, all glittery and romantic.

In reality I am a widow. I am lonely. I don't know where I will stay or for how long. I don't speak the language well enough to be anything but comical to Parisians or possibly the object of scorn.

I take his card, say, "Yes, perhaps." And put it in my pack.

NOVEMBER 25, 1990–JANUARY 12, 1991
Paris

One reason Paris is more romantic than America: here we speak of arrondissements rather than zip codes. I have taken a room in a tourist hotel on the left bank near the Eiffel Tower, a hotel in the seventh arrondissement.

Hotel Eiffel Kensington, 79 Avenue de la Bourdonnais. Room, basic; view, none. But step outside, pay however many francs it costs so you can sit in the café with your café au lait, your journal, your fantasies, and drink it all in.

Though I am relieved to be alone, I'm also terribly homesick and more than a little anxious. As though being with friends, my own tribe, reminded me of who I am—or at least who I am when I am with others. Being alone in a foreign country where I don't know my way and don't speak the language, I am another person, a stranger even to myself. Sometimes it's as if I'm an imposter or an actress playing the role of me as written by someone else.

Many write of travel as a way of finding themselves; I am beginning to believe my journey is an attempt to integrate my many selves, including those I am just beginning to make acquaintance with.

"My goal," I write in my journal at a small table in the first of what I know will be many small tables in many small Parisian cafés, "is to find a place I can rent for a month, even six weeks or more." I'll be here for the holidays. Amy will come for Christmas, and letter exchanges have suggested the on-again, off-again man might come too. That relationship is so tenuous.

I want a place like I had in Budapest. Not in the suburbs, as was the Cseka's home on that tranquil hill overlooking the Danube, or out in the suburbs of Paris where Camille house-sat a few years ago and where Amy and I came to visit and explored this seductive city. I want to be in the heart of Paris, to let my heart beat to the pulse of the city. The calling is different than in Greece. There, it was something deep and mysterious, even soulful.

Here the call is all romance and I'm the romantic; already my language is taking on that coloring. (*Let my heart beat to the pulse of the city*? Really?) The call is also to be still after a time of activity and sensory indulgence—laughter, tears—to the point of overload that I experienced in the Soviet Union. Paris will be another kind of indulgence, but one tempered with solitude.

I've been snugged in bed since early evening under the covers in my pink sweats, and I'm grateful for them. It's cold in Paris. I've read the weekend *International Herald Tribune* and *The European*. I've eaten the second half of my sandwich à l'américaine, which I brought home from a café after an exploratory outing. Beside me sits a cup of tea made with the little electric device Bruce gave me as we left the Soviet Union—a simple coil that you insert in your cup of water. Plug the thing in and *voilà!* in just a few moments you have water hot enough to steep your tea.

I was only truly lost once today. I kept turning right instead of left and going around in circles. I crossed the Seine to George V for the Sunday AA meeting at Saint Joseph's Church just on the other side of the Arc de Triomphe where a McDonald's intrudes on all that history. Having a coffee at a McDonald's in Paris or Budapest or Copenhagen is like going to another country—the same too-bright orange and white, clean and cold country that has raised its international flag in every city and town and country I've visited except the Soviet Union and some of the farther reaches of the Greek islands. But especially here in Paris I'm certain having coffee at a McDonald's is a sin, and bless me but this is the kind of sinner I am, selling my soul for a cheap cup of joe.

During the AA meeting I hear a few muffled notes plucked from a guitar, then some sweet young voices from a room below and recognize the words, *Lord help me, Jesus / I've wasted it so help me, Jesus* . . . the Kris Kristofferson song "Why Me." How strange to hear it being sung so sweetly by a Sunday-school choir when I bet he wrote it when he was deathly hungover, one of the reasons Tom loved it so much.

After the meeting I tour the Champs-Élysées to Avenue Montaigne. The City of Light outdoes herself at the holidays. Twinkle lights twinkle everywhere like thousands of tiny white stars, so different from the garish reds, greens, and golds that delighted me as a little girl in St. Jo, Daddy driving us around on those blue December nights through neighborhoods that were known for their extravagant holiday presentations.

Strolling these boulevards with their exquisite displays, surrounded by all those fairyland lights, I am transported; I can't help but grin as I amble along, and I forget my self-conscious stranger-in-a-strange-land-ness and am simply present in the present moment. A woman of a certain age sauntering along the magically lit streets of Paris, grinning like the kid she was and who is still within her. It takes so little to make me happy for a few moments.

My route this afternoon: Montaigne as it angled back and connected with George V at the Seine, then across Pont de l'Alma and along Quai d'Orsay to Rue Saint-Dominique to Bosquet to Grenelle—I love saying those words, trying to shape them correctly in my mouth, writing them in my journal with more flourish than I might write *Third Avenue* or *Broadway*—and stopping for another café au lait, expensive for my budget but all this beauty renders me expansive. This drink is vastly different than a necessary coffee at McDonald's. Here the coffee is served in a generous ceramic cup, not a small plasticky foam thing; it's rich and sigh-inducing.

This is Paris these last days of November 1990—late afternoon and already dusk, the magic of the lights, their abundant yes to beauty. A warm café, an attentive waiter, the generous cup with its thick handle and matching saucer with a small insignia of pale green scripting the café's name, a small piece of chocolate leaving its melted kiss against the warm cup. Shaded lamps glow softly on pale tabletops. Windows look out to a lamplit street where three- and four-story buildings rise, elegantly ornate, with wrought iron balconies and crowns of terra-cotta chimney pots.

Even here in this make-do bed in this two-star hotel under the covers in my pink sweats, bread crumbs on my sheets, I sigh as I fold open my city map and trace my finger along the streets I explored today.

Romantic that I am, I could fall in love here.

Sunday night and I vow to have a place by Tuesday. Propped up in bed, thin pillow against my back, dim bulb on the bedside table, I tell myself to visualize it.

I want a place with a kitchen with a table where I can write. I want to stack books beside a chair and read into the afternoon, rich golden lamplight beside me bringing warmth and color to what I am learning are brief gray days.

We are far north of the thirty-third parallel of my home in Southern California. Paris is at the forty-eighth parallel and the earth is turning toward midwinter and it is cold. The kind of wet cold that seeps into the bones. I want a tub where I can soak deep into hot water and a bathroom that holds the warm steam.

Memory offers a picture of my mother during the long Midwestern winters, hanging clothes that sometimes freeze stiff on the line. Her hands red and chapped.

One of my favorite sentences ever is from *My Ántonia* by Willa Cather: "Winter comes down savagely over a little town on the prairie." Here's my mother at her clothesline in the wicked cold, pinning up wet towels and sheets and the many school dresses of three little girls, all bound together with wooden clothespins to a frozen line. My father is telling her of California, but she keeps hanging wet clothes until, until . . . whatever he said or did that convinces her. I don't know what he told her, but I'm grateful he said it and she listened.

I won't be hanging clothes outside; I'll be going to the laundromat, the dry cleaner's. I don't know yet how you say these things in French. I know they'll sound better than in English. I'll go to charming small shops to buy cheese and eggs and another for fresh produce; I'll find bread at a patisserie where everything is just-baked and smells delicious. I'll find a small market in the neighborhood for necessities, toiletries and such. There'll be a flower shop nearby. "*Fleuriste*," I practice saying the word aloud.

At the women's meeting at the American church I meet Leafy from Boston, a taller-than-me redhead with a wide, generous smile and a steady handshake that will become a friendly AA hug before long, I just know it. I also meet Anne and Genevieve and Deb and so many other women; Americans, Brits, other English-speakers from other countries, some like me traveling through and others here for the long stay. One woman, Julia, an opera singer, came nearly fifty years ago and never left. I understand how that could happen.

I like women's AA meetings; the same open trust that I've experienced in other women's-only meetings going way back to the consciousness-raising sessions of the seventies in LA. I like the laughter, that howling laughter you hear whenever a group of women gather and tell their stories, laughter I first heard as a little girl crawling under the Formica-topped, chrome-legged kitchen tables at the veterans' housing complex where my mother and other young mothers pulled their chairs close for the ritual daily coffee klatches.

Here's what I know about women in AA: mention that you're new in town or new to a meeting or newly sober and after the meeting you'll have phone numbers thrust at you with invitations to "Call me," or "Come to our Wednesday meeting; it's a step-study," or "Let's have coffee." When I was new in the program all the welcoming hands and hugs and phone numbers intimidated me—now I know how important they are and I'm among the first to offer mine. Or I will as soon as I get a place with a phone.

The studio apartment in an old four-story building at 27 Rue Quincampoix in the Marais, a semiboho, *très* historic neighborhood, is truly funky with a loft bed, huge windows that look onto a cobbled square, scuffed wood floors, a tiny kitchen nook, and an even tinier bathroom with a tub that's half my size. But I love it. And I like Christine, a lovely young Frenchwoman with softy curling tawny hair whose English sounds exactly how I would want mine to sound if I were an alluring young Frenchwoman who spoke good English. Christine and her husband, Frederic, live in the country but she keeps the Paris studio and rents it out longish-term to travelers like me, listing it on the bulletin board at the American church where I discovered it.

As Christine shows me around, though you can more or less stand in one place and see the entire apartment, I visualize candles and flowers, the radiator warming to a toasty temperature that encourages reading late in the high bed and, in the morning, lingering with coffee and writing at the round oak table with its generous wicker chairs. And there's the telephone, a white one that rests on the second step (of eight) that lead to the loft bed. I say, "Yes!" and pay for the first month. Tomorrow I'll bring my bags from Hotel Eiffel Kensington in the seventh, across the Seine on the Left Bank to the fourth on the Right Bank. Forgive me, but I can't help but sigh writing these words.

I put my things in their places and hang my clothes in the mirrored wardrobe that's crowned by a delightful goose lamp—not a gooseneck lamp, but a lamp in the shape of a goose, white with orange feet and an orange beak. My toiletries are stashed in the tiny bathroom. Christine left flowers and fruit for my arrival. Long-stemmed mums and bright ranunculus in the bath, and on the table a huge platter of fruit that included a pineapple, a papaya, and lychees. *Lychees.* Exotic and so graciously French. I like how the bed is high enough to make space below where a big mirror is balanced on a storage cabinet. Atop the cabinet, more flowers. On the table between two large windows is another small lamp and a radio.

So many mirrors and windows in this little studio. The floor-to-ceiling windows look out over the bare branches of plane trees to the Pompidou Center—with its exposed pipes and ducts and wiring, appearing for all the world unfinished—and across Rue Quincampoix to where Place Edmond-Michelet is squared all around with iconic French wrought iron lampposts and inviting benches.

Before she left, Christine took me around the neighborhood to the laundromat (*laverie*-the shortened version of *laverie automatique*) and the dry cleaner's (*nettoyeur à sec*), the small supermarket (*super-marché*, that one easy to remember), and the closest stop for the bus that will take me to meetings at the American church. She pointed out places with good things to eat—the butcher, the cheese shop, the charcuterie; told me about this restaurant, that café, the vegetarian place—saying it all in her enticing accent. She's an actress, she told me, just returned from making a film in Spain in which she played the role of lady-in-waiting to the queen. I try to explain myself but get tangled up. I tell her I'm staying in Paris for the holidays before continuing on to India and, well, wherever else I'm going. We laugh easily together; I try some French and she corrects my pronunciation but with much good humor. We could be friends, I sense. I hope so.

Later I busy around, organizing my things. My journal and pen placed on the round oak table with the chair arranged so I can look up from my writing and gaze out the windows, a few books unloaded from my bags and stacked on a shelf that parallels the bed. As I straighten up, the telephone rings. Strange, as I haven't given the number to anyone yet. It could be Christine, something she forgot to tell me.

A man speaks French. We struggle to understand each other. Finally, in heavily accented English, the man says, "How much do you cost to fuck?" I laugh, also in English. So much for romance.

Leafy calls this afternoon and invites me to the hammam at the Mosquée de Paris, France's oldest place of Islamic worship. The mosque is located in the fifth arrondissement near the botanical gardens, a short metro ride for me. But just because it's close by doesn't stop me from getting lost. I'd been obsessing on getting a coffee pot for the apartment and took the wrong metro exit.

Coming up out of metros, no matter which city I'm in, causes my directionally challenged senses to awake and blink, wide-eyed. How often have I gone the wrong way—in Paris, London, Budapest, Athens. Whether a familiar city and a familiar route or not, I must always take my bearings, consult my map, or, if I can speak the language, ask a stranger. I have spent a good deal of my life lost, which isn't always a bad thing, but this afternoon I'm to meet Leafy and I want to be on time.

The mosque is an impressive structure with its minaret rising imposingly into the Paris sky. I locate Leafy in the courtyard and we enter through a scrim of curtains, past the tearoom with its intricate tiled walls and delicately carved teak, and come into an inner sanctum—a sacred place.

"Wow," I say.

"I know," Leafy says.

We enter a great marble-floored room with a tiered fountain in its center and walls adorned with brightly colored tiles that appear as mandalas or many-petaled rare flowers. Pillars of deep cobalt and a watery, silky green bordered in patterned gold rise to a balcony and decorative carved screens. Higher still, the ceiling curves into a graceful sapphire dome aglitter with light-sparks from a massive crystal chandelier. The air is heavy with the scent of a mixture of oils: rose, jasmine, lavender, and—what else?—Sandalwood. And something deeper, musky. The fragrances mix and blend into a lush, sensuous aroma. The murmuring of women's voices and the plashing of the fountain echo off tiled walls and high ceiling.

Situated on ledges around the fountain are mats covered with various fabrics in patterns and solids, some in vivid yellow and orange, others soft rose or muted green. Women in varying stages of dress and undress recline or sit or stand, some in bikinis, some in bras and panties, some only panties. Traditionally visitors to the hammam disrobed completely except for a loincloth; this bit of modesty is retained, albeit in skimpy, lacy versions.

Leafy and I are given space on the mats and begin to undress. No matter how many locker rooms I've undressed in or group showers I've taken, though I attempt a casual attitude, I am still self-conscious of my naked body, especially with strangers. Clearly Leafy doesn't experience the same shyness. She undresses while continuing to talk, asking if I'd like a massage later.

"Maybe," I say, remembering the masseur at the baths in Helsinki and the deep well of sorrow his touch released.

We arrange our things on our mats and wander into another room, a shower area where women are receiving massages and gritty, soapy rub-downs—the *gommage*—by hefty-looking women in white clothes.

"You can sign up for one at the desk if you want," Leafy says. I'm not sure about this either.

Another room offers more vibrantly tiled walls and benches and ledges where more women lounge. Are all the women truly that splendid, or is it the veiled mist of fragrant steam that makes it seem so? The contrast is stark between my experience in Helsinki with the very white, mostly old, intricately wrinkled Finns, and here where gorgeous women with glowing skin—shades of oiled tan, brown, black, and olive—and every one, it seems, with gracefully flowing, long, dark hair, the kind of hair I have always wanted and swear in my next life I will have. Of course I compare myself unfavorably. The tan I earned on the Dalmatian beaches and Greek islands is now faded to a memory, and I'm acutely conscious of my forty-eight-year-old body.

Five marble-lined rooms succeed each other, each getting warmer as we pass through. In the final room we come upon a large platform, about knee-high and squared by more pillars, next to a shallow pool, empty now. All along the perimeter of the room are more ledges, bare of mats and glistening damply.

"How about here?" Leafy asks, gesturing toward one of the vacant ledges. This is where we situate ourselves.

Dimly lit and haloed by steam, the air is hot and wet and heavy. We don't make conversation, but I do emit audible sighs of relief, the kind I make every time I get into a hot shower or lower myself into a hot tub. Yes, this is pure indulgence; a moist sensuality as seminude women rub down their bodies with loofas.

Every now and again a woman brings a hose out to rinse where one woman leaves and another comes to take her place. With the steam and the ever-rising temperature, I become too hot and find relief by leaning against the coolish stone wall, its ledge hard and ungiving under my near-naked bum.

After a while, along with the increasing heat, the sounds in this expansive marble-floored, misty room become disturbingly loud as women come and go and voices rise on the steam and echo off the walls.

Apparently Leafy has noticed this, too, as she joins me. "Do you want to try another room?" she asks. Her already curly red hair has gone corkscrew-y in the humidity.

"Yes, let's," I agree, and we return to the room where we left our mats, each of us finding a place to lie down, lengthening out our damp, relaxed bodies.

I don't know, can never know, what it's like with men—in the steam room, for instance, or other private, intimate settings. We've all seen clichéd scenes in movies and on television. Deals are made, assignments given, most often by towel-wrapped white men who sometimes smoke cigars.

But for Leafy and me and the dozen or so other women in this room of the hammam, we stretch out on our mats and share that kind of lazy, rambling conversation women make when they're nearly naked together, open from the heat, the steam, and the pure sensuality and intimacy of the baths. We talk about our bodies, what we'd like to eat, maybe an idle fantasy. This companionable sharing has always been as much a part of the traditional baths as the ritual ablutions of cleansing and relaxing the body, an Islamic tradition that dates back as far as the seventh or eighth century.

After the baths we take the metro to Leafy's apartment, where we have tangerines and tea and sit on large pillows on the floor near an altar she has arranged beneath a window. She shows me carvings she's made, graceful shapes in dark, polished wood; a crystal her therapist gave her, "For clarity," she tells me; and what she says is a "call to prayer" bowl, which she makes sing as she circles it with a small mallet. A pure resonating sound enters my being, and I fall into it as I did in Salzburg when Julia curved that dowel around the small brass bowl in the sound exhibit. For just that moment, in the fading colors of the Paris afternoon in this apartment with my friend, I give myself over to that single pure note and vow to have a prayer bowl of my own once I am where I will be.

A week has passed since I moved into the studio on Rue Quincampoix; the passage of time marked by the flowers Christine left for me, which are wilting. I wake up and it's still dark, so I snuggle down and sleep more as I have each day so far in this safe apartment that is my temporary home. Daylight doesn't come until well past nine, and even then it's not a shining light but cottony and drab.

When I finally rise I make toast with bread from the patisserie, choose fruit from the ever-dwindling supply Christine arranged, sit at my table, drink coffee from the coffee maker I finally located at a neighborhood shop, and write.

Sounds come up from Place Edmond-Michelet and draw me to the windows. Below, some kind of a demonstration is taking place. Several dozen people are gathered, chanting. I can't translate the signs or their words—for or against immigration or what is happening in the Middle East. Watching from two stories above the street, instead of feeling the anger of the crowd below, I am sad.

Some of the old sorrow has returned. Grief for Tom and his too-young death, but something more too. I come upon a quote from Camus: "There is no love of life without despair of life."

After breakfast I climb the stairs back up to my loft bed with the *Elan* section of the weekend *European* and read about filmmakers and playwrights and poets and artists. Given my present mood, rather than being excited about the work these artists do and checking dates so I can witness their creations in person, I revert to the too-human thing of comparing myself and my life to all of theirs and, of course, come up lacking.

I go on and on in my journal, as self-pity allows, writing in a sloppy hand of half-cursive, half-printed self-talk I've been taught in meetings and by therapists. I soothe myself by writing that it's okay to rest here and be sad and to express the sorrow and regrets about missed opportunities and choices made and not made.

I fully acknowledge my emotions and don't worry that anyone will find my journal and discover what a pitiful woman I've become. I write and I cry and the ink smears and I keep writing until I am emptied and my hand aches.

Finally I close my journal, blow my nose, and go down the eight steps from my bed. Something has changed outside the windows. The protesters with their signs and shouting have gone, and in their place two guys in too-large overcoats perform some kind of goofy act, slapstick and silly. A small crowd has gathered and the occasional rush of sound comes through the windows as their laughter rises in unison. This, too, is how my moods come and go, not unlike the weather these early December days in Paris. Dreary days but then suddenly, surprisingly, the sun breaks through and everything is shining again.

Shopping is a challenge when you don't know the language, when you can't ask for what you want, don't understand the money, and don't know where to find what you need. Travel books don't help much, at least not when all you want is a frying pan. To lessen my anxiety, I approach shopping as an adventure, like searching for hidden treasure or a scavenger hunt.

Today I explore beyond my neighborhood and venture to Forum des Halles, a vast underground shopping mall not far across Rue de Rivoli. Here, among the kinds of shops you might find in any large American mall, I buy a new lipstick. In Greece I wore bright pink, a color from the sixties that I continued to wear in the Soviet Union, but here in Paris I want something softer, more French, a more subtle shade. There's an air about Paris that—what? This is hard to define. It's the thing that allows Parisian women to wear a plain dark skirt and sweater, flats, and a silk scarf tied just so and the whole thing looks so sophisticated. I don't know how they do it, but a more subtle shade of lipstick is a good start and I choose a soft rose matte. I also buy two pairs of warm woolen socks—my feet get so cold trudging the concrete and cobbles of Paris streets—a pair of dangly earrings, a tall brass candlestick and a supply of taper candles, and two more green houseplants in terra-cotta pots. More and more I fill this already warm and inviting apartment with items chosen to please the part of me that loves these special touches.

I return home with a bag of groceries and frozen toes.

Partly to warm my bones and partly for the pleasure of it, I have a lovely soak in the funky little tub, hot water sprinkled generously with lavender bath salts, which I purchased on today's shopping adventure. The tub has little bum bumps that keep me from sliding completely underwater and allow me to lean against the slanted end. A tall ivory candle burns in its new holder, creating a circle of mist that surrounds the flame. In the other room the transistor radio plays a jazz station I found that always goes soft and sexy in late evening. Perfect. Except the tub is so small that in order to fit I have to fold my legs crisscross, which is not the sensuousness I am aiming for. No languorous stretching out to full length. Still, a cold night in Paris, my body in the hot water, the steamy, lavender-scented mist haloing the candle flame, the music—a girl can dream.

Snugged in my bed with a cup of tea, I write this quote by Thomas Crum in my journal and ask it of myself: "What would it be like if you lived each day, each breath, as a work of art in progress?"

I have always escaped into books. Or gone there for pure joy, to experience a life different from my own. Nothing gives me more delight and fulfillment than being so deep inside a story that I am outside myself.

In every city where I have stopped for more than a few days I've

found a special café and a bookstore. In Paris I find both in one: Tea &
Tattered Pages, 24 Rue Mayet, Montparnasse. The bookstore with the
red door is smallish, but the shop offers a great variety of reasonably
priced used books in English (the owner is American) and a delectable
selection of pastries. There is no better place to go on a cold winter
afternoon.

I take a long time choosing books; my Libran self, forever comparing and weighing decisions, interferes with any kind of efficiency.
But then who wants to be efficient in a bookstore? Today's bounty:
a new Margaret Atwood (*Bodily Harm*), another by Louise Erdrich
(*Love Medicine*), and an anthology of American poetry.

At my window table I open the *Herald Tribune*, nibble my almond
croissant, read, and eavesdrop. At the next table two women are having
afternoon tea and discussing family back in America using names
they both know—the one in the brown coat does most of the talking
and the other nods and *mm-hmm*s as she sips her tea. Their chat isn't
really worth listening in on; a discerning eavesdropper hopes for
something enticing, maybe a little juicy. Meanwhile at the counter, the
proprietor talks on the phone while she rings up a customer, juggling
phone, money, the book, and a smile. As I watch, I imagine myself as
proprietress, wondering how I'll adapt to the role when Camille and I
open our café. I've never worked with the public before—never had a
job in food service or retail. To tell the truth, I don't even like baking
all that much and know even less of how to do it.

I once tried to make a cobbler during a bountiful harvest of
peaches from our orchard in Jamul. Well, I actually did make the cobbler—mixing the dough, making a mess of the kitchen, spilling a tin
of cinnamon on the counter. We'd invited Pine Tree Bill to come for
dinner and promised cobbler for dessert. Pine Tree Bill was from west
Texas and said he knew a thing or two about cobbler. I don't know if I
laughed out of embarrassment or just in general when he tried to cut
the crust with his fork, couldn't, picked up the piece of cobbler, and
knock-knocked it on the table. Even then it didn't crumble.

I sleep late, not only because of the sweet comfort of my bed and the late rising of the sun, which hasn't yet broken through the gray, but because I stayed awake finishing *Utrillo's Mother* by Sarah Baylis. So late and so lost inside it; sometimes I force myself to put a book down and turn off the bedside lamp, but last night I just kept reading. I love that delicious, tension-filled place between wanting to keep reading and not wanting the story to end.

Sometimes, for days after closing the cover on a book I've been deep inside, living with characters I've come to know well and to care about deeply, a kind of melancholy comes over me, and I miss the people I have been so intensively involved with.

What a luxury to be in this apartment for a while, bringing home all the books that call my name (*Judy, Judy, Judy,* in that Cary Grant voice, which I understand he never really said, but I like the way it sounds in my ear). I love the luxury of stacking them on the shelf that runs alongside the loft bed, on the table and on the chair beside the table, taking one with me as I go out into the day, because who knows where I might find myself with time and a place I can simply be—a woman alone, reading a book.

But first, coffee and my journal at the table with the occasional glance out the windows across the square to the Pompidou Center, all glass and metal and those various colored pipes and ducts climbing the walls. In comparison, the row of old buildings along Quincampoix are full of character and all the inconveniences that go with it—the dim lobby, the dank staircase, the smell of mold and stale wine.

Camille calls and after we talk about all the things we always talk about, she shares with me that every one of the evaluations from our trip to the USSR recommended me as a future trip leader. What a surprise. I saw myself as part of the group, a follower. Interesting how others see us versus how we see ourselves. After I got hired at Project Concern International many years ago, Quinn the HR guy told me one of the reasons I got the job was my self-confidence. That surprised me too. How do I project that on the outside when the inside is often so insecure? This self-confident self is apparently another of my many selves. *How,* I wonder, *do I integrate that outside with the inside so I become more of who I am, or maybe simply realize and express more of who I am?*

Camille and I discuss the ways we spend our time—her days are so different now that she's in a relationship. All those things she used to do to fill her time—long hours in her gray chair by the window, reading, listening to music, and writing in cafés. All that has been replaced by time spent with her new partner. She says she likes it better. She used to say she loved her life exactly the way it was and didn't know where she would fit in a relationship. Now she knows.

Priorities change. I, for example, have hardly lived alone in my life and am now here with this grand desire for solitude.

I hear Kati Mati's voice that evening in Budapest when she told me about her withdrawal into her garden. So, too, have I withdrawn into the garden of my inner life—can I say that without sounding too mannered? I know it's vital to have solitude and time for writing, yet I also need other people. As always, the answer is balance. So the question is: How do you do that?

Finally the sun! Place Edmond-Michelet is alive and lively—people, dogs, the ubiquitous green "clean" trucks that sometimes wake me in the morning. I dress to go out into the welcome sunlight, first putting on my warmest socks and boots, knowing how cold my feet get. I don't know how the Frenchwomen stand it in their thin stockings and thin leather shoes.

Today I am a flaneuse, strolling across the bridge at Pont Saint-Michel to visit Shakespeare and Company. For a long moment before I pass beneath the green awning, I pause in the brick entryway and breathe in literary history. This shop is not the original Shakespeare and Company that Sylvia Beach opened and where, in the twenties, Hemingway, James Joyce, Djuna Barnes, and others gathered. That one closed during the German occupation of Paris. This site opened in 1951 and was later named Shakespeare and Company in tribute to Sylvia Beach's legacy.

I wander aisles, explore tightly packed nooks and crannies, climb stairs so narrow they cause browsers and shoppers to turn sideways when we pass one another. Here are slender young literary types in turtlenecks and jeans who've come, as I have, to pay homage. We're tourists with our cameras, wanderers, romantics, historians—all of us coming to Shakespeare and Company like art lovers enter the Louvre or fashionistas along Avenue Montaigne enter Dior and Chanel.

I pull books from cluttered shelves and inhale their aroma, read a few lines, and replace them. Dare I wonder, for a heartbeat of a moment, if one day a book that bears my name will be among these dusty stacks found by another curious flaneuse who pages through it, weighing the purchase.

I have books at home, I tell myself, savoring the word *home* and its close relationship with the word *books*, and try to resist buying more. I can always come back. Yes, and I can always come back to Paris. So I leave the fabled bookshop without adding more books. But I have experienced it, breathed the smell that is uniquely used bookstore, and honored the literary legacy of this particular bookstore. As I go back into the bright Paris afternoon I take one last deep breath and leave with the comforting knowledge that here, as at Tea & Tattered Pages, is abundance. Bury me in a coffin of books.

More ambling, more flaneusing, through the streets and passages of Saint-Michele as I aim my wandering way toward the Louvre. Though I visited the museum on a previous trip to Paris, I've yet to see the Pyramid.

The Louvre is covered in scaffolding and draped for a grand refurbishment. At the front of the museum squats an ungrand mess of construction. But there it is: the Pyramid, an exact replica of the Great Pyramid of Giza but made of glass and metal, all agleam in the winter sun. Designed by I. M. Pei as the new entrance to the museum, the addition has caused much controversy. Too modern. A disfigurement of the classical architecture. Even rumors that the structure is evil because of the number of glass panes—the number is actually 673, but it's commonly said to be 666, which is the number of the demon/beast in the Book of Revelation.

In spite of the draping and the construction, the Louvre Pyramid and its three smaller adjoining pyramids appear strong and powerful and clean. Grand fountains rise on either side and pools of water seem level with the benches that surround them, suggesting, from my viewpoint, that those seated there are actually balanced on the water; a stunning optical illusion.

Continuing my rambling, lazy afternoon, I cross through the Jardin des Tuileries toward Place de la Concorde, my feet so cold I'm somewhat distracted from the beauty of the scene, captivating even in the frigid, bare days before the winter solstice.

A little way off the central walkway in the Tuileries, a fire burns among the trees. Not a wildfire but a keeping-warm fire, I suspect. Smoke rises and fills the air. The sun, now weakened by a misty haze, filters through the bare branches. I left my camera at the apartment today; sometimes it's better to be present than to view life through the lens of a camera. But the scene before me—the black-trunked trees, bare in the cold winter day, the smoke, the pale filtered sun—would be a magnificent photo. I stand on the gravel path and memorize the image.

By now my feet are so cold that every footfall on a small rock in the path results in a shooting pain. I'm afraid someone will step on my toes or run over them with a bicycle. I imagine all sorts of horrible, painful things happening to my toes—weights being dropped on them, small animals attacking them. They feel brittle, as if one misstep will break them completely and cleanly off my foot or shatter them into splintered, bony shards.

Still I keep walking. I'm in Paris.

The ringing of church bells in the distance, like the echo of a faraway train whistle, evokes a yearning for something nameless. This Sunday morning Saint-Merri's, just across Place Edmond-Michelet from my apartment, sends out its refrain, which for some may be a call to worship or prayer but for me calls up a familiar desire. Today I want other than what I have, though I know I should heed a warning from long ago: *Be careful what you wish for.*

Sometimes when Tom and I both lived and worked in our home in Jamul and all our time was spent there, together, I felt crowded. Even though we lived on more than an acre and our closest neighbors were in their own homes on their own acreage, the shared space could sometimes feel confining. This wasn't caused by disagreements or the buildup of minor resentments that can come with any marriage; still I would sense the reality of not being free or independent. I'd find myself leaning on the deck railing, gazing off into the canyon and wishing for time and space and solitude; for something different. It wasn't Tom and it wasn't Jamul or the life we'd created—this same disturbance interrupted, or maybe *disrupted* is a better word, my other marriages as well. It's this same restlessness that had me sell everything, get on a plane, and start this journey.

I know when Amy comes in a few weeks I'll revel in our time together. Being in Paris with the lights and magic and goodwill of the holidays with one of my favorite people in the whole world will be a joy.

This cycle of involvement to the point of craving unstructured aloneness, followed by the debilitating loneliness that besets me when I get what I wish for, sends me back to examining my Libran personality—the constant seeking of balance. I envy the lady who is the symbol for Libra—Lady Justice who holds in her hands perfectly balanced twin scales, the serenity of her face. My wish should be phrased as wanting "balanced living where involvement and solitude are in equal measure."

I hear my mother's question, *Why do you always make things so complicated?* and respond, Oh, Mother, if only I knew the answer to that.

Anne, a friend from the women's meeting, and I are in her apartment in Montmartre one Sunday afternoon when the snow begins. We're drinking tea and talking of our lives—she's a university professor at a liberal arts college in the eastern US. Me, well, I begin as I always do . . . *I'm um, I'm not sure, I'm* . . . when I spot snow out the window and stop mid-umming.

"Oh look! It's snowing!" I say. I could be six years old, the way my voice sounds.

"Let's go out," Anne exclaims, forgetting tenure and the politics of academia. She's excited too. You'd think neither of us had ever experienced falling snow before.

Coats, mittens, boots, and out into the snowy swirl we go, where we're serenaded by the biggest snowflakes I have ever seen. Wondrous in their size. The kind of snowflakes Paris deserves. I imagine each flake exquisite in its own design.

From Anne's apartment we climb the hill to Sacré-Cœur and gaze down upon Paris, snowy and fogged in. I can barely discern the outline of the Eiffel Tower.

We enter the church, where the light is smoke-hazed from scores of wax candles and the air infused with the heady scent of incense. Stained glass windows watercolor the walls. The small chapels set aside for prayers are full; the place is crowded with tourists and worshipers.

I stand, feet apart for balance, and gaze up at the mosaic inside the great dome. The heart inside the figure of Jesus appears to be glowing. This may be caused by the effect of hundreds of candles flickering against golden tiles or some kind of trick the artist used in his design, which causes an optical illusion when the light is just right. Or conceivably an illusion manifested by the fervent wishes of a seeker.

On our way back down the hill we stop at a café in Place du Tertre for an omelet. All around the square the work of various artists—painters, sketchers, illustrators—is exhibited. The snow has nearly stopped and the few flakes that float down melt as soon as they land—as if, regardless of their size, they are too delicate to withstand the blow of hitting brick, tile, stone.

Anne is one of the few people I've met in Paris who has a car. She drives us to a meeting at the American church by way of the Champs-Élysées, where we stop to admire elegantly decorated Christmas trees. All along the boulevard holiday decorations do their bright conjuring.

Whether the illusionary trick of light inside the dome of Sacré-Cœur or the enchantment of twinkle lights, I am easy prey for such magic.

I'm thankful daily for my blue Greek coat and matching scarf, which I wear around my neck, not wrapped around my head the way the saleswoman in the shop on Corfu dressed me with that gaudy brooch holding the scarf in place. Though now, on these cold days in Paris, wearing it that way would surely help keep my ears warm.

I'm also grateful for the wool socks I bought at Forum des Halles and often wear both pairs when I go out. Drying them on the little radiator in the bathroom after washing them at night brings a smell of toasting wool that harkens memories of our little-kid mittens being dried on the radiator when we lived at veterans' housing in St. Jo after Daddy came home from the war. I'm transported back to that two-bedroom duplex that shared a front porch with the one next to it and connected in a line of four or six others that faced each other across a patch of yard with a central sidewalk. The hardwood floors, the linoleum in the kitchen, that scratchy brown couch where a wider world was revealed to me and set me dreaming. Look at me now, Daddy.

Still, double wool socks or not, tramping all that concrete and cobble, I'm certain my toes could crack right off like the icicles that hung from the eaves of those veterans' homes in Missouri.

Today, a particularly toe-freezing day, I head down Rue Saint-Dominique, looking in shoe store windows for a pair of shoes with thicker soles and happen upon a guy in a bedraggled jacket working a knife into a large piece of cardboard that leans against a trash container. Already cut out from the cardboard is a jagged but perfectly shoe-shaped hole, and I see he's sawing away at a second one with his knife.

How clever! California woman that I am, I never considered liners for the inside of my shoes. Not cardboard, but something soft and warm like the inside of slippers. Something cozy, like kittens or bunnies. Not the whole animal, just the fuzzy part. Made, of course, of fake fur. Surely someone makes such things. I would search for them.

The metro ride to Porte de Clignancourt, north of the city, takes a while. It's early and I'm glad to finally arrive and meet Leafy and Genevieve for café crème and an almond croissant before we begin our ramble through the tables and booths at the Paris flea market.

Les Puces is the world's largest flea market. It began in the Middle Ages when entrepreneurial merchants gathered and sold old clothes and flea-ridden rags. The name *flea market* continues to this day. The French name sounds fun and even a little romantic, so much more so than what we in San Diego call a *swap meet*.

Les Puces is street after street, row after row of mostly antique dealers, including some very high-end stuff, far from flea-ridden. There's also clothing, knickknacks, old records, photographs, postcards, dishes, and all manner of household goods. I've been to flea markets in any number of grand cities, including Athens and London, and in smaller wayside towns: Paducah, Kentucky, and beachside Leucadia near San Diego. No matter the location, in my experience the smells are pretty much the same—something old (used books, moth-eaten jackets, not-quite-clean skillets), something cooking (popcorn, cinnamon rolls, hot dogs), people (perfumed and unbathed alike), and sometimes animals (birds in Athens, chickens in Paducah, kittens in Leucadia). And though the music is different and the language varied, there is still a flea market sound and a certain energy of anticipation on the part of the buyer, hopeful for a bargain, and another kind of anticipation on the part of the sellers.

The energy of anticipation is high the morning we enter Les Puces, exuding from professional shoppers and the dealers to the curious tourists like me; housewives, families, the wanderers, and the purposeful. Some apparently know exactly where they're going; they have their favorite stalls. Others, like me, roam the aisles and wait for inspiration to strike. All manner of items spread out from booths and tables and into the narrow walkways as well as along the main avenues.

"Watch your purse," Genevieve warns. "Pickpockets."

I tuck my pack under my arm.

We walk together for a while, then Leafy suggests we each go our own way. "Meet at the juncture of Rue Pierre-et-Marie-Curie and Rue des Rosiers in an hour," she says.

Off I wander, up this aisle and down that row, not looking for anything in particular but interested in so much, especially the old jewelry and vintage bags and clothes. In one small booth filled to bursting with small statues, old jewelry, and fancy—if chipped—china, I pause to examine the detailing on a small oval mirror encircled by an embossed brass frame that rises from a brass pedestal. Along one side of the frame is the graceful form of a woman. She leans into the mirror, gazing at herself; her flowing gown trails into the decorated frame. She has about her a deco style, the low back of her gown draping a slender figure. The mirror itself is held in place by small decorative screws on either side so the view can tilt this way or that.

Of course I buy it. I don't even bargain for it. My French is next to nonexistent and I can't remember any of the words for numbers anyhow. The seller, an old man with a scraggly mustache and well-worn hands, smiles, is glad to sell it to me for full price. There's something precious about this mirror; I can intuit stories inside the brass as I pick it up and wonder who I'll see when I gaze into its glass.

The man wraps it in old newspapers and stuffs it in a paper bag that barely folds over the top and hands it back to me.

I thank him with *merci*, the word I've used most often in Paris, and hold my prize against my chest as if adding emphasis to my *merci*. Now my story will be added to the others, held inside much as the two brass screws hold the mirror in its frame. For some reason I don't know, perhaps thinking of all those who have owned it before me, I wonder: After I'm gone where will it go? Very probably it will be sold at a garage sale by my son and daughter, who'll have to go through my things and sort them and release them to the world. Or it may find its way to a granddaughter I've yet to know, or even a great-granddaughter, who might someday tell the story of the time her grandmother stayed in Paris one winter and found this mirror at a flea market and brought it home with her.

I continue my roaming, carefully wrapped mirror in my pack and—surprise!—a stall selling shoe inserts made of shearling perfectly cut to fit my shoes. Soft and warm and fuzzy and a cushion for my feet on the frozen cobbles and bricks of Paris's winter streets, its paths and alleyways that lead to so many surprises.

One afternoon, as I travel home on the metro, a man stands at the end of our car. He's not a boy but not very old either—a young man in a black jacket, plaid scarf wound the way Europeans know to wrap them. Next to him, the door with a glass window. As the car bounces and jiggles, the dark window reflects his face as a mirror would. He looks at himself in the glass, tugs at his skimpy mustache as if willing it to grow, and stares into his own eyes for a long moment.

I recognize myself in him. I do this: stare at my reflection, though not in public. I remember one of the common cautions back in the days of smoking marijuana: "Watch out for the mirrors; they'll capture you."

Straight and sober all these years, I sometimes still stare at myself in mirrors, deep into my eyes. This is not vanity. This is not adjusting my hair or pulling the skin of my cheeks back to see how I would look if I "had some work done" (though yes, I do that too). This gazing into my own eyes is a search. If the eyes are windows into the soul, who do I see when I stare so intently?

I have never been able to say, "I see you; I recognize you." My stare, almost as if hypnotized, always asks the question: "Who are you?"

I meet Rip at an AA meeting at the American church and he invites me for lunch the next day. I like how he shared his story in the meeting—thoughtful, articulate, and he didn't go on too long—so I say,

"Sure." *Why not*, I'm thinking. Later I tell Camille this on the phone and she says it's a date.

"No it's not," I say.

We meet at the Arc de Triomphe, smile and wave when we see each other. I admit to taking a little care when I dressed for our not-a-date. A white sweater with pink flowers embroidered across the breast, feminine but warm, and black wool trousers that fit well enough even with the weight I've lost from all my Paris explorations. Black boots with the fuzzy inserts, which make them a bit tight but better that than frozen toes.

Rip is not a tall man, our gazes meet pretty much at eye level. He's from Cape Cod, in Paris for a business trip, he says. I don't know his business. He's American East Coast attractive and carries himself with a kind of sophistication that's different than Southern California guys. He wears an expensive leather jacket and gloves. California men don't have gloves like Rip's. California men have to buy gloves like that specially for journeys to cold places; Rip wears his with ease. His plaid wool scarf warms his neck; he knows how to dress for the cold. His longish blond hair is pulled back in a ponytail. Cute. We cross the street and have lunch at le drugstore.

From lunch we go to Notre-Dame. The Christchurch Cathedral Choir from New Zealand is performing a concert of sacred music. Neither of us knew this was scheduled; we were going to Notre-Dame because that's what you do when you visit Paris.

I've visited the cathedral many times. My excursions often take me across Île de la Cité, and sometimes if I've been out for a while and am cold and worn down from the noise and stimulation of the city, I go inside, light a candle, and rest amid the quiet.

Rip and I find a place on the old pews and settle in with others who are equally dressed for the chill. All around the murmur of people taking their places, the shuffle of feet on the old stones, the sounds hushed and absorbed into this vast and holy place. The choir enters: pure white robes, scarlet red at the collar; men first, to the back row, and another after them, then two rows of women. The choir director takes his place and soon holy music saturates the cavernous space. I thrill with the sound, the harmonies that rise and resonate. I slide my arm through Rip's and cannot stop the tears. The glorious music fills me as if I'm holding my breath and also breathing deeply along with the voices that rise, fall, go soft, then rise once more. The music isn't familiar, but somehow I know it all as if from some old forgotten place, a time out of time. Afterward, for some moments, I don't dare look at Rip, nor am I able to speak.

It's dark as we leave Notre-Dame, though still early, and we walk companionably though quietly through the flower market toward my apartment. I buy a bright poinsettia in a foil-wrapped pot and tuck it under my arm. We stop at a patisserie for a pastry to go with the coffee we'll have in my apartment; I've invited him up.

I place the poinsettia on the oak table and set about making coffee. The radio plays its moody jazz, the goose lamp offers its warm glow. Outside, streetlamps have come on and silhouette the tall windows.

We drink our coffee and share the pastry, which I've served on a white ceramic plate, tearing off small pieces with our hands. We talk and tell stories and probably a few lies. Rip notices the loft bed, a presence I try to ignore. He smiles. I consider he may be counting the steps up. I don't catch his eye but go on with whatever I'm talking about.

"It's good to talk to a man," I say. "My friends in Paris are all women; we talk of different things."

"Men, too," he says, "when they're together. But I like women. I like to be with women."

Then he tells me he's thirty-six, and, "I discovered some time ago I like older women."

"Oh," I say. I don't tell him my age but wonder how he sees me. "I guess that's a compliment?"

"I mean it that way," he says. Smiles. I like his smile, his full bottom lip—which, just now, has a tiny flake of crusted sugar near the corner. I like having a man sit across the table from me. The apartment seems to like it too. The candles lend richness to the warm wood, the music is especially smooth, the kind of after-dark jazz you want on a winter night in Paris as you're drinking coffee and eating sweet food at a cozy table. I know what he has in mind and look at what I've done with the candles and the sexy music. But for some reason, in spite of my setup, I don't have the same thing in mind; I just want the romance. I keep talking and he's polite enough or patient enough or respectful enough to let me.

After some time we go to the tiny four-table restaurant on the corner, dim and smoky of course, as Parisian restaurants should be. We're led to a place next to the window and order onion soup and good bread.

"You're an intense woman," Rip tells me. Candlelight shadow-dances on the white tablecloth. "But you have a guard up."

"Really," I say. "I do?"

"If I could just put my hands over your eyes," he reaches across the table toward me, "touch your forehead," he touches my forehead lightly, "I could ease that tension."

"I don't think I'm tense," I say, and consciously relax my shoulders. Maybe I am, a little.

"I knew someone like you before," he says, "and when that intensity translated into sex it was so good."

There it is.

I like that he's attracted to me. I like the tension of it. It was the same with Marty, the Canadian I met in the Netherlands who slept in my bed in Room 24 at the Bali Hotel, the mutual attraction. But I know I won't have sex with Rip either and consider how different for me, for the me I was when I was young—especially during those excessive years of drinking and smoking dope before Tom. Not having casual sex somehow makes me feel clean and strong. For now I like the tension better. The energy it gives me. As if I, too, am patient with, even respectful of, myself.

Rip walks me back to my apartment. We hug, share a brief, clumsy kiss, not a kiss that would invite going up the stairs to the apartment and then up the stairs to the bed. We kiss again, missing each other's mouths.

"Well, goodnight," I say. "See you at the meeting tomorrow?"

"Maybe," he says and turns and starts down Quincampoix, where he'll cross to Rue di Rivoli. I watch him walk away, hands in his pockets, that little ponytail.

Leafy is going back to America. She comes to the apartment so we can say goodbye, share our last tea and conversation together.

"I want to go and I don't want to go," she tells me.

We sit with our cups and our sighs at the table, books and poinsettia pushed aside. I've made tea, a mix of chamomile and lavender that I found at the vegetarian restaurant around the corner.

"I know," I say. "I've felt that way in virtually every place I've gone. I even felt that way as I made plans to make this trip."

"There's so much I want to do. My business. My girlfriend." She sighs, sips her tea.

Leafy and I, friends from that very first AA meeting in Paris and how many since then. She and Anne have been my closest friends and confidants here. Anne has already gone back to the US. We've promised to stay in touch and I hope we will.

Leafy has been one of the women with whom I've shared the intimacies of secrets, of the self I hold back until trust is built. Friendships such as these are born of a trust that's known through some psychic telegraphing not measured by the limits of time but recognized on a deeper, more soulful level.

"Leafy, do you think I carry a lot of tension?" I ask. "Am I an intense person?" Rip's comment from a few nights ago surfaces.

"When I first met you I did notice a certain tension about you. You were," she hesitates as if picturing me then, "you were moving fast. That's one of the reasons I invited you to the baths that day. I thought it would be calming."

"It was," I say. "The baths that day was exactly what I needed. And I know I'll go again. I wish we could go together."

"Who knows," she says, and takes her purple scarf from the back of the chair, wraps it around her neck. I like how the color contrasts her russet hair. She wears a leather coat, too, another East Coast person who knows how to dress for the cold.

"I've never been to Boston," I say as we hug goodbye.

"And I've never been to San Francisco." Her breath tickles my ear. "That's where you're going, right?"

I've told her about Camille and our plans for Café Britska. "That's the plan," I say with a confidence that feels real.

I watch out the window as she leaves the building; I want her to turn and wave goodbye, but she doesn't. I turn back to my empty apartment, put away the tea makings, rinse our cups.

Over three weeks in Paris and Amy arrives tomorrow. But today I go to the Indian embassy to get a visa for my stay there. *Take a number,* the sign orders. But there are no numbers. There are crowds of people and the place is cacophonous and chaotic and colorful. After an hour-and-a-half wait, my visa application is accepted. Next, a cholera inoculation to complete the process, and I will be welcomed in India when I arrive sometime in mid-January. A month from now.

The day moves along with a trip to the papeterie at Saint-Michel, then Tea & Tattered Pages, and the 7:00 p.m. AA meeting before returning home. One more night alone and my daughter will be here. I haven't seen her for nearly six months.

A package arrived in the mail today from Jill in London with more pages of her story about Max and Beatrice and Duncan and Libby. I like trading pages with another writer and talking about writing in our exchanged letters. I read Jill's story upstairs in my bed, then stay up late with Isabel Allende's *The House of the Spirits,* stunned by the characters she creates: beauties with green hair, women who know the future, mothers whose heads fly off at death and daughters who find them. Lovers and strong-willed prostitutes. Sex-starved spinsters who fall in love with their sisters-in-law. Old mothers who die awful deaths amid rotting appendages and dirty sheets.

These are not the kind of characters Jill created, nor the kind of characters I imagine ever creating. But wow! I am in thrall to Allende's writing.

I meet Amy at the terminal at de Gaulle and, after she passes through immigration and all the other passing-through one must do upon entering one country from another, finally here she is. We grin, we hug—long, tight hugs—we laugh, we're both crying, too, but laughing, and my throat aches with love and gladness. She brings with her packages and cards and enough light to fill the gray Paris days—a light that has always filled my heart.

From the very beginning, from that first afternoon in Sharp Memorial Hospital—the Stork Club, they called the maternity wing there—that Thursday afternoon in January when she was born (her father on a photo assignment on an aircraft carrier documenting the arrival of a fighter jet on a great ship out in the Pacific), when she was placed in my arms and I kissed the top of her newborn head, I knew this was one of the best things that ever happened, not just for me and her father and her big brother but in the world. Nearly twenty-five years later I still believe this is true.

She seems unchanged—still those lovely green eyes, still that bright smile, her hair a shade darker than mine, but both of us wearing it short. People say we look alike, they say they know right away we're mother and daughter. I see it sometimes, too, but not as clearly as others do. How we see ourselves is always different than how we look to others and all I've ever seen of myself is a mirrored representation or a photograph. Still I always take it as a compliment because in my eyes Amy is always beautiful. And never more so to me than today after missing her presence these last months.

We sleep late the next couple of frosty mornings, wake to drink coffee and talk, catching up on all the details that can't be relayed in long-distance phone calls, and after a while, enter the world. We explore—Montmartre, the Abbesses, Sacré-Cœur, more coffee at a funky little café named Banana, its awning decorated with images of the bright yellow fruit. Banana Café makes us laugh. It doesn't take much to make us laugh. Tramping through the skim of snow on the ground, we come upon a couple of jaunty red-hatted snowmen built on round snow-pillars and pat them with mittened hands. We go to Shakespeare and Company and I buy a book about trekking in Nepal. (Linda and I are planning another trip together, and she's suggested that after we tour India we could go to Nepal; I don't think I want to go trekking.) We talk more, sometimes telling stories, sometimes mother-daughter talk. We shop. We eat gyros at a café in Saint-Michel and plan a jaunt to the country for dinner with Christine and Frederic. Amy's delighted with the prospect of going to the French countryside, even if it's only a short train ride out of the city.

Amy has always been one for taking us somewhere else. Two years ago we traveled around Europe—for me, the first visit—London, Rome, Vienna, Venice, and finally Paris, where we caught up with Camille and had a riotous time, once laughing so loud our next-door neighbors at the Hotel des Grandes Écoles knocked on the wall and told us to quiet down. We motor-scootered to Monaco from Cannes and got caught in the rain on the way back. We packaged ourselves up in clear plastic trash bags so that we looked like someone's lunch and putt-putted down the highway, laughing so uproariously as to make the journey even more hazardous.

Christmas Eve Day Amy and I sleep late after being up until three. We'd gone to see *42nd Street* at Théâtre du Châtelet, lots of singing and dancing. If there's one thing Amy and I do well, it's go to the theater or pretty much any kind of performance—stand-up comedy, cabaret, musicals, movies.

Last night, after we finally went to bed, I had another dream. In this one my second husband appeared, only it wasn't him; this person was more a combination of him and the on-again, off-again boyfriend who'll be coming to Paris after Amy leaves. In the dream, as I opened the door to my apartment to let the cats out—apparently in this dream life I had cats—this man, the ex blended with the sometimes-ex, came out of a room down the hall and was waiting to meet me. I didn't want to meet him, but I knew I was supposed to, and so I went down the hall.

Over coffee I tell Amy about the dream and she says it sounds like I felt I had an obligation toward the on-again, off-again that I didn't want to keep.

"Yeah, I've been sort of thinking that myself," I say.

We finish our coffee and I clear the table while she uses the tiny bathroom to dress, then my turn, and after all the "How's this?" and "Is my hair okay?" and "Will I need another sweater?" we finally set out. It's Christmas Eve and we're in Paris.

First we have sweet crepes from the crepes man on the corner, then go to the Pompidou Center for *Art & Pub: Art & Publicité 1890–1990*. This is an exhibit Amy wants to see because her day job is as a graphic designer at the *San Diego Daily Transcript*. Another of my daughter's talents: illustration. As a little kid she was always drawing and cutting and pasting, scraps of paper clinging to her socks and following in her footsteps like so many breadcrumbs.

After Pompidou we wander and flaneuse, following Rue de Rivoli to the Concorde then along the Champs-Élysées. We have pizza for dinner and decide to see *Rocky V* at a movie theater near the Arc de Triomphe. The French-Indian ticket seller surprises us with free admission. Because it's Christmas Eve, he says, and we're Americans, and because he's excited about flying to Boston next week.

After the movie we journey along the Champs-Élysées with all its bright gaiety and crowds of people; it's a gala evening and the City of Light is brightly lit. Being completely American tourists, we stop for ice cream at le drugstore and for photos of L'église de la Madeleine—Paris's Greek-columned church, which is under restoration—with a lifelike painted screen ashine with violet spotlights. We take pictures of magnificent flower displays in a window along Rue Royale. I'm in my blue Greek coat, my fuzzy inserts in my new kinda-cowboy ankle boots with embroidered flowers on the toes I'd bought on an impulse-shopping stop. Amy looks hip and could pass for French in her brown leather jacket and jeans. She knows how to wrap a scarf.

Passing under the arcades on Rue de Rivoli, a group of young Parisian men approach, buoyant with the general joie de vivre of the evening. One young man stops in front of Amy, "*Joyeux Noël*," he says and kisses her on both cheeks, laughing. We're all laughing. "*Joyeux Noël*," we all say.

The disco where all the trendy young Parisians go—La Scala—still rings loud at this late hour; energy seeps out the door and flows along with us, then gradually fades into the night. Finally we are in our neighborhood and all is quiet and dark except for streetlamps, misty in the December night, and the glow from a few apartment windows. On the grating above the Châtelet metro stop a man sleeps, wrapped in a blanket and curled around his shoes.

Who knows how many miles we covered tonight as we turn on to Quincampoix and climb the sour-wine-smelling stairs.

"Those boys," we say, grinning and shaking our heads. It's 2:30 a.m. Christmas morning in Paris. We climb up to the loft bed. "Those boys," one of us says again as we snuggle in and, still smiling, close our eyes and drift off.

Christmas day we gather with Deb, a friend from the Friday-night meeting, in her apartment. Other women from the meeting are there, a few men too. We carry in boxes of cookies from our neighborhood patisserie to share and exchange both-cheek kisses as is the lovely way here. Friendly and easy, and I'm grateful to have made so many friends in the month I've been in Paris and glad to introduce Amy to them so she'd know references in my stories. I hope another time, another year, my son and I can travel to some far and distance place together too.

Who can ever tell what their future holds?

DECEMBER 25–26, 1978
Cardiff-by-the-Sea

I arrive home from dinner with my family and find a bottle of Tom and Jerry holiday drink mix, a concoction of eggnog and brandy, tucked between the front door and screen. The *Jerry* on the label has been crossed out and *Judy* written in its place. Tom called a few days before Christmas and asked if he could take me to lunch. He said he'd been paid for the production he'd voiced for me, and he always took a client out to lunch after he got paid. I didn't know if that was true, but I would've said yes if he'd just asked, "Want to go to lunch?" I would have said yes if he'd just said, "Want to . . .?" I vividly recalled the dream I had after he auditioned for the gig—he wore a white *Saturday Night Fever* suit and stood center stage, a spotlight shining down on him, striating his dark hair with auburn. I also remembered a certain electricity in the booth at the recording studio, sparking both sides of the glass between us as he read the script for the show I was producing and the eye contact between us that contained subtext to the direction I gave and the questions he asked.

We'd made a date for the day after Christmas; he'd stopped by with his gift a day early.

He was late picking me up the next day, arriving at my house on the hill in Cardiff-by-the-Sea in his long indigo Buick Electra, an enormous car that took up the entire space—mailbox to juniper tree—in front of my house. He'd been up all night, he said, playing pool and hanging out. I didn't know what to make of what he'd said, but with that voice he could say anything; I just wanted to hear him talk. And he did. A natural storyteller, he was smart and funny, and besides that I liked the way he looked. He wore a turtleneck, a tweed sport coat, and jeans. His thick hair a little disheveled, which I liked, too, and wire-rimmed glasses, that one squinted, wonky eye. All this made him altogether interesting and very sexy.

We drove down the hill to The Hydra, a restaurant on the beach side of Pacific Coast Highway. The day was sunny and warm enough to sit on the patio, the ocean close enough to hear the susurration of waves on the shore. He drank martinis; I had bloody bulls. We must have eaten. He told stories; I listened. We drank. The sun crossed mid-sky and hung in the west over the black-suited surfers in the water.

He'd just left his wife the day before, he said, that was why he was out all night. "She wanted to make omelets and I wanted to go to Mexico."

I didn't believe all of what he said, but I liked the way he said it, and anyway, in those days nobody I knew was much concerned about anyone's past. It was the seventies, a *let's get stoned* time, and *let's dance*, and *let's have another drink*.

"Let's go to the mountains," he said after enough alcohol that our legs were touching under the table and our conversation was immersed in innuendoes. "We can get a room with a fireplace."

"I have a fireplace," I said. "Why don't we just go to my house?"

And so we did.

The next morning he brought in a few things from his car—apparently he actually had just left his wife the day before—and we stayed together in that house on the hill in Cardiff-by-the-Sea until, a year later, both of us sober and in AA, we moved to the first floor of a three-story condo in Ocean Beach right at the edge of a cliff.

❧

The day after Christmas in Paris I woke up sick with some kind of respiratory thing, pain in my chest when I coughed and pain between my shoulders when I took too deep a breath. Amy and I stayed in bed until three, slept off and on. Then we drank coffee and talked, Amy doing most of the talking, until we finally decided to go out to do laundry and run errands. She'd be leaving in a few days and wanted to begin packing. She smiled a lot as she talked; she was ready to go home. Exciting things were happening: she and two other women were doing sketch comedy in a group they named "Beyond Therapy" and were performing at clubs around town.

At the laundromat I read a letter from Al JaCoby, my old boss at the *San Diego Union-Tribune* and my first mentor. He'd enclosed a copy of an excerpt of one of my letters that he'd submitted to the travel editor at the paper. He'd done some minor editing, changing my description of my apartment from *très funky* to *très fancy*, which upgraded my circumstances, and told me to send my social security number in the event the piece was accepted and I'd be paid. I was Beyond Thrilled. Imagine, Amy somewhere performing comedy, and me somewhere writing.

We fold clothes, talk more amid the whirling and swishing soundtrack of the laundromat, the late-December afternoon pearling outside the windows.

Before Amy leaves and after Rex (the on-again, off-again) arrives is a partial day and complete night crossover. The studio is crowded with the three of us banging around, suitcases everywhere, the tiny bathroom, and only two chairs at the table, so for that night I get a room at a nearby hotel for him and me, leaving Amy in the apartment to complete her packing.

I began seeing Rex less than a year after Tom died. Someone in AA introduced us. Rex is different in so many ways from Tom. Physically, first of all. Where Tom was tall and rangy, Rex is stocky and muscular. Tom had a gorgeous head of dark auburn hair; Rex is nearly bald, what hair he does have rings his head in silver-gray. Tom had dark eyes; Rex's eyes, his most striking feature, remind me of the color seen underwater off tropical islands. Tom was brilliant smart; Rex is an educated man. Tom was all about doing; Rex is all about romance, and at that time, I needed romance in my life. Or thought I did.

Rex and I had been living together in the condo by the estuary when the idea came that I would take this journey around the world, alone, a plan conjured by a need I couldn't express and didn't understand. For some time I'd been restless, searching for that unnamed, unidentified *thing*. Seeking some solace to the—I hate to use the word, but here it is—*angst* that had beset me. The deepest inside part of me, if I was honest enough to acknowledge it, knew the life I was participating in wasn't the life I was meant to live and that Rex was not the man I was supposed to be with. So, along with selling most everything and buying an around-the-world ticket and packing my single unwieldy suitcase, leaving him was a necessary part of running away or running toward, escaping or searching, whatever was happening.

Much of my journal writing these months away has been an examination of my relationship with him. Though we'd been in frequent contact—letters, phone calls—this planned holiday in Paris would, I knew, result in my breaking off completely with him.

After taking Amy to the airport Rex and I return to the apartment for lunch and he takes my usual chair at the table. Oh, I notice. I take the other.

We make an itinerary; we'll fill our days with sightseeing. We make a list of things we both want to do, to see. It's his first time in Paris, so we'll return to a few places I've already paid homage to, but I'm more than willing to go again. Time will go fast, I know that. The ten days with Amy went by in a flash as bright as the lights along all the grand boulevards. Here she was, in Paris with me, filling my space with warmth and laugher. And now here I am with him. He's loving and kind, but I'm separated from him.

Separate.

In the morning we sit at the table drinking coffee and eating cranberry cake that his mother made. He again sits in my usual chair and I take the other one, again saying nothing, but I notice I'm scraping candle wax off the tabletop with my fingernail.

We go out for a day of touristing:

Sainte-Chappelle glows blue in memory. The sapphire of sculpted ceilings starred with fleur-de-lis and cerulean stained glass windows five stories high to catch the majesty of the limitless universe. Musée d'Orsay: railway station in a ball gown. Grand arches of glass—light and space filled with art. Renoir. Degas. Monet. Manet. Sisley. Pissarro. Toulouse-Lautrec. Rodin. Gauguin. Cézanne. Van Gogh. I do love Vincent's swirled skies and yellow stars. And that grand clock of the old railroad station, black hands and numbers in clear glass panes— we stand silhouetted by time, and I am exhausted by too much art.

Later, tired but hungry, we go to the vegetarian restaurant Christine took me to that first day, and to which I've been many times over my month in Paris. The food is fresh and flavorfully good—baked goods, earthy spices, and rich stewy concoctions.

I can tell Rex is tired as I sit across from him at one of the communal tables. His eyes are not quite as bright, and there's a kind of droop to his broad shoulders. Jet lag takes a while to recover from.

We place our orders and talk about our day. He reaches for my hand across the table. His hand, always warm, soft, unlike Tom's large, knuckled hands that evidenced a working-in-the-orchard, digging-in-the-dirt ruggedness.

"What's going on?" Rex asks. "You seem distant."

"Tired, I guess," I start circling around, my usual way of not talking about what I need to talk about. I've taken my hand from his and I'm making circles on the table with my water glass. I set it solid on the table, put my hands in my lap.

"I am a little, too," he says, "but it's something else. It feels like you're holding something back."

I have been holding back, letting moments go by without saying anything, moments that are laden even to me, and turning away from him after our lovemaking rather than finding our usual way of staying entwined—his arm around me, me nestled into the curve between neck and shoulder. Bodies sated and at rest.

Our meals are served and I'm glad for the distraction. Napkins to lap, forks in hand, eyes on the plate and not each other. A few tentative bites.

"Good, yes?" I say. "How's your veggie chili?"

"Good," he says.

More silent eating. I swallow a bite of salad; it goes down hard and I take a drink of water.

"We've talked about it," I say, "in our letters, on the phone. You know how I've been feeling. Being alone all this time, doing what I want when I want, all the thinking and considering I've been doing."

My throat is tight. I take another drink of water. We're quiet for a moment then I begin again, not sure what I'm going to say or how it will come out.

"I've told you how sometimes I'm so damn lonely I don't think I can stand it, but when I think about . . . well, when I consider being with someone . . ." I don't say *you*, but it's clear I mean him. "I mean sharing a day-in, day-out life, I just don't think that's what I want right now."

He looks across the table at me. His eyes fill, which emphasizes their color, now even more aqua, even more like the water of a tropical sea.

Just then another couple comes to our table. "May we?" the man says, gesturing to the open bench.

"Of course," I say, then, "bien sûr," my accent even more terrible than usual. Rex and I slide ourselves and our plates over slightly to make room.

Rex has used his napkin to dab his eyes. His response tells me that he might finally understand what I've said so many different ways in our letter exchanges and expensive, extensive phone conversations. That I don't want to be "coupled," that I don't believe I can be in a committed relationship in which you make plans together, do the world in tandem, where you're—if not always physically together—at least psychically linked.

More moments pass. I'm uncomfortably aware of the others just a few feet away. The man on the same side as Rex, facing the window, and the woman like me, facing the interior of the restaurant. They don't look at us; they may sense the emotional content of our conversation even if they don't understand the words.

"I know what you've said," Rex says, "what you wrote, but I thought it was something you just needed to work through. Something you were working through."

"Maybe so," I say, "but that's how I have been feeling." I offer the tenuous *maybe* as a way of making it possible for us to get through the next days, making a concession so he doesn't have to get on a plane back to California tomorrow. Though in my mind it's final, I'm willing to continue talking about it, for us to follow through on the plans we've made for his holiday. It's not as though I'm angry at him, or wouldn't consider continuing a friendship, or who knows. It's not as though I never want to see him. But now that I've said the words out loud—in his presence, to his face—I *know*, and the part that knows is at peace for the first time in many months. Who can say how the next ten days together will be. But at least I know I'm not pretending to myself anymore.

The next morning we don't talk much. We take turns in the tiny bathroom, I make coffee in the tiny kitchen, and we find our now-usual places at the table: him in the chair at the center arc of the table, placed to have the perfect view out the window and into the Paris street scene. I take the other chair, the one that looks through the door into the kitchen nook. I say nothing, but I am experiencing so, so much.

He's a Leo, born under the sign of the lion. Every Leo I know has big energy. Their energy can fill most any room they enter. Not an outward, aggressive energy but a kind of a psychic energy. Rex's presence is like this. Again, he's taken my place at the table and his energy emanates from that place and takes over the air in the room.

This morning I want to strangle him.

But I am Libra, the peacemaker. I am all Venus—love and beauty. I don't confront; I negotiate. I am also my mother's daughter. *Don't you use that tone of voice with me. Don't you look at me like that. Don't you talk back to me.*

I don't know if it's the messages I received directly that make me hold my tongue and hold my anger inside, or if it came from watching her and other adult women of that era be subservient, acquiescing, quiet. Domesticated. Probably both, coupled with my own nature, which tends to avoid conflict and confrontation. Apparently in spite of all those consciousness-raising meetings of the seventies, my subscription to *Ms.* magazine, my leadership positions, I've not had enough therapy, not been in enough codependency groups, not evolved enough to be able to ask for what I want. I haven't yet come into myself enough to state my feelings and leave the other person to his own. Instead, in a thousand instances—more—I have behaved in this manner. Allowing Rex to take my place at the table, which he does naturally, without thought, is just today's example.

This is one of the many differences I've noticed between men and women. An assumption by the man to take the head of the table, the driver's seat in the car, the outside of the bed, just as it is the "assumption" of women to acquiesce the head of the table, the driver's seat, the outside of the bed.

I gaze at his profile as he casually writes, takes a drink of coffee, glances out the window, my resentments festering until I just can't bear it.

"Hey," I say, "you know that's my usual place you're sitting in." I don't say it in anger, of course. I sublimate my resentment, trying to make it easy.

"Oh," he says. "Really?" He pushes back his journal, puts down his pen. "I'm sorry. Why didn't you say something?"

He really is sorry; I can tell by the tone of his voice, the sincerity in his eyes. He really didn't know. His apology is authentic. Of course he'd been oblivious to my feelings, and not because he's selfish or self-centered. He generally has a sensitivity toward others; I know this about him. But he didn't know because I am so well practiced at hiding my truth. Decades of practice that probably started in the crib.

"I don't know, I just didn't. But I am now. I've been sitting in that chair, writing, looking out the windows, eating, reading, listening to music, talking on the phone, letters . . . everything," I say, "since I've been here. From that chair."

"Here," he says and gets up, "let's do this." He moves the table just that much to the right, six inches or so. "Get up," he says. I do, and he places the chairs not side by side but at angles at the table. He stands behind one and looks toward the windows, then moves to the other, stands behind it, and looks out the window. "There," he says, and exchanges coffee cups, writing materials, books that we've each had beside us, one for the other, then passes behind me and takes the chair I've been sitting in, leaving "my" chair for me to take. Which I do. Smiling.

"Thank you," I say. "I never thought of that."

I settle into my chair and gaze out the window. How wonderful, how amazing. Here in this *très* funky apartment on a winter morning, the placement of a simple wicker chair at a plain oak table serves as a metaphor to open my eyes to a view inside myself that is every bit as fascinating and clear as the view out my window.

Rex's simple solution fixes the situation with the table and chairs, but I know the issue goes much deeper than the view out the window.

The true issue is what I've done all my life—relinquished my independence, my solitary selfhood, my sovereignty, for someone else's comfort. Time and again in my relationships—with my husbands, at work, in any and maybe most situations and circumstances—I have allowed someone else's wants and needs and desires and even unconscious assumptions of right to overtake my own. Oh.

New Year's Eve is a bright winter day as we visit a fellow AA from San Diego who also happens to be in Paris for the holidays, someone I know only from meetings but is a friend of Rex's. He's staying in the Saint-Germain area and the late-afternoon sun is resplendent on the steeples of Saint-Sulpice.

Holiday lights that decorate a fountain blink on as we leave our friend's building and cross to Saint-Germain-des-Prés, where artists hang their work on wrought iron fences. Rex and I are easy enough with each other. We talk about what we're seeing as we stroll along and of people he's met at meetings. Anything more to be said between us, and most likely there will be, will come as it comes. For now we stop for coffee and pastries and sit in the warmth of a café until we have to rush to make this evening's meeting on time.

Afterward we join the group at Marilee's home near Luxembourg Gardens, along with Kent, an expat from London, and Ian from Toronto, who came to Paris for holiday and has fallen in love with the city. "Swept off my feet," Ian tells us. He wants to stay, like so many others who've told me stories of coming for months and staying for years. John and Sue from Denver are with us too. John is an insurance salesman turned Le Cordon Bleu student. Sue has her own business as an accountant. She and I lean on the cluttered counter in Marilee's kitchen.

"You can't claim all the money you make," she says after I tell her about plans I've made with Camille for Café Britska. "And find out about skimming." But before I can ask what she means, she continues, "You have to be there all the time, either you or your partner. If you're not, your employees will rob you blind. It's a cash business so you have no way of knowing."

Skimming and employees robbing you blind? These are details of running a business I know nothing about. I don't like the way it sounds. I'm glad the group is gathering up coats and gloves and getting ready to "storm the Bastille," as someone says. We're off to celebrate the New Year, Paris-style.

We race the steps of the new Opera House where more people are gathering—expats and tourists like us mostly but most, unlike us, drinking. The Paris police are out in full force, busloads with riot helmets and guns. They're drinking wine in the buses as they keep an eye on us revelers. At Saint-Michel several young men scale the fountain to much cheering from the crowd below. It's an altogether gala night with fireworks and singing and much kissing of both cheeks. *Bonne année, bonne année,* we repeat. And yes, Rex and I kiss at midnight, and it's a good kiss, the kind of kiss you want to have when you're celebrating New Year's Eve in Paris. It would be a good kiss with a stranger. Perchance, in some ways, even better.

NEW YEAR'S EVE, 1986
Jamul

Our Jamul AA friends—the group from the Wednesday-night meeting—Davinia, Pine Tree Bill, TV Tom, and a few others gather at Davinia's house in Lyons Valley for a potluck. Tom and I drove there in the rig. By now he'd probably just as soon live in the camper with its cab-over double-bed, the little booth table where he can sit with a cup of coffee and look out the small window at his land. For him it may feel safer than the big house, where the more frail he becomes the more precarious it seems.

He doesn't come inside for dinner with us. He isn't eating much anyway—basically drinking cans of Similac, which we buy by the case. Taking the necessary pain meds—morphine, which I have learned to inject in his arm. Bone-thin and pale, lips pulled tight against the constant pain to which he never gives words, nor does he need to; I witness. I see. I know.

After dinner and one by one, our friends go into the camper for time with him, each one saying what they need or want to say.

There is no shooting off of fireworks or guns, though Davinia has a couple stashed away. Tom and I don't even stay until midnight. We drive home in the dark of the last night of 1986. For us New Year's is not a celebration. Goodbye to the old, but neither of us wants to welcome the New Year. It won't be long now, and even if I am in denial of that, Tom is not.

༄

I don't know whether there's been a lull in the tensions of the Gulf over the month I've been in Paris or whether I've not been reading the news with the same interest, but the days continue to pass peacefully enough. Rex and I stroll through Parisian gardens and neighborhoods, visit museums, stop at cafés, share the morning table with our coffee and journals and books. All this time I am two people. I am the fellow tourist, the companion, the occasional lover—finding myself turning away more and more—and the playmate who accompanies and sometimes instigates. At the same time, under the outer layer, I am the solitary woman I've come to know so well. She who is my true companion for the journey. The restless woman who, after all this time, all these places, all these experiences, may still be uncertain of exactly what she is seeking but does know that she wants to be separate from this man, or, right now, any man. She wants her independence and her freedom, and she craves solitude.

The big suitcase with my heavy winter clothes will go back to San Diego with Rex. My blue Greek coat, lavender Swedish mittens, Canadian mukluks, along with my sweaters and warm socks, my kinda-cowboy ankle boots with flowers embroidered on the toes. Saving only a light jacket, jeans, and a sweatshirt, everything else goes—it will all be too heavy for the south of India, where I am headed next.

Standing at the big windows that overlook Place Edmund-Michelet, Rex and I say a tear-filled goodbye in the apartment, and I ride the train with him to the airport. This breakup is the right thing to do and I know it, but that doesn't make it any less sad. It is a little scary, too, in a way. Knowing we are really off-again with no on-again in our future, at least none that I can imagine, means I don't have that psychic defense of feeling like I am "with" someone even though we are separated physically.

On the train ride back to the city I recall that session with my therapist, Charlie, who took me back through the loss of everyone in my life until I was all alone. The dusty train window reflects an image of me as that little girl in the middle of a long empty road, standing by myself with no one to call on, no one to find me, no one to come.

Charlie's final question, *And then what will happen?*

I will die, I said.

You will? he asked.

Would I?

There is something of the human spirit—no, not just human but the spirit of all of life—that wants to live. Why else the push of the jasmine vine through the seams of the stairs to our deck in Jamul, why else the little kitten that dragged herself home to my doorstep at the condo after being hit by a car, her tiny legs crushed. Why else our treks through the wilds, our desperate calls in the night, our prayers to a God we may not believe in?

Breaking off with Rex is nothing like those desperate situations, certainly nothing compared to the loss of Tom. How dare I even compare the two? Still, every emotion has its levels of intensity, and after the delight of Amy's visit and now this separation from Rex, I ride back into the beauty of the city with a familiar loneliness, a loneliness that has taken on its own kind of desperate beauty.

Tonight is my last Friday night in Paris; next Friday night I'll sleep on a train on my way to Frankfurt.

I didn't write much while Rex was here and hardly wrote anything at all during Amy's stay. It's one of the reasons I know I need to be alone, to have the solitude I am hungry for. When I am with others I don't take the time, don't *set aside* the time to be quiet and to quietly write. I miss the process and the effort and the results. I remember a quote by Henry James I read somewhere, "Anyone who want to be a writer must inscribe on his banner the word 'loneliness.'"

Tonight, table cleared after dinner, I can write, and write, and write, with candles burning and the good jazz station on the radio.

I make plans for India and read the travel books I picked up at Tea & Tattered Pages and Shakespeare and Company. It's time to move on, and I'm cold and have been cold for so long. Much as I love Paris,

I'm weary of bundling up to go outside, wearing coats and scarves and mittens; putting those fuzzy inserts in my shoes. But I also don't want to go. After seven weeks in Paris, the longest I have been in one place since I moved out of my condo last June, I have grown comfortable and it's familiar. A place that has been my own, the people in the neighborhood who recognize me—the young man at the money exchange who flirts with me as I flirt back; the crepes man on the street by the Pompidou who knows how much apricot to layer in my warm crepe, just enough that it slides down my arm in a sticky trickle; the madam at the flower store who sings her *bonjour* when I arrive and always takes, what seems to me, extra time with my bouquet— she may take that much time with all her customers, but I feel a part of the neighborhood because of her care.

My anticipation about going to India is the same as I've experienced as I readied to leave for other places—attraction and fear that arrives as dread. It's been safe here, especially in this studio by myself. Being alone is the most comfortable now. This may be selfish, but for now, I like it that way.

Even with these mixed feelings I look forward to being on the beach in Goa, where I'll go after Bombay, then on to Delhi, where I'll meet Linda. I can be a true tourist in India, clearly I'll look the part. I want to go to shrines and temples and markets.

I write an itinerary in my journal—India. Thailand. Bali. Hawaii. Back to the US by spring. I've made plans to be home by April, but what if I want to stay in Bali? I remember that impulse when I was there all those years ago, believing I could stay for a long, long time.

I read Paul Theroux's *The Great Railway Bazaar* and Pico Iyer's *Video Night in Kathmandu*. I have always loved reading travel books, not the "go here, see this, stay here" kind of books, though I've consulted my copies of *Frommer's* and *Let's Go Europe* frequently throughout my journey and am grateful for the information they offer. The books I love are part memoir, part travel, part—what? Philosophy about travel, which is to say, about life. Especially Mary Morris's *Nothing to Declare*,

Henry Miller's *The Colossus of Maroussi*, pretty much anything by Jan Morris, and Beryl Markham's *West with the Night*, which was published the year I was born but I didn't find until the year before I left on this journey.

Imagine: me sitting beside my dad on that brown couch, turning the pages of his oversized world atlas, and all the time Beryl Markham's book was out there, an adventure story more than a travel book, this woman who grew up in Kenya with wild animals, the first person to fly nonstop from Europe to America, the first woman to fly solo east to west across the Atlantic. What adventures might I have had if I'd known Beryl Markham as an early model, rather than the fictional Brenda Starr. I might have been more independent, less of a settle-downer and more of a brave adventurer. Who can say? But tonight I am in my high bed, wearing my warmest nightgown, reading about India and imagining the hot, drippy humidity of Bombay and the sun-stroked beaches of Goa, longing to be wet with sweat and know the burn of sun on my bare skin.

Genevieve came by for tea today, and I got calls from Leydee and Christine. These gracious Frenchwomen saying their formal goodbyes. Earlier, riding the metro, my last time at the Châtelet stop, a performer with his guitar was singing riffs from "La Bamba." Imagine "La Bamba" making you cry. But it did. Most anything does today.

I'm packed, back to my single bag, jam-packed and heavy. The studio is cleaned and a bright pink, full-throated azalea in a gold foil–wrapped pot awaits on the round table for Christine. No fruit bowl. I ate the last of a grapefruit and some leftover pizza today. Only a half-full jar of apricot jam and some butter left in the fridge, a few partially filled boxes of tea in the cupboard, including the jasmine I decided I didn't like. Otherwise all the books, all the candles, all the evidence of me was given away or tossed out.

Tonight, January 11, 1991, I leave Paris on an overnight train to Frankfurt, and tomorrow I board a flight to Bombay.

JANUARY 10, 1987
Jamul

It was a bright, sunny day. Tom had been making plans for the ongoing remodeling of the house with Jesús. Tom hired a contractor for some tasks Jesús and the other hardworking but untrained men didn't know how to do. There were problems with the large open space in the office downstairs—a pillar needed to be constructed to bear the weight of the house above—and some other complications that hadn't been anticipated, as well as additions Tom wanted to figure into the seemingly never-ending project. Maybe on some level he felt that so long as work needed to be done, work could be done, and nothing would end.

But that Thursday something changed. He was in more pain and it was in a new location in his body. He needed more morphine. Carol, our friend Jim's wife whom we visited in Baton Rouge, is a nurse who worked in oncology. When I'd asked about treatment for end-stage cancer, compassion softened her voice as she said, "You just try to manage the pain."

Tom went to bed that afternoon, something he rarely did. He'd take what he called "wolf naps" on the sofa in the den—twenty minutes, a half-hour at most. But that afternoon he fell asleep in our bedroom, in the bed he'd had made for us of redwood, a soft wood that bruised easily.

He slept all that afternoon and into the night. I'd check on him every now and again, and each time it appeared as though he hadn't even changed position, lying as he was on his back, long legs stretched full length, bedcovers in a straight line across his chest.

That night as I was preparing for bed he stirred, then awoke. Never one to wear pajamas, he slept in only his underwear, boxer shorts that hung precariously on his narrow hips. He used the bathroom then asked me to give him another injection, which I did, measuring the amount of morphine going into the vial, tapping the glass, pushing the plunger until a clear drop appeared at the tip, cleaning his arm with alcohol, then carefully inserting the needle precisely into his vein, and pushing the drug into his body.

He slept once more. His still-glossy hair dark on the white pillow-slip, sheets and blankets pulled up to his neck, covering his thin shoulders. His face, cheekbones like something honed, lips thin against the pain. Eyes closed—that one wonky eye—his glasses close by on the nightstand.

Am I, in some way, betraying him as I write this? He told me he never wanted people looking at him as he lay dying. This most intimate and vulnerable time, this most brutal time. "Don't let them say, 'he looked so peaceful,'" he'd told me.

Tom may have been sleeping, he may have been put under by the morphine, but he was not peaceful. He did not want to die and he most adamantly did not want an audience to his death. Writing this feels as if I am inviting an audience to watch. People who never knew him. Strangers. How dare I! But still, I remind myself, I am writing my experience, telling my story, and Tom's dying is part of my life, as mournful and anguished a part as I ever want to experience, but it is, nonetheless, mine.

He slept the night through and into the next day. As the long hours passed I grew more and more anxious. On Friday afternoon I called his doctor, who was, I was told, away for the weekend. "Here's the number of the doctor who's on call."

When I finally reach this stranger-doctor and give him the update, voice shaky, hands shaky, anxiety like a live animal in my body, I ask, "Is it possible to have a nurse come for the weekend? Someone who can help until we can get to the office on Monday?"

Arrangements like that must be made in advance, he tells me. "We don't have nurses who can come and stay on such short notice." And then he asks, "Does he want to die at home?"

"He's not dying!" I'm quick to respond, and I hear the defensive panic in my voice. "He's sleeping. It's just that he's been sleeping for so long and I don't know what to do." I'm crying now. It's hard to get the words out.

It's decided that I will call in the morning. Somehow I'm reassured that we will make it through the night. I hear that old Kristofferson recording in my mind, the one Tom used to play, and hear Tom's voice in my ear—*Hold your warm and tender body close to mine.* I'll help him make it through the night, and things will be different in the morning. Things will be better.

∾

JANUARY 12, 1991
Frankfurt to Bombay

The Frankfurt Airport is mired in military. Men, boys really, decked out in full camouflage uniforms lug duffels nearly as large as they are. They're deploying to *the desert*, as they called it at Sandy and Bill's house. The *International Herald Tribune* and *Time* magazine are filled with other proper nouns: Iraq, Saudi Arabia, Kuwait. Sanctions have been laid down. The US Congress passed a joint resolution authorizing the use of military force in Iraq and Kuwait.

The clamor of comings and goings, of bags whomping against counters, of airline announcements—gate numbers, flight numbers, arrivals, and destinations—barrage the sterile café where I eat a breakfast of cheese omelet that would be passable were it not for the sharp crunch of eggshell cooked within. I munch dry toast and try to shut out the chaos and cacophony by imagining myself in the sun wearing the teal-and-purple bikini I bought last summer in Dubrovnik. I am stretched out on a towel, the warmth soaking into my bones, my bones melting into the sand of a beach I don't know at an ocean I've yet to see.

I don't know where I'll stay when we reach Bombay. I can't imagine India, only movies and books, only Forester and Theroux and *Frommer's*. Instead of allowing any anxiety of going to this new place to build up, I go with the fantasy. I know beaches. I know sun on naked skin, body spread belly-down on warm sand. I know the *shush-shush* of ocean lapping, waves breaking, the squawk of seabirds.

Our flight is delayed and delayed. We board, finally, at seven. We'll arrive in the early morning, and hopefully this time I will sleep on the plane, though I rarely do.

JANUARY 11, 1987
Jamul

Somehow we do make it through the night, though I hardly sleep. I've left the bedside lamp on, and with each awakening I look at Tom. So still. He hasn't moved or changed positions all night. I lean close, watch the vein in his neck, a watery pulse.

In the morning he does awaken. I tell him I'm afraid, that I tried to get someone to come but there is no way we can get last-minute weekend help. I tell him his doctor is away for the weekend; I talked to the doctor on call.

He sits on the edge of the bed, bare feet on the carpet, leaning slightly forward. I can scarcely bear looking at him—every bone, every knuckle in his spine exposed through thin skin. And yet I long to look at him.

"Do you want to go to the hospital?" I ask, surprising myself with the words.

"Yes," he says. "Yes." And I know the depth of pain and fear he must be experiencing to admit this.

I find him clothes—a long-sleeved cotton shirt with pearl snap buttons. Jeans. Those big-heeled boots that carry the smell of dirt from the orchard. He goes into the bathroom. I hear water running, toilet flushing, while I call our friend Mary Joyce and tell her I'm taking him to the hospital.

She doesn't make me ask. "I'll meet you there," she says, as I knew she would.

I call the on-call doctor. Tell him.

Down the stairs and into Tom's car.

It's not far to Grossmont Hospital from our house in Jamul. Tom's oncologist's office is near there; we've made the trip many times. Usually Tom drives, but this time I do.

The business of checking in, getting the room, the paperwork, all done, all done. Mary Joyce meets us in the lobby. A wheelchair is brought for Tom.

"Before I go to my room," Tom asks the attendant who will take us up to the fifth floor, "can we just go outside for a moment?"

One last time out in the fresh air, is that what he's thinking?

We're shown the way to an outside patio in the back of the emergency area. The square-shouldered attendant in navy pants and shirt pushes Tom in the wheelchair. Mary Joyce and I follow.

"I'll come find you in a few minutes," I tell the attendant. Okay, he nods. This kind man must know too.

After the hospital noise inside, the florescent lights, the buzzing and dinging and cliché smells of antiseptic and illness, the patio is quiet though bare, a rough blacktop without plants or chairs or any prettifying. The blank brick wall of the building and opposite, a few feet away, a cement wall that blocks any view. Rising above the wall, the dark straight trunk of a tree, its green foliage spread toward the sky.

"Got a cigarette?" Tom asks Mary Joyce.

Of course she does. She's one of our few friends who still smokes. She doesn't act surprised. She doesn't say, *Are you kidding? You're dying of lung cancer and you want a cigarette?*

I don't say anything either. Of course he wants a cigarette. I want one too. All those years I used smoking to ward off emotions and in relief of their absence. We all want a cigarette.

Mary Joyce simply and generously—*compassionately*, I want to say—takes her cigarette pack out of her purse, shakes one out for him and one for herself, and clicks her lighter for each of them. He inhales and lets out a long line of redemptive smoke.

Nobody talks.

Mary Joyce leans against the brick wall. I glance at Tom in the wheelchair. He's wearing his glasses, of course, his snap-button shirt, jeans, boots, that beautiful hair. His cigarette smoke rises into the cloudless January sky.

∾

JANUARY 12–15, 1991
Bombay

I stand among the Indian women in line at customs and immigration at Sahar International Airport in Bombay. We're crowded together close enough that I can look down at the head of the woman directly in front of me. Her hair is deeply and solidly black with no hint of another shade, even in the cool fluorescent glow of the airport. Black-black, a deeper black than I've ever seen. They wear their hair long, some with ropy braids halfway down their backs, these comely women with skin the color of the deepest tan I yearned for as a teenage girl—turning and turning on my sandy towel at Mission Beach—a color I could never attain. How different we are outwardly. Though not tall, I'm inches taller than these women and fair, especially after my Paris winter. My hair short and fine and blond. My eyes the same bright blue as my father's. But they don't stare at me, these women. They are busy with their bags and bundles, graceful in their saris of many colors.

The taxi ride to Juhu Beach is madness. My driver, an old man with a grubby turban round his head, is unsure where to find the Citizen Hotel. He asks me a few times, and each time I give him the address. Each time he nods and continues the wild driving. I'm reminded of that early morning in Athens upon my return from Santorini, the taxi driver who couldn't find my hotel in the Pláka and finally put me out on the empty dark streets. Even in daytime I don't want to be put out on the teeming streets of Bombay. Though in some ways it might be safer, or at least less terrifying, than the ride itself.

Why this driver doesn't hit someone or something, I don't know, unless it's some kind of divine intervention. Me in the back seat, clinging anxiously to my backpack, thrown this way and that as he honks and passes yet another car, honks and comes nose-to-tail-end of a bicycle-drawn cart, honks and barely misses a pedestrian. I'm jerked around helter-skelter, trying to catch my breath and a few times stifling squeals.

Every book or article I have ever read describing India says virtually the same thing: the roads are incredibly crowded with every means of transportation—cars, buses, taxis by the score, both four- and three-wheeled carts, bicycles, trucks, and pedestrians. Swarms of pedestrians. The idea apparently is to honk and simultaneously forge ahead. My driver is adept at this as he keeps both hands on the wheel, the thumb of his right stretched to hold its ready place on the horn.

The sun is bright and hot. If Paris is a moody black-and-white film in an art theater, Bombay is cinemascope technicolor in a megascreen multiplex. We pass street after street lined with tent homes: dirty shelters that stream back from streets overflowing with humanity. "Expect poverty," the travel books tell me. My expectations are exceeded not by the level of poverty—I know about that from years of working for Project Concern International, wandering the dump in Tijuana, Mexico, with my camera, weeping and taking photographs of little kids picking through smoldering trash, grubbing for anything of value; mothers with infants tied to their breast in ragged, make-do carriers, bent over, breathing the stench. So it isn't the heartbreaking poverty here but the sheer quantity of impoverished humans.

On the terrace at the Citizen Hotel, a few steps up from the beach, a small wall separates me from the Sunday-afternoon population. Beggars approach the wall, including young girls with even younger children hoisted onto their hips. A man with crutches, one leg missing, sits on the sand just below, staring up at me, attempting to make eye contact. Another man with a performing monkey stops by and offers to put on a show. I struggle to maintain my distance behind the walls—the hotel's physical one and the psychic one I've established for myself. Otherwise I fear I could be consumed by the thronging humanity of the scene.

It's a relief to look farther out along the shoreline where camels are led along the sand, their long necks stretched in resistance to the reins that urge them forward, their awkwardly jointed legs reluctantly slow. On their backs, two-seater saddles atop red fabric draped around their bellies, bright in contrast to the dun of the sand and the gray-green sea. Riding one camel is a lone child who appears scared but fascinated, too, as I would be. On another, an entire family has climbed aboard, parents each holding a child on their lap while another child rides behind, holding fast to father's waist.

Horses trot along the hard-packed sand beside the receding sea, riders astride; some galloping like racehorses, tails streaming, backlit by the metallic setting sun. Occasional squeals of thrilled children carry over the sound of gentle waves breaking on the shore. Fresh ocean scent mixes with camel and horse dung, which mixes with spicy incense that comes from I don't know where.

Shaggy ponies pull carts decorated with brilliant yellow and magenta streamers and filled with grinning kids. Little girls in frilly dresses and boys in shorts and thin shirts on their skinny bodies. Couples stroll together along the shoreline. More children frolic behind, kicking up brief whirlwinds of sand, turning cartwheels, scrawny brown legs pointed upward for a brief moment before tumbling backward into giggling heaps. Here and there clumps of women stroll together, holding hands or their arms around each other, touching in a friendly way that we American women grow out of by the time we pass adolescence. Another sort of grace left behind.

A couple sits together on the sand, his handkerchief spread beneath him, her on one of her flowing scarves. They talk earnestly, leaning in to each other. Young couples flirt with one another, one woman coyly playing with her scarf as the wind catches it and billows it out behind her—a gorgeous butterfly, a bird on the wing.

Perched on the terrace with a cool drink, I'm comfortable in my loose teal skirt and T-shirt, wearing short sleeves for the first time since when—Greece last October? The tropical air brushes my bare arms. Compared to the women on the beach in their undulating scarves and long lengths of colorful fabric wrapped gracefully about their bodies, I'm underdressed, too casually American.

The colors and designs of the saris capture me with their silky swirls, like being lost in an abstract painting. Every imaginable shade and tint— blues in the colors of the Arabian Sea itself, from indigo depths to hazy blue-gray waves and seafoam greens of the surf as it breaks toward shore. The bright orange-red neon ball of the setting sun is repeated in the sinuous silk of one sari. Deep reds and purples and fuchsias, the green of new buds on spring trees, and some shy, quiet colors too—rich cream, buttery yellow, the seashell pink of the sky at dawn.

Many saris are plainly sewn, color their only decoration, with combinations that merge subtle shadings and gradations of tone, others that play against each other in loud, luminous contrast; others are intricately designed with mosaics of stitching and geometries of weaving. These magnificent saris make even beggar women look regal as the wind caresses the rich fabric away from their outstretched arms. I long for a palette of colored pencils to capture the many shades in my journal.

The parade goes on beyond sunset and I take a few photos of camels silhouetted in the sinking light before a coolish wind drives me from the terrace. I buy a bottle of mineral water from the little shop in the lobby and ask about taxis and trains and check-out time. I won't stay here long.

Upstairs, the air conditioner is too cold and there's no way to adjust it; still I'm glad to be in the room, its polished floor and red-stained furniture with contrasting pink upholstery. More Indian color! The shower is refreshing, too, after nearly two months of the tiny bathtub in my Paris studio. I stand under the lukewarm water and let it pour over me, washing away the loud colorful day. Tomorrow I will go into Bombay. I'm almost ready for the city. Just one more night of good sleep.

JANUARY 13, 1987
Grossmont Hospital

Tom is sleeping. Morphine drips into his arm, oxygen flows through a thin clear tube. He stays in one position on his back, a pillow beneath his head, the bed raised at a small angle. *No extreme measures*, the orders read.

A few feet away on a cot the staff brought in for me, I try to read, then get up and stand beside him. My back aches. I haven't slept well. The cot isn't comfortable, but it's not that. Of course it's not that.

A few friends have come by. He didn't want—he specifically said—a bunch of people standing around his bed, watching him die. Always a strong man, always in charge. They wanted to come, those few closest friends, but I am his protector. Mary Joyce and I talk about it. She gently guides. "Okay," I say. "But one at a time." They group in the hallway outside the closed door and talk softly, awaiting their time to say goodbye.

I don't call Peg, Tom's mother in Toronto. She would have been here, and while he hadn't said specifically not his mother, just *people*, I believe I'm protecting him, protecting his privacy, protecting the intimacy of his dying. But I also know I don't want to be forced to interact with her, because it would not be just for the ten minutes the few others come into his room but for who knows how long—days? And then, after? It isn't because she and I don't get along; we do. I like Peg, "Peglet," is Tom's name for her. She's bright and funny and has lived a life that makes for great stories, and she tells them well. She's also a strong, opinionated woman and could take over any quiet, tender time Tom and I have left. I don't want to make conversation. I

don't want to hear her opinions about his care, the room, the nurses—
anything. I just want the private, precious hours with him to myself.

Though he's deeply asleep most of the time, I believe he's aware
of my presence. I talk to him, though he doesn't respond. Sometimes
I read aloud from the book I brought with me, *A New Pair of
Glasses* by Chuck C., one of those people we AAs call gurus. His
words are what I need now. "Some part of every one of you is going
to be with me for the rest of my life," he wrote. *Some part of you,* I
send a thought to Tom, *is going to be with me for the rest of my life.*

I leave the hospital only briefly. Mary Joyce stays with Tom while I am
gone. This afternoon I go to Jamul to shower, to change and to breathe
some fresh air. I want to bring back the scent of pine and citrus to his
room. I want to go down to the grove and pick some oranges or a few
tangerines from the tree at the farthest end of the row. Tom and I used
to stand beside that tree, mouths full of sweet fruit, juice sliding down
our chins and wrists, and see who could spit seeds the farthest into
the canyon.

After my shower, the phone rings.

Mary Joyce: "You better come quickly. We're losing him."

And I do rush back and dash up five flights of stairs to his room,
the elevator too slow.

He's still alive. Still breathing. Still the drip of morphine, the drip
of liquids into his vein. The oxygen. And he is still beautiful. Mary
Joyce has brushed his hair, full and thick and dark with that glint of
auburn. I lean over his bed, touch his face, take his hand.

"You were such a good husband, Tommy," I tell him, choosing the
scarcely used diminutive I once heard his grandfather call him. "How
I have loved you."

He doesn't respond.

∽

Crowded is such an inaccurate word, even a wimpy word, to describe
Bombay. *Crowded* is five people in an elevator, *crowded* is the mall

parking lot during Christmas shopping season, *crowded* is my local Trader Joe's on a Friday afternoon. To describe the sort of crowded found near the Gateway of India sends me to my thesaurus for words like *bursting, crammed, packed, massed, congested,* and still none of them completely captures the experience. None of them can conjure not only the sheer numbers of people but the sounds, the scents, the colors, the utter aliveness and humanity of it all.

Today I saw a cow on the sidewalk, munching hay, just as I was led to believe I would. Still, knowing in your mind doesn't prepare you for the reality. Especially for a woman who grew up in the Midwest and who, for a few years, lived on the outskirts of town in an old farmhouse next door to a herd of black-and-white lumberers who slowly grazed and who sometimes stood in the muddy pond in water up to their knuckled knees.

Here on the Bombay street, black-haired women in their gorgeous saris unload rocks and dirt from road construction. There are blind beggars and beggars on little rolling boards—men whose stick-legs are tucked under them on small platforms the size of a Southern California teen's skateboard. One woman rolls by with only stumps for legs and arms that stop just below the elbow.

People set up housekeeping with clotheslines, mats, and boxes. Tent cities and cardboard lean-tos crowd (there's that word again) congested sidewalks, where there are sidewalks. Barefoot children tramp the dirty, dangerous passageways. Women and girls with shiny metal pails and copper jugs pick their way through trash-strewn streets to fetch water from the nearby bay.

The massive arch that is the Gateway of India, originally constructed as a symbolic ceremonial entrance to British India, opens to the harbor. Tourist boats await to take visitors to Elephanta Island, where they can tour cave temples enshrined with religious carvings depicting Hindu mythologies. Under the arch of the Gateway itself, a man with a costumed monkey offers a show. The monkey wears sunglasses. His little balls hang out through a cutaway in his somehow-still-elegant purple outfit.

As I try to record the details—the colors, the smells, the sounds of the streets—in my journal, I catch glimpses of myself in the mirror that hangs over the desk in my room at the Hotel Godwin where I've returned for respite from the day. I'm wearing my abalone shell earrings. I haven't worn them since those sun-soaked weeks in Greece. I stop writing and really look at myself like the young man on the metro in Paris. I don't see tension in my face, but someone else might. I may have become accustomed to seeing myself this way. If I could compare photos of myself before and now, would I see a difference in my face before this trip? Before I sold the house and the business. Before I left Jamul. Before Tom died. Before we even heard the word *adenocarcinoma*.

Looking into my eyes, I don't see the same anxiety that was there this morning before I ventured out into the teeming world of Bombay. Then I move closer. Yes, there it is. Sadness and loss. Not fear though. Instead, a certain weariness. India, at least what I witnessed today, which is only a tiny part of all that India is, will wear you out. It will also break your heart.

Bombay is nine hours earlier than Washington, DC. Tomorrow, January 15, is deadline day—the allied forces have drawn a line in the desert sand: withdraw from Kuwait or else! Will there be a strike at dawn?

My room comes with a large-screen television, but I resist the urge to turn it on. I remember once during a partial eclipse of the sun wearing no special glasses, and fearing to injure my eyes, it was nearly impossible to resist the urge to look at the celestial phenomenon. This is the same impulse I have to turn on the television. What injury would I suffer if I knew we were going to war? What would I do with the information?

Instead I dress for the day, pack my backpack, and go back out into the streets to wander until my train for Goa leaves later this evening.

A man on the corner holds out a metal tool that looks like a drill bit.

"You have corns on your feet?" he asks. "Troublesome toenails?"

I glance at my well-worn, scuffed huaraches, my feet bare inside, unprotected by the warm woolen socks I wore in Paris. *What does he do with his strange tool*, I wonder, *and does he do it right there on the street corner?* I shift my pack on my shoulder and continue on.

A half dozen men shovel a hole in the street, filling large baskets with debris, which is transported fire-bucket-style by a line of women who pass it, woman-to-woman, to the last woman, who dumps it into a wheelbarrow. The men wear dirty white trousers rolled up at the ankles; the women wear their ubiquitous saris.

A little girl turns tremendously graceful cartwheels right in front of me, her cotton dress flying around her head. We passersby drop coins into her tin bowl.

I make only a short foray into the street before I become too hot and too inundated with sensory stimulation—the crowds, the noise, the cars and buses, the carts and bicycles, the incessant honking. The bright sun turning the already intense colors into something beyond technicolor. The smoke from cook fires, brush and trash burning. And the odor of decay—something so awful I can't find words. I've read descriptions of dead things by better writers than me, of decomposing corpses and rotting animals. This is a stench so strong it surely will kill the more delicate receptors in my nose. After this, I may never again be able to smell the faint fragrance of a violet or the sweet scent of a tree-ripened peach.

The café in the luxurious Taj Mahal Palace offers refuge. I order an iced coffee and drop into a chair at a table by the window. I'm still reading Pico Iyer's *Video Night in Kathmandu* in anticipation of my upcoming journey to Nepal with Linda. Iyer writes about low-budget travelers, backpackers and the like, which I'm definitely not. Their credo, he writes: "Thou shalt not plan. Thou shalt not hurry. Thou shalt not travel without backpacks, on anything other than backroads. And thou shalt not ever, in any circumstance, call thyself a tourist."

As I drink my coffee, read, and make notes in my journal, a man sits down at the table just opposite me. He wears a pale loose shirt that contrasts with his dark skin. Like many men I've seen in this city, he's thin to the point of malnourished yet has about him the righteous air of a man whose rightful place has been taken by a woman.

"You wouldn't do that at home," he says, "in your own country."

Clearly he doesn't know me and the hours I spend at cafés with notebook and pen. And besides, I've been at the window table, which he obviously wants, for less than half an hour, a legitimate time for any iced-coffee drinker on a hot afternoon's respite at the Taj Hotel.

He continues to watch me. I try to ignore him, but it's well nigh impossible to ignore someone when you know they're staring at you, sending unpleasant thoughts, maybe curses, maybe imagining doing all sorts of horrible things to you—breaking my fingers as I hold my pen, smashing my head into the table, or through the very window he wants to sit beside. I remember the man on the corner with the drill bit and his offer to have a look at my troublesome toenails.

Finally the man gets up. "Now you can start on your IR20," he says as he leaves, "your income tax form."

The embarrassed hostess comes over to apologize for him. But in spite of Pico Iyer's commandment to never "call thyself a tourist," this must be how I appear to others here. Of course, physically, I am from elsewhere—my fair skin and blue eyes, the way I dress: my skirt and T-shirt and beat-up huaraches. But I really don't want to be a "tourist." All along this journey, I have viewed myself as a traveler, a journeyer. A visitor in some cases, a pilgrim in others. But a tourist only occasionally.

Back outside the lovely young girl who turned those wonderfully acrobatic cartwheels has been joined by a young boy in shorts—I assume her brother—and his dog. The boy climbs up on five tin cans of graduated sizes that he's stacked atop each other. He balances on one thin leg while his sister turns more cartwheels around him. I put more coins in their bowl. They earn their money, these children, as well as any buskers on the streets of Paris or Amsterdam or the magicians back home in Balboa Park.

A man catches up to me and matches my steps. He leans close and says in my ear, "You are my mother-sister contact," and then moves on.

I recall the man in Rome (*Remember me from twenty years ago?*), the man in Dubrovnik (*Do you know this song?* as he hummed "Lara's Theme"), and wonder what this is, these random contacts with men and their unique messages.

At the Gateway grounds which is seemingly off-limits to the hawkers and the beggars, I take a seat on a stone bench, unmolested, as families lounge here and there, fathers and mothers on benches like mine, children playing nearby. A small gathering of boys stands close and some of the boys stare at me; other children come to gaze.

Though most of my life I've been one among many, those times I was "other" stay with me. Sometimes uncomfortably, especially as a young woman having to pass a collection of workingmen, construction workers, as cliché as that sounds. Those times I was seen as a sexual object. Here I'm merely an oddity, a curiosity, and one of the privileges of being a child is the gift of staring. Our mothers scold it out of us soon enough, but for as long as we can get away with it, we stare. Of course we do. We're curious. We're learning. We're gathering information. That's one of the reasons I loved taking photographs on the job with those complicated cameras and all their lenses; I could look as long as I wanted. And I did.

A humid breeze lifts the hem of my skirt. It's nearly sunset and the park has gone shady as the sun goes behind "the Taj" where crowds of men gather. I don't know what has happened today, but the way the men line the street, restless, agitated, gives off dangerous energy. Something about the Gulf conflict, the metaphorical line drawn in the literal sand? The park begins to fill with men and boys. I gather up my pack and leave.

JANUARY 14, 1987
Grossmont Hospital

I awaken early on my cot in Tom's hospital room. Nurses come, do what they do. After, I stand next to his bed, touch his face, which is slightly whisker-rough. I don't know how to shave a man's face, but I could try. His eyes are closed, dark lashes brush thin cheeks. I touch his hair, brush it off his forehead. He doesn't respond to my touch. His breath is steady, the pulse in his throat, the one I use as a measure, is steady too. In his arm, pale on the white covers, needles carry the hydration drip, the morphine drip.

When another nurse comes in I take a few moments to slip down to the cafeteria and bring back a cup of coffee. Details fade. What remains is the sight of the urine bag that hangs from the side of the bed, the beep of machines when they do something, record something; I'm not sure what the various sounds mean. The room is rife with sounds and smells, air that holds our breath, mixing the two— his, oxygen-filtered, and mine, labored with dread.

Outside his closed door, in the hall, at the nurse's station, in other rooms, is activity: conversations, paperwork, decisions being made, people leaving or arriving. But here in our room there is just Tom in his bed and me standing next to him, me in the chair beside his bed, me staring out the window at the eucalyptus across the parking lot, me on my cot, reading/not reading, glancing over my book to look at him until I can't anymore.

Time passes slowly in this room. Sometime after lunch—I ate a little from the tray I ordered for Tom—Mary Joyce arrives to stay with him while I go home to shower and change, to be alone, to breathe

255

the fresh January air, to rest my gaze on something besides the room and all it holds.

I barely arrive home before Mary Joyce calls.

"You need to come back now," she says. She need say no more.

I don't take time to change but grab my bag and rush downstairs to the car. But before I can drive away, Jesús catches me.

"Por favor," he says. "I want to see Tom. Please." And something else in Spanish I don't understand. "I take the truck."

The look on his face, imploring. For these last years Tom and Jesús have worked side by side in the orchard, laid irrigation to the new avocado trees, lingered early mornings in the trailer where Jesús and Lucy live, scratching out plans for never-ending construction projects. The two men have become close over their time together.

"Yes, yes," I say. "Hurry."

We form a two-vehicle procession. Me driving Tom's car, Jesús and Lucy following in the old black pickup. I don't know if Jesús has a license, though he drives the truck around Jamul, picking up this and that for the orchard and the house remodel. But he doesn't drive well, nor does he know the way to the hospital, so I must go more slowly than I want, than the urgency that's pushing me.

The curves along Jamul Drive make driving tortuously slow. The stop sign at Steele Canyon Road steals time. My gaze is as often to the rearview mirror as it is to the road before me. Time passes as we proceed on the freeway, reach the hospital, find a place to park, traverse the long sidewalk to the entry, the two of them hurrying to keep up with me as I nearly run. Inside, the elevator doesn't come and doesn't come. My stomach clinches with impatience and anxiety. I must be breathing—it's what the body does—but I hold myself so rigidly I don't know how breath can enter or escape.

On the fifth floor I rush down the hall to Tom's room, not considering Jesús and Lucy; they'll follow or not.

Mary Joyce steps away as I take my place at the left side of Tom's bed. On the right is the apparatus that holds the hydration, the morphine.

He looks the same as when I left him less than an hour ago. Eyes still closed, those lashes, those cheekbones, that rough skim of overnight whiskers. His lips look different though: they're not held tight against the pain as they have been over the last months. They appear softer, almost relaxed.

His hands lay crossed atop his chest. Those hands I fell in love with exactly eight years ago—long fingers, prominent veins, the gold wedding band that's been on his finger only three of those eight years. I take his hand and lean in to him, my back rigid. The pulse on his neck that has been my measure is still beating, but in slow, gentle waves, barely moving.

"I love you," I whisper. I can hardly speak, my throat closed tight, thick with the emotion my body wants to express. "My darling man."

As I watch, his watery pulse ceases; a small half-breath escapes his mouth. His eyes are closed still, but with that breath, barely noticeable, the smallest flutter of his eyelids. Just that and that is all.

‿

JANUARY 15, 1991
Bombay to Goa

I climb the jammed stairs at the Churchgate station, lugging my pack. I'm to meet up with Andrew, a young Brit, also traveling to Goa. We met the previous day when I came to purchase my ticket and agreed to make the twenty-four-hour journey together.

The day is bright and hot, as I've come to expect, and the flight of stairs to the top level is elbow-to-elbow, body-to-body men and women. Although still morning, it's already sweating hot, especially with the humidity, my pack, the stairs. Then there's a hand on my behind. The sort of touch that's not an accident in the crush of people but a deliberate grope of the kind most women have experienced. Unwelcome, uninvited, crude, and arrogant. I turn sharply and even in this teeming sea of humanity I see the guilty man. A middle-aged Indian man wearing a traditional long shirt, loose trousers, and a smirk. He looks me in the eyes and I boldly shout, "Keep your hands off me!" He doesn't look away. He has no shame. I push ahead, rudely elbowing others as I get as many steps ahead of him as I can given the solid-yet-moving mass.

At the top of the platform, our agreed-upon meeting place, I am still bristling when I meet young Andrew.

"That son of a bitch," I say. "That man grabbed my butt on the stairs." I turn to point him out but there's no finding him in the throng that's separating and coming apart like so many giant amoebas.

Andrew is twenty-two years old, younger than my son, tall and dangerously lean with a noticeable Adam's apple and large teeth. In London he's an accountant who has earned an advanced degree in his field. He, too, is traveling alone and is also a bit anxious on his first visit to this continent. Like so many other strangers who find one another while traveling, we're glad for each other's company. But as we ready to board our train for the first part of our journey, a short ride from Victoria Terminus to Dadar, we're told he must travel on the men-only car while I'm sent to the women-only one; his car is as congested as the stairs leading to the trains, while mine, blessedly, is nearly empty.

I know this seeming privilege is another example of the inequality of the sexes, but to tell the truth, sometimes I'm glad for these separations, and, having seen the crowd in the men's car and still feeling the ugly imprint of that man's grope, I'm especially glad today. I tell a disappointed Andrew, "It's only a short ride to Dadar; then we'll have twenty hours of one another."

I take the seat next to a woman whose cheekbones I envy; she's dressed in a sari of the palest pink, like the inside of a Finesse peach rose in my Jamul garden. She says she likes to talk to foreigners and begins by telling me of relatives who live "abroad." She isn't married, her father died of cancer and, she says, "I have to take care of my mother."

How I love listening to her lovely accent, the way she speaks English. We talk in an easy way, though I keep the details of my life to myself. I'm hesitant to say I'm a widow. I still don't want to talk to strangers about Tom's death. So instead of revealing my own story, I ask questions: about women working in India, her own job, as well as wage equality and our own struggle for it in America. I ask her if wearing a sari is comfortable.

It's when I tell her how pretty her sari is, how lovely I find all the saris, that I begin to cry. We look away from each other as she witnesses my response: a throat-swelling, eyes-filling, spontaneous—I don't want to say *eruption* because the sensation comes more slowly than that. It's the same upwelling of emotion I felt in Greece at the Sanctuary of Athena in Delphi, as I experienced standing before Van Gogh's *Starry Night* at the museum in Amsterdam, and on the light-filled night at Tivoli Gardens. Unexpected, unexplained emotion that I believe comes when some part of me touches the mystery of the divine, a soul-filling of beauty. I wonder if this tearful response to beauty is when I understand the depth of who I am—acknowledge my own beauty—beneath the protective layers I've created to survive.

At a session I had with Carol the psychic reader in early summer just before I left, she talked about the healing I was to do in India. She spoke of "the mother wound," which I'd only vaguely heard of. We sat in her apartment in San Francisco, Carol in her rocking chair, pregnant with her first child. "It's passed down mother to daughter to daughter," she said and explained that the *wound* is the pain that comes in response to generations of women living in patriarchal cultures. "We develop ways of coping that don't serve us, that diminish us and our power."

I'm curious about my attraction to the women in India, my fascination with their clothes, their hair; how I'm drawn to their inquisitive, dark-eyed children, staring right back at them as they stare at me, each so curious about the other. There must be some deep connection I can't interpret intellectually and can't fully express otherwise. (The man on the street, *You are my mother-sister connection.*) I'm hesitant to write of things that have no basis in fact or science but are about something more elusive, especially for one who can't say she's a believer in anything for certain. And yet there are these physical responses to an emotion that doesn't appear to have a basis in any present event or circumstances—these may be spiritual breadcrumbs along the way to a deeper understanding of the mystery.

Andrew and I find one another at Dadar Station, board our train for Goa, and begin the long, gorgeous journey. We look out the windows and talk of everything and nothing. The train stops along the way but we don't disembark. Vendors line the platforms at small stations and offer food of all manner through open windows; a few leap aboard, singing their wares, disembarking as the train starts its slow movement. Andrew and I eat what we've brought with us—I have some naan, a few pieces of fruit; Andrew shares his "Bombay sandwich," filled with boiled potatoes and cucumbers and other delicious ingredients. We find ourselves in tiny bunks on cramped train cars with rattly overhead fans that do little to cool us. We continue and continue, twenty hours through winding valleys, rolling banks of forested hills, at one point passing the thundering Dudhsagar waterfall, which crashes down a rocky hillside.

JANUARY 16, 1991
Colva Beach

On the west coast of the Arabian Sea, Colva is known for its powdery white sand and its long, graceful length of beach lined with coconut palms, where sunsets smolder for hours, staining the sky a smoky burnt orange. The town is small, its businesses and shops primarily catering to vacationers and tourists. I find a room at the Silver Sands Beach Resort and Andrew goes on to a guesthouse, less expensive and farther down the beach. We promise to catch up with each other in the morning.

The Silver Sands is modern and clean with a pool, a coffee shop, a restaurant, and a telephone—comfortable and a little too cushy for Andrew, who's on a grand adventure. The air is sea-fresh and welcome after the humidity of Bombay.

Under Portuguese rule from the 1500s until 1961, when it was annexed to India, the surrounding area is still home to old Portuguese villas and ruins. The Igreja de Nossa Senhora das Mercês (which I translate to *Church of Our Lady of Mercies*) stands ornate and pillared in the main square. While Hinduism is the religion of most Indians, every October the town is inundated by the faithful who come for the annual *Fama* Festival, during which the miraculous statue of *Menino Jesus* (Baby Jesus) is unlocked from its vault in the church and paraded through town on its way to be dipped into a nearby river. *Menino Jesus* is believed to have healing powers and pilgrims anoint themselves with water from the dripping Baby Jesus.

Travelers from abroad as well as vacationing Indians normally flock to Colva in mid-January. The weather is mild and humidity not so high as during the hot summer months. Tourists from the Middle East and Europe, especially Germany, fill budget hotels like the Silver Sands as well as guesthouses and hostels, and the beach is rich with all manner of visitors. But this year the Silver Sands is nearly empty, as are the many other lodgings, grand as well as modest. I wonder what has happened in the Gulf. I've still not heard the news. On the train a young boy asked where I was from, and when I said America, he said something about a war but I didn't get any details.

In the hotel's modern, clean restaurant, having my first coffee of the day, I revel in the quiet of the place, the open space. In the six days since I left Paris, I have had six sleeping locations, including the uncomfortable bunk on the slow train from Bombay.

I want to relax, warm my bones, to open my entire body to the languishing warmth of the tropical night. But I'm experiencing another bout of homesickness too; that word that carries so much meaning. Sick from wanting home, from missing home, without knowing exactly what *home* means. This is a sickness of the psyche or the soul, an ineffable longing that can't be named.

Writing the date in my journal, I recognize that this sadness, this inability to express myself, must come from some intuitive recognition of the anniversary of Tom's death, January 14, which fell on the day in Bombay that I was unable to find a place to be at ease.

That night I dream my father died of alcoholism alone in a hotel room, my sister committed suicide, and an old family friend was being beaten by her husband, something that had been going on for years. In my dream room nothing worked—no lights or electricity, and there were bugs or worms in bags everywhere.

Later, standing at the desk in the lobby of the hotel, I hear about the bombings in Bagdad.

I'm of the generation born in the days building up to America's entry into the Second World War. We're known as the *Silent Generation*, those born between 1928 and 1945. My father joined the navy in 1944 and returned home just a few days after my third birthday. Unnamed fears were part of my earliest experience. What must a young mother feel when her husband goes off to war and she's left behind with three small children? That fear must have influenced us daughters in ways we can't identify. All my life I named my mother as fearful, and most certainly her anxieties were part of her long before the war or my father's leaving. She was born in 1917 during World War I, and the very next year the Spanish flu—the great pandemic—struck, killing fifty million people worldwide; she grew up during the Great Depression in an already poor family. Who can say what effect the chaos and suffering of the world has on any of us, and how it's transmitted, mother to daughter to daughter? More effects of "the mother wound."

The veterans' housing we lived in after my father returned home was repurposed from a former military base in St. Joseph: Fort Rosecrans. All the families' fathers had served in World War II, what became known as the "Good War." The Korean War, begun in 1950, hardly affected us, at least as far as I know. I scarcely remember talk about it in our home or at school. But then came Vietnam, which I do remember and which I protested and which still, when I think of it or read references to it or see it in films or plays, sickens me.

And now I am in India, at the western edge of Asia, and across the Arabian Sea, America is again dropping bombs, cruise missiles are rupturing the sky, and fighter jets—I don't know all the words for the ways we inflict our damage.

Several of us gather around the hotel pool and report what we've heard—facts, gossip, exaggerations, rumors, suspicions, even imaginings: twenty-eight tons of bombs dropped on Baghdad, two-hundred thousand Muslim Indians want to fight for Saddam Hussein in retaliation, someone says there's rioting in the cities.

"I feel guilty lounging beside a pool when there's a war going on," says Kenny, a young Canadian with bright red hair and an abundance of freckles. His eyelashes are a paler shade of red. He's a young gay guy who works at a tuxedo shop in Winnipeg.

I love Canadians. A broad general statement, I know, but I do. I enjoyed meeting them all the times Tom took me home to Toronto, to

Vancouver, and to Edmonton, where he worked on the Commonwealth Games and the sky stayed light until midnight. Anyway, there's something about Kenny's Canadian-ness I connect with, that and the concern in his dark eyes.

"What should we do?" I ask him. "Should we be protesting? Where would we go?"

I don't know what action to take. Protest? How? Where? To whom? We are a small collection of foreigners here. So far as I know I'm the only American. Kenny, Canadian; Andrew, British; there are a few Germans; a handful of others. Hardly anyone has come to Goa this season. I read that tourism is down by 60 percent. India is popular with Middle Easterners too. But they aren't here this year. They're having a war.

Our group slowly scatters and soon Kenny leaves. I'm alone at the patio table. The servers huddle around the bar, talking in low voices. The last of the loungers gathers her things and goes inside.

I send out silent prayers for peace. I drink my iced tea and ponder what peace even means, how it cannot seem to last. On the other side of the pool there's a ruckus as a gray cat attempts to capture a bird in a palm tree.

Time is surreal these days, lounging with iced drinks by the pool, wandering the shopping streets of Colva, strolling along the shore of the gently lapping Arabian Sea. All the ingredients of a blissful holiday—except, except.

At the edge of the sea I look out to the far horizon. If I could see only a little farther, I would witness a world being torn apart. If I went to a city, especially Delhi, I would witness hundreds of thousands of Indians rioting, protesting what is happening across the sea. But here I am on this picture-postcard palm-lined shore where, farther out on the aquamarine water, fishing boats keep their slow pulsing movement, a rhythm I know from before birth.

When it's hottest I lounge by the pool, my teal-and-purple bikini covered by a thin gauzy coverup I found at the outdoor market down the street. Empty chaises at the poolside, empty cafés along the beach, empty rooms at the hotels.

Kenny and I go to his room to watch the news on the small TV. Or we go to a makeshift thatched-roof bar down on the sand and listen to the news from the BBC. Flights into and out of Delhi are cancelled. Americans in the Delhi area are told to go home. The bombing continues.

One evening at dinner at some seaside eatery with Andrew—all scarred tables and lopsided chairs and the freshest fish imaginable— he tells me about Bangkok. He especially wants to talk about Patpong, the notorious red-light district that caters to international travelers.

We're on the deck, a few steps up from the sand. Below, a circle of boys play in the sand; farther out, fishing boats line the shore, in for the night, and family members—boys, girls, women—unload the catch into large round woven baskets.

"I don't know what to think about it," Andrew says. He's young, even for twenty-two, and a little shy, making eye contact then looking away. "If I hadn't been with those others, the Australians, I would have gone with one of the girls. I wanted to," he says, "but the doctors warned us against AIDS." He picks at his naan with long fingers, and I picture him tallying accounts on a calculator.

He tells me about the old men there and how it seems perverse for them to hire girls for sex but somehow seems okay for young men like himself.

"What's your opinion?" he asks.

Andrew likes everything to be in order, labeled. He doesn't like not knowing what he thinks about something. I'm sure he considers me an odd sort of mother figure; my guess is he wouldn't talk to his mother about such as this. I know my son would not.

"There has always been sex for money," I say. "It can be a fair trade if the one selling is making their own choices. But young girls being forced to put on shows, to have sex for money, money they don't even receive—and being controlled by men, kidnapped, some of them.

Sold. This is wrong," I tell him. "It's shameful and immoral and just . . ."
My anger rises, knowing what happens to those innocent, vulnerable
young girls. "I know it can be titillating and exciting, but consider
what you're contributing to. Consider what you're purchasing.

"You're an economist," I say. "Consider the implications of the
exchange."

The next day I hire a taxi for the drive to Panjim, the capital of Goa
about thirty-four kilometers from Colva. Although I haven't been
able to reach her for several days, if Linda's going to meet me in Delhi
in ten days I need to see about getting a ticket and to find out if it's
true what I've heard about flights to Delhi being cancelled, the reality
of the danger there. And if all flights are cancelled, then what? Do we
meet someplace else? I have no idea what will happen in the next ten
days. Or even tomorrow.

There's an AA meeting scheduled in Panjim this evening. A meeting will be a good thing after all this unrest and uncertainty, very little
news, and lots of rumors. I haven't been to a meeting since I left Paris
a little over a week ago.

I don't like to bargain with taxi drivers for the fare; it puts us in
adversarial roles, though I know it's the custom. Here, I've found, you
bargain for everything but food and lodging. The shorts I bought at
the flea market, the cost of a massage to which I've yet to treat myself,
and the prices are already so low. Still we come to an agreement—the
driver knows his part and I know mine.

The drive to Panjim is stunning—green valleys along a winding
road, lush planted hillsides and occasional grand houses, Portuguese
in style, painted bright colors with pillars and fancy window adorn-
ments, half-hidden behind walls and gates and verdant greenery.
Smaller homes exist, too, surrounded by farms and orchards.

I'm reminded of Bali. The green, green rice fields, the palms and
tropical growth. Yes, I say to myself, after India and Thailand and
Nepal, I'll go back to Bali. That gentle, peaceful place.

On Panjim's terraced streets are more lovely Portuguese-style

buildings with balconies and red-tiled roofs, along with some broad avenues filled with traffic—both on wheels and on foot—all hushed by the
generous and fully leafed banyan trees. I locate the Air India office and
go in to ask about a ticket. This takes some time. The office is congested
with a disorderly queue, if the confusion can be called a queue at all.
Finally, a ticket to Delhi for next Tuesday in hand, I go back out onto the
street, stop for a snack and tea at the Perfect Confectionery Café, then
find my way to the AA meeting in a building near Don Bosco School.

The meeting room is dark and smoky with a dozen Indian men
around a long table. They seem surprised to see a white woman of a
certain age, casually dressed and obviously American, join them. I
don't know if AA meetings are segregated like railway cars and I have
committed some terrible cultural faux pas or if there are no women
alcoholics in India. In this conservative society drinking is, if not
forbidden, at the very least considered not acceptable behavior for
women. And if there are women alcoholics, and odds are there are,
I imagine secrecy and shame keep those who might have a problem
from admitting it, probably even to themselves. But here I am, a brash
American woman, crashing the smoky sanctity of the men's AA meeting. I take my place, introduce myself, but don't share beyond that.
Nobody presses me to do so.

After the meeting, glad to leave the dim room with all that smoke
and disapproval, I find a public phone in a quiet hotel lobby and try to
call Camille. Blessing upon blessing, I finally get through.

"You sound sad," she says.

"You too."

"And far away."

"You too."

I'm self-conscious, fearing that some of the few others in the
lobby might be eavesdropping; I'm certainly guilty of that, and so I
assume others do it too. We talk of the war. I don't want to cry, don't
want to admit aloud how afraid I am. Confused. Homesick.

We don't talk long; I give her my phone number at the Silver
Sands and ask her to give it to Amy and Linda.

"I'm planning on being home by Easter. Just nine weeks. Not long," I say and wonder why I should not just go home now.

Back outside I answer my own question: It's not that I don't know where home is—I do, sort of, as I'm holding on to the idea that I'll live in San Francisco; Camille and I will open our café. But the physical place I'll return to is only part of it. This self-diagnosed *homesickness* is more than that or not only that.

All my life I've done the next indicated thing: go to school, get a job, get married, get divorced, get married again—go on to the next job, the next man. Never have I been at a crossroads where there is no clear next indicated thing. It's as if finally, as I near the half-century mark, I'm acknowledging a deeper need, the sort of soul-longing that has sent so many on an odyssey to we know not where. This is not a search for a certain *where* to be found on any map. It's a process of finding for ourselves—within ourselves—a home, and we may not even know we're there until we awake one day and discover ourselves welcome: the wished-for guest we have been waiting for.

A phone call wakes me early. The hotel phones are unreliable and our connection is bad.

"There are reports of terrorists in India," Amy tells me. "The news says Americans are urged to return home." The phone breaks up. Or maybe it is her voice that is shaky. "I've been trying to reach you for three days," she says. "Please. It's time to come home."

"I'm safe," I say, trying to reassure both of us. "This is a small place, out of the way. Just a tiny beach area. People are fishing. There are families. Kids." I don't know if either of us believes me. "Is Linda still coming? Do you know?"

She tells me she talked to Linda the day before, and yes, she's still planning to come.

"But—" Amy keeps talking, but the connection worsens and then cuts off completely. I hang up, get out of bed, and try to orient myself to the morning. Of course it is another bright day—every day is bright, the sun high, the birds going like mad. I take an orange from the table and go outside to my balcony, peel it, and drop the peels onto the ground—let the birds have them, or the squirrels, or whatever critters want to share with me. I hear snatches of radio from below: it's in English, probably the BBC, but I understand few words. Past the scrabble of town is the beach, across palm trees and tile roofs and out onto the road where smoking buses honk their incessant horns. Never mind the signs that warn, *Avoid a fine—don't honk.*

Downstairs I order breakfast, a chicken-and-cheese sandwich on white bread, crusts trimmed. The Silver Sands, like all the hotels and guesthouses and resorts, caters to tourists. I'm not experiencing India; I'm in India experiencing tourism. A few nights ago at dinner with Andrew, he chided me about not renting a bike, joining him on excursions. But right now I'm not adventuresome or curious. I'm confused, homesick, and anxious. I keep hearing my daughter's shaky words: *Please come home.*

Yet there is the plan. Linda will come. We'll meet in Delhi. I already have my ticket. We'll experience India together. We'll be travelers, not tourists.

I eat my white-bread breakfast and wonder about finding a shop where I can buy another book, get a newspaper. Then I'll come back and lie by the pool. Right now that's all I can do.

I find a newspaper at a little shop down the road that also sells locally made clothes, cheap bangle-y jewelry, jute bags, souvenirs, and packaged sweets. I bring back only the newspaper, find a place in the shade by the pool, and order a cool mango juice. Only one other guest is here this morning, a man I haven't seen before, American or German or Australian or some other kind of tourist. He's stretched out in a chaise, round belly over madras shorts, straw hat pulled low over his face.

The news isn't good. The war escalates. What was Operation Desert Shield has become Operation Desert Storm and the US has deployed Patriot missiles to Israel and Saudi Arabia. More flights are cancelled. More trouble in Delhi. I put the paper away, lean back in my chaise and try to relax. *Breathe*, I tell myself. *Be present*. But anxiety and restlessness won't leave me alone. I dress and cross the street, where I find a reliable telephone connection and spend forty dollars on a call to Linda.

"Are you still planning to come?" I ask.

"Yes," she says. "I have my ticket to Delhi."

I tell her what I have heard about the riots in Delhi. The American Express office there was bombed.

"Maybe we should meet in Bangkok," I suggest, an idea that came to me as my mind arm-wrestled alternatives.

"Okay," she says. She sounds glad. "See if you can get a ticket and call me back."

Back at the hotel the little black-and-white TV in the lobby is tuned to the news. It's *x* number of fighter jets. It's so many soldiers. It's President Bush. It's Prime Minister Margaret Thatcher. It's the UN. It's facts and rhetoric and fuzzy black-and-white images of smoke and rubble. It's reactions from newscasters. It's what we humans do to one another, and I need a friend.

I search out Kenny, and his good humor and reasonableness calm me down. He tells me he may go to Bangkok too. His Goa/Bombay flight was cancelled. We decide to go to Panjim the next day to investigate possibilities.

At the little bar down on the beach where we go in the evenings to hear the BBC news, we meet Harold, a Brit who doesn't understand why I would leave India. "Everyone's overreacting," he says.

"Tell that to the soldiers," I say. Is death an overreaction to war?

Kenny and I had planned to leave early, but the morning is so quiet and peaceful we decide to go down to the beach first. This is the way travel is supposed to be—you make a plan and then you do what beckons, and this morning, in the midst of it all, the sea calls to us.

The tide has receded and we traipse along the shoreline on the still-wet, hard sand. Scattered loosely out on the green water, fishing boats do their sea dance, up and down and to and fro; Crayola-colored boats moving with the breath of the sea.

"It's good to remember yourself," I tell Kenny as we stroll, "your body, what it notices." Being so close to the ocean day and night, you can forget to notice the smell of it, its fresh green scent, and the air so different than farther inland where mist and sea salt are lost to the earthy smell of lush trees and planted hillsides. Kenny and I stop our aimless amble for a moment; both of us breathe in deeply.

Farther along the beach we come upon two young Indian kids, a teenage boy and his lovely sister. They tell us they're on holiday from Varanasi. "I'm seventeen years," the girl tells us. She's been in the water. Her sari's burnt-orange hue has gone darker and fairly glows against her skin. She's at ease in her prettiness, as some young women can be. Her brother is tall and lean but easy in his body, too, his small, tight-fitting electric-blue bathing suit vivid in the morning's sun. He takes us over to meet his family and introduces us to his mother.

"May I take a picture?" I ask, holding out my camera.

"Yes, yes of course. Thank you." She's polite, with little half bows and a large smile showing a gold tooth.

I want to capture their grace, their generosity. Something that emanates from them that briefly lets me forget the madness across the sea and chaos in the cities, the doubts I have about our inability to care for each other. For these few moments there is only the beauty of the morning, the warmth of these two young people, and the way they want to include their mother in our small circle—the boy, his sister, Kenny, me. This small moment of connection and friendliness and sincere interest in one another warms me more than even the morning's sun.

In Panjim I am not surprised to discover my flight to Delhi has been cancelled. I can't get a confirmed ticket to Bangkok until February 5, nearly two weeks away, but I can get on a wait-list for a flight to Bombay tomorrow. Linda will be in Bangkok in just a week. If I can get to Bombay, I may be able to find a ticket to Bangkok from there. I put my name on the wait-list.

Later that evening Kenny and I have dinner on the deck of a seaside restaurant. He sits across the table, smiling that smile that crinkles his cheeks and hides some of his map of freckles as we talk of plans made, changed, remade—the way of travelers everywhere. The frustration of the day is forgotten or set aside for the time. Here we are. Expats and tourists and travelers lounging around the rickety beach cafés and bars and restaurants among the coconut palms, all of us in floppy cotton shorts or shirts or loosely tied dresses of Indian cotton. Silvery bangles on our arms, circling our ankles, in our ears. Tattoos on men, long hair still worn in sixties ponytails, ex-hippies or travelers on the road. Young people living as cheaply as possible, and it's possible to live very cheaply here in Goa on the beach. In another time I could have easily stayed here.

This is me, we say as we gather, *this is who I am, where I come from*. Among millions of people on this earth, we create companion-ship with one another, here and for now, in this place where we find ourselves, sometimes surprisingly.

We eat our fresh fish and rice, drink our drinks, and talk; candles on the table flicker as candles do at night outside by the ocean. Above, in the space between the beams and the thatch roof of the restaurant, a spider spins her web, linking a beam on the left to a beam on the right, joining this side to that, the candlelight making her perfect sticky strands glisten.

Linda is hesitating to come to Thailand now. She's heard warnings of terrorist activities in Bangkok.

"Do you want to continue the trip?" Linda asks, phone voice tinny.

I hesitate. "Do you want to come here? To India? To Goa?"

A longer hesitation from her.

"Let's do it some other time," she finally says.

Our plans are off. By the sound of her voice, I doubt we will ever go to Thailand or Nepal together or see Agra or Delhi or any other place in India. And, I realize, neither will I. Not now anyhow. Not with the uncertainty of the war, the dangers of traveling, the warnings to Americans.

The sudden realization comes as though a stuck door has opened and light breaks through. The decision so bright I blink against its glare.

"Will you please call Amy and let her know?" I ask. I know my daughter will be relieved. I'm relieved too. "Tell her I'm coming home."

I don't know how I'll get back to the states. How I'll get out of Goa. There's the slim chance of catching that flight to Bombay the next afternoon; I'm third or fourth wait-listed. Only forty-four passengers; still I don't like my chances. I remember the anxious queue at the Air India office in Panjim days earlier when I got my ticket to Delhi. Everyone wants to leave. But the decision is made and that's a relief. From here on, it's a matter of trust.

The next day, I meet Andrew on the beach and tell him of my decision to go home. It's another hot day at Colva Beach. We wear shorts and loose shirts. Andrew's long legs, knobby and thin. Me, tan from days poolside. I've been in Colva just over a week, though it seems longer—time out of time in a surreal contrast of poolside chaise longue with icy fruit drinks and news of the war across the sea.

"I'm wait-listed on the Vayadoot flight to Bombay tomorrow," I say as we follow the curve of the shoreline. "Fourth in line."

"I went to Panjim yesterday," Andrew says, "I have a reservation on that flight." He pulls a card from his pocket that shows his reservation.

"Here," he says and offers me the card. "You take it."

"Really?" I look at him, this sweet young man in all his Britishness, his lanky bones and big-toothed smile.

My hand is trembling as I take the card. I know my eyes fill, but I don't pay any attention. This thin card, a little larger than a business card—this is all it takes to set me on my way, and it appears like that. Like magic.

"Wait," Andrew says and takes the card back. Magic act—the disappearing card. He fumbles in his shirt pocket. "Do you have a pen?"

"Pen, paper, anything. Rupees." I locate a pen in my pack and give it to him.

"No, no rupees. I haven't paid for the ticket yet. I just have this."

He takes my pen and writes something on the card and hands both back to me.

On the card he's written that he is transferring his reservation on tomorrow's flight from Goa to Bombay to me. My name—Judy Reeves—is written in his neat accountant's handwriting. Just my name. No *Miss* or *Mrs.* or even *Ms.* preceding it, nothing that labels or limits me (*I'm Judy Reeves and I do PR; I'm Judy and I'm an alcoholic; I'm Judy Reeves and I'm a widow*), just my name: *Judy Reeves*. I can be any of these or all of these and more. I recall the line from Walt Whitman's "Song of Myself": *I am large, I contain multitudes.*

I can't say I'm this or I'm that and be only this or only that. I change, I transform. I'm all the selves of myself. Like the poet, I contain multitudes, and I will sing the Song of Myself in my off-key voice, sometimes tremulously, sometimes confidently, and sometimes loud enough for the world to hear.

I hug Andrew, this sweet twenty-two-year-old who was a stranger a little over a week ago, a young guy who also happened to be going south. I hug him with gratitude that spills out of me in fat tears and a runny nose, thankful for his generosity and also for the sudden understanding that unconditional trust opens the door to unlimited possibilities.

"Thank you, Andrew. Thank you. Thank you." I'm sloppy and messy and I don't care and neither does he. He hugs me back. Hard.

I don't sleep much that night, my last at the Silver Sands, and not just because of the mosquitoes that dive-bomb me when, in my restlessness, the sheet comes off. I'm unsettled and excited and also anxious—holding a small fear that nudges trust aside with the idea that they won't let me go, they won't accept the precious card that I've tucked inside my passport packet.

As I pack I vow that I'll come back to India one day and complete my around-the-world journey; next time I'll travel to the north and cross into Nepal and then Thailand. I'll continue on to Bali—and Tahiti, too, because Gauguin and the way the name satisfies my mouth.

I'm a traveler; I love the journey and the surprises and the strangers I meet who remind me that I'm one among many, that we humans are alike in more ways than we are different. I'll do it for my father who never got to fulfill his own travel dreams and for Tom and the many more road trips we might have taken together.

JANUARY 1987
Jamul

I hadn't dared look into the cardboard box I brought home from the mortuary that Saturday afternoon. Carried protected in my lap and held with both hands securing it against sudden stops or accidents as Davinia drove, it was heavier than I expected—though what I expected I can't say—and wrapped in plain brown paper like any common package you might get in the mail, neatly folded edges sealed with wide cellophane tape. Once home I didn't know where to put this odd and laden container—upstairs in our bedroom where I'd sleep with it resting on the bookcase or the headboard, on the hearth of the fireplace that opened to both our bedroom and the cozy room where he used to take his wolf naps on the leather couch? Downstairs on his desk? On a kitchen counter? On the glass-top table by the sliding doors that led to the deck then down to the orchard?

The moon is in its final quarter the January night we scatter his ashes. Just those few close friends, mostly from our Jamul AA group—Pine Tree Bill, TV Tom, Davinia, Duncan the Scotsman, a few others. The same friends we'd spent New Year's Eve with just a few weeks previous. We gather inside and tell Tom stories—some of them, who could ever tell all the stories? We laugh, of course; it's what we must do as we bear our sorrow, especially those of us who have "traveled the road" together, and through our many meetings shared the depths of our pain, marveled together at the joys that often take us by surprise. And we cried too.

Outside and down the steps to the orchard, a few stars and the dying moon above, me carrying the box I'd opened with a knife in one clean cut, folding back the paper and loosening the tape around the clear plastic bag inside with its contents that made the package so unexpectedly heavy. The air carries the scent of damp earth. The stone-fruit trees are bare now, but farther down the citrus are heavy with ripe fruit. The avocado trees on the hillside rise in dark silhouettes.

I stand near the top edge of the orchard, holding the open box as our friends reach inside and take what their hands can hold—first one hand, then the other—and wander off among the trees to say their private goodbyes. I watch as they go; occasionally I hear a quiet sound—a sniff or muffled word.

Down and down into the orchard, I bend under low branches, open my palm, release his ashes close to the trunks where I imagine there are roots, hungry and alive, underground. Only when I reach the far terrace where the row of citrus grows just before the hill slopes down into the avocado grove do I dare look into the box I carry in the crook of my arm. As I reach inside, my fingernail hits upon something hard and sharp, and my breath catches. A chip of bone? A shard of tooth?

I open my hand, look: dull gray speckled with white, taupe, tan. By the faint glow of the quarter moon, I imagine shades more than actually identify them. Particles that could have been ashes from a fireplace, or granules of fine sand from the beach where we used to live, catch in the creases of my palm, along the Heart line the palm reader told me carried many breaks. Another breath of wind lifts the ashes from my hand and releases them into my hair, across my shoulders. Some find the wet trace of tears on my cheeks. I taste them on my lips.

Goodbye, Goodbye, I tell the trees.

∾

Kenny rides with me to Goa International Airport in Dabolim, about twenty kilometers along a winding road that takes us between rice fields and palm trees. I never tire of the light and the colors and the people on these roads. What nerve the bicycle riders and motorbike drivers have. Cars and buses and trucks whiz past them, horns blaring, but they don't wave. They drive or pedal on, never a backward glance. They trust, too, these fearless travelers—that they won't be overtaken, run down, crushed by whatever honking thing is looming behind them.

The airport is noisy; the large, high-ceilinged room echoes the whooshing of many fans and the chatter of those gathered here. It's not as crowded as I thought it would be, but then most flights have been cancelled, both coming in and going out, and not just here but all across India, in Thailand, and elsewhere.

My flight is called. Kenny and I hug goodbye. He lets me keep his Canadian maple-leaf pin I've been wearing since the war broke out. We kidded that it was my disguise; no one trusts Americans. We hug and hug and tell each other we'll be in touch, Kenny and me, for as long as we can sustain our shared memories and separate lives. I roll my bag toward the door and turn once more to see him, his bright red hair, his easy slouch. Yes, we'll be in touch; this is the kind of friend you want to keep. He must have that sense too. He turns and waves, throws a kiss and a smile before he disappears around the corner.

Soon most of the others have boarded the plane and I sit near the boarding gate, waiting, anxious. Yes, they will honor my reservation, the man at the counter tells me, but they have no "stock." Stock? He says for me to trust him. So I remain where I am told to sit, waiting for another plane to arrive with more "stock." I'm not exactly sure, and I don't ask, but I believe he must mean the actual ticket—that multiple-layered piece of paper that will have my name and the flight number, the time, and destination.

We wait and we wait, we few apprehensive travelers, while outside on the tarmac is our plane to Bombay. I hope it will wait for us.

Finally the "stock" arrives and I'm called to the counter to purchase my ticket. But they won't accept credit cards or American Express traveler's checks.

"I'm sorry," the man at the counter says. "Cash only. Rupees or American dollars."

I'm in a jam. I have only half enough rupees and no American dollars at all—I haven't had any dollars since I landed in London last July.

Then a kind fellow—another stranger, a traveler from Nigeria with the complicated name of Mr. Patrick Boone Eruemolar Ikehi—saves me by paying for the other half of my ticket in US dollars.

"I'll pay you back when we arrive in Bombay," I promise, barely resisting the urge to hug him. These strangers who, time and again, have offered their kindnesses—the man at the post office in Paris who stepped forward and translated my mailing instructions for me; Julia at the sensory circus in Salzburg; Stephen, my fellow traveler in Leningrad, who stood with me at the end of a frozen row of mass graves as I emptied my grief; Kati Mati, my Stranger at the Crossroads in Budapest, who shared her wisdom; the Greek woman who gave me the flower as I trudged up the hill atop the Acropolis; Marty, the Canadian who stayed with me in my single bed at the Bali Hotel and held me in my sleep; Sandy and her family, who shared their American Thanksgiving with me in the Netherlands, whose sons had been sent to *the desert* in preparation for what was to come—the war that is now sending me home three months before my planned return.

Here we are, finally, seated next to each other, Mr. Patrick Boone Eruemolor Ikehi and me, on our flight to Bombay, where I'll exchange money and gratefully repay him for his generosity—at least as much as money can say *thank you*—and we'll part ways, never to see each other again.

JANUARY 24, 1991
Bangkok to Portland

I drift in and out, in between places, not here, not there. Flying above some sea I can't see because of cloud cover, because we are so high, because I am here and not here. I listen to Simon & Garfunkel sing "Homeward Bound" on my headphones. The music and their harmony awakens a longing for the comfort and safety of my Paris studio and the round table where I wrote and looked out the windows. For my apartment on Tourmaline in Pacific Beach, roaming the boardwalk along the ocean, trying to get used to the idea of life without Tom. And for the condo on the bay, where the idea to make this journey was born on the balcony overlooking the estuary nearly nine months ago, watching the tides come in and go out, like the tides of every sea all over the world.

I picture dawn breaking over the mountains in Jamul: gray, then mauve, then pink. The outline of the hill outside our bedroom window, past the deck, to where wild rabbits forage for food. The big bed that Tom built from redwood spread with my books and journal and early-morning coffee. Tom already out in the orchard, whistling as he ambles among the trees—the stone fruit, the citrus, the avocado.

I am homeward bound and I still don't know where or what home is, but I trust I'll find it even without an absolute idea of what it is I'm trusting in. I trust in something unnamable and unknowable, like the bird trusts the air to lift her wings, like the peaches in the orchard trust the sun to ripen them, like my pen trusts the page beneath it to catch and hold the words it forms.

EPILOGUE
AUGUST 1991
San Francisco

As I waited for a bus on Geary Street, dressed in jeans and a leather jacket and still chilled inside and out, I knew San Francisco wasn't home. The idea that Camille and I would open a café hadn't become a reality, nor would it. After just six months in the city, I packed up my belongings one more time and aimed my U-Haul truck south.

Back in San Diego, it wasn't long before life became full once again: I was part of a lively community of like-spirited souls, active in a writing group, leading journaling workshops. Income from the sale of the business continued to support me in a limited way, and I lived life day-to-day, week-to-week, with no real plans for any kind of a future. I wasn't unhappy, I wasn't lonely, but still something was missing.

One chilly night in November 1992, the little studio above a garage I'd taken as a writing space felt especially cold. To warm my bones, I did what I'd learned to do in Paris: I drew a steamy bath, lit a few candles to fragrance up the misty air, and climbed in. Leaning back and uttering that sigh that always comes, I closed my eyes. *Ahh.*

Suddenly! And it was just like that—*suddenly!* I was struck with an idea so clear and so complete and so powerful that its arrival literally knocked a candle from the edge of the tub and into my bath.

Open a writing center!

More specific: create a place where writers of all kinds can come together in community and support each other and work together.

Unlike the message that came to me not two years earlier as I sat on my balcony overlooking the estuary to *Go. Just go*, this message came with direction, almost ordering me to take action. I immediately climbed out of the tub, wrapped myself in towels, grabbed my notebook, and, still dripping, began writing:

This is what you will do—writing classes and workshops and writing groups and readings and open mics; this is what it will look like—even to the arrangement of furniture in the salon; this is the kind of funding you'll need—it will be a nonprofit; you'll have memberships, charge fees for services, you'll get grants. Notes and notes and notes, pages and pages and pages of notes.

Less than a year later, on my fifty-first birthday, The Writing Center was born in a live-work space in San Diego's Gaslamp Quarter, and in November 1993, we commenced the first writing session—the Brown Bag Writing Group. We were three at that noontime meeting: my dear friend Davinia, a guy who saw our sign in the window and walked in off the street, and me. But I knew I'd found the answer to Kati Mati's question. This was what I would finally do.

I found teaching, or teaching found me; I became a workshop leader and I could finally say, "I'm a writer." The Writing Center had a lively five-year existence with a diverse and expansive writing community, and in 2004 I was thrilled to be one of the cofounders of San Diego Writers, Ink, a nonprofit literary organization which thrives today. Brown Bag Writing Group, the first group formed at that old building in the Gaslamp Quarter nearly thirty years ago, still meets weekly, with writers gathering together, opening their notebooks, and writing. A practice I continue even now.

ACKNOWLEDGMENTS

Who can say what book, when? There I was revising the novel when the memoir I intended to write "some day," declared itself and everything shifted. Thank goodness I kept my old journals.

Thank goodness, too, for my family, friends, and writing community. Without their love, support, and deep well of patience, my story may have never emerged from those first scribbled pages to finally become the book you hold in your hands.

Those first scribbled pages were written as I sat at the dining room table of my good friend and writing companion, Jill Hall. Jill, your encouragement and support continues to help in more ways than I can name. What a joy to share this journey with you. I am forever grateful.

Dian Greenwood, you have been an inspiration and a grounding source all these years of friendship and writing. Camille Soleil, you were on the journey with me then and how grateful I am that we continue to travel the road together. Thank you, Roger Aplon, for your undying belief in me. Steve Montgomery, I wouldn't want to do any of this without you.

When it comes to family, I am one lucky writer. Amy Boyd— daughter and friend, companion and playmate, inspirer and delighter, heart-filler and joy-bringer—what a gift you are. Thank you, Chris and Stephanie, Jackson and Craig, and Kathleen (KMM). Thank you, Sharon, you were part of those early memories and your role as family historian was invaluable.

My gratitude to Tia Meredith for our long conversations and your deep insights. Divine Grace, your special gifts answered my questions and settled my heart. Thank you, Gina Cameron for all the time we spent together sharing our lives and our writing. Thanks, Amy Wallen for your encouragement and support. Leslie Johansen Nack, you're the best.

Thanks to San Diego Writers, Ink and friend and colleague, Executive Director Kristen Fogle. The Tuesday Memoir Group—Janice Alper, Carrie Danielson, Barbara Huntington, Connie Henry, Rose Lochmann, David Reed, and Marilyn Woods—our time together made my life and my writing better. David, thank you for your help in identifying the many trees that populate my descriptions. Remembering with gratitude my writing group who graciously supported my transition from novel to memoir. Thanks Betsy Marro, Libby Brydolf, Steve Rodriguez, Erin Sanchez, and Frank DiPalmero. Thank you, Frank for all the before and after and in between talks and commiserations.

My thanks to the Wild Women of Ajijic for our time together and your generous support. I can't wait until our next time.

I wish I could acknowledge individually all the writers in my community in San Diego and elsewhere who have been a part of my journey from then to now, but if I did the pages in this section of the book would easily outnumber those in the story it contains.

I am indebted to friend and colleague Jennifer Silva Redmond for professional knowledge and expertise as both early- and late-stage editor and for all-around cheering on. Thanks, Beth Kephart, for your review, for your books, and teaching about memoir, all have influenced my work. What a gift for my editor at New World Library, Georgia Hughes, to review my manuscript. Thank you, Georgia for your always insightful thoughts. Thank you, Gina Walters, you're the kind of copy editor every writer needs. My gratitude to beta readers whose generous response made the book better. Thank you, Jill Hall, Gina Cameron, Rick Geist, Roger Aplon, Leslie Johansen Nack, Carol Brennan, and Tom Larson.

We writers have so many options to take our stories from birthing place into the public realm. She Writes Press is a shining example of how creativity, innovation, and professional knowledge can open a brilliant new world of opportunities. I am honored to have my book ushered into the world under the guidance of founder and publisher, Brooke Warner. Thank you, project manager Addison Gallegos, and gratitude to the entire She Writes team and community.

Daddy, thank you for opening your world atlas that long-ago afternoon and for nurturing my dreams all the way into the universe and beyond.

Tom, the joy and the tears, then and still.

ABOUT THE AUTHOR

photo credit: Jenny Siegwart

Judy Reeves is an award-winning writer and teacher whose books include *A Writer's Book of Days* (named "Best Nonfiction" by the San Diego Book Awards and a "Hottest Books for Writers" by *Writer's Digest*); *Writing Alone, Writing Together*; *The Writer's Retreat Kit*; and *Wild Women, Wild Voices*. Her fiction, nonfiction, and poetry have appeared in magazines, literary journals, and anthologies, most recently in *The Great Book of Journaling*. She has edited several anthologies and chapbooks, including those born out of her Wild Women writing workshops. A long-time teacher of creative writing, she previously taught at University of California San Diego Extension and has led community-based writing practice groups for thirty years. She continues to teach at writing conferences internationally and at San Diego Writers, Ink, a nonprofit literary center she cofounded. Her awards include those from the San Diego Writers and Editors Guild, San Diego Writer's Festival, and The African American Writers & Artists Association. Mayor Jerry Sanders declared July 24, 2010 "Judy Reeves Day" in San Diego. Judy lives and writes in San Diego amid bulging bookshelves and an ancient Underwood typewriter that claims its own social media fan base. You can catch up with Judy on her website www. judyreeveswriter.com, where you can sign up to receive her monthly newsletter, "Lively News from the Lively Muse."

SELECTED TITLES FROM SHE WRITES PRESS

She Writes Press is an independent publishing company founded to serve women writers everywhere. Visit us at www.shewritespress.com.

Travel Mania: Stories of Wanderlust by Karen Gershowitz
$16.95, 978-1-64742-126-7
After flying to Europe at seventeen, Karen Gershowitz became addicted to travel and adventure—and went on to visit more than ninety countries. In these engaging stories, she reflects on the amazing ways in which travel has changed her life.

Bowing to Elephants: Tales of a Travel Junkie by Mag Dimond
$16.95, 978-1-63152-596-4
Mag Dimond, an unloved girl from San Francisco, becomes a travel junkie to avoid the fate of her narcissistic, alcoholic mother—but everywhere she goes, she's haunted by memories of her mother's neglect, and by a hunger to find out who she is, until she finds peace and her authentic self in the refuge of Buddhist practice.

Brave(ish): A Memoir of a Recovering Perfectionist by Margaret Davis Ghielmetti. $16.95, 978-1-63152-747-0
An intrepid traveler sets off at forty to live the expatriate dream over-seas—only to discover that she has no idea how to live even her own life. Part travelogue and part transformation tale, Ghielmetti's memoir, narrated with humor and warmth, proves that it's never too late to reconnect with our authentic selves—if we dare to put our own lives first at last.

Finding Venerable Mother: A Daughter's Spiritual Quest to Thailand by Cindy Rasicot. $16.95, 978-1-63152-702-9
In midlife, Cindy travels halfway around the world to Thailand and unex-pectedly discovers a Thai Buddhist nun who offers her the unconditional love and acceptance her own mother was never able to provide. This soulful and engaging memoir reminds readers that when we go forward with a truly open heart, faith, forgiveness, and love are all possible.

Just Be: A Search for Self-Love in India by Meredith Rom
$16.95, 978-1-63152-286-4
After following her intuition to fly across the world and travel alone through the crowded streets of India, twenty-two-year-old Meredith Rom learns that that true spiritual development begins when we take the leap of trusting our intuition and finding a love within.